Dearly Beloved

Letters to the Children of My Spirit

VOLUME TWO

1964 - 1973

by
Catherine de Hueck Doherty

MADONNA HOUSE   PUBLICATIONS
Combermere, Ontario   Canada   K0J 1L0

PRINTED IN CANADA

ii

Cover: Catherine at the shrine on her island where these letters were written.

Nihil Obstat: Rev. Robert D. Pelton

Imprimatur:

J.R. Windle
Bishop of Pembroke
Aug. 15, 1990

The Nihil Obstat and Imprimatur are a declaration that a book or pamphlet is considered to be free from doctrinal or moral error. It is not implied that those who have granted the Nihil Obstat and Imprimatur agree with the contents, opinions or statements expressed.

Canadian Cataloguing in Publication Data
Doherty, Catherine de Hueck, 1896-1985
Dearly beloved: letters to the children of my spirit vol. 2

Includes bibliographical references.
ISBN 0-921440-10-3 (v. 1). –
ISBN 0-921440-11-1 (v. 2)

1. Christian life – Catholic authors.
2. Doherty, Catherine de Hueck, 1896-1985.
I. Title.

BX4705.D64A3   1988   248.4'82   C89-090000-0

MADONNA HOUSE   PUBLICATIONS
Combermere, Ontario   Canada   K0J 1L0

DEDICATION

To all the Children of my Spirit,
those who are with me now and those
who are as yet unborn.

INTRODUCTION

Readers of Volume One have sent us comments and suggestions. We thank them for their letters. In reply, we have added a section at the end of Volume Two, *Helps for the Reader.* At the end of Volume Three, we hope to print an *Index* to all three books. One of the most frequent requests is that we place Catherine's Letters in a broad historical setting. We do so here, briefly mentioning events which Catherine would have experienced.

* * *

At the beginning of Volume One, the world-at-large is still recovering from the Second World War, and is starting to deal with the implications of the Cold War. *During 1955-1957:* The Korean War ends. Austria becomes an independent nation. Eastern Bloc countries sign the Warsaw Pact. West Germany joins NATO. Japan becomes a member of the UN. Cardinal Wyszynski (Poland), Cardinal Mindszenty (Hungary), Archbishop Makarios (Cyprus) are released from their prison cells. The Hungarian uprising is suppressed by Soviet troops. Castro lands in Cuba with a guerilla army. The USA explodes a hydrogen bomb in the Bikini Atoll. The Russians launch the world's first artificial satellite, Sputnik I.

In the USA: 1955 is a watershed year. Elvis Presley signs a contract with a major record company and rapidly acquires international fame. The first 'deep freeze' units, to store fresh food, are sold to families. In Montgomery, Alabama, the segregated bus system is boycotted by the black population. Martin Luther King emerges as the new leader in their march toward desegregation.

In Canada: It is only in 1947 that Catherine and Eddie move to that country. By 1951 (the year that the village of Combermere gets electricity) a few volunteers have gathered around Catherine. By the spring of 1954, there are sixteen Staff Workers in residence. Catherine sends three of them to the Yukon, to open the first Madonna House mission. In 1955, a mission team is sent to Edmonton. More followers continue to join her, so in 1956 Catherine accepts fieldhouses in Arizona and in Oregon, and opens them in 1957.

Catherine is faced with the double task of training new staff in Combermere, and maintaining contact with outlying mission teams. She feels the need to communicate her ideas, so she starts to write a monthly letter to her followers, beginning each one with the words: Dearly Beloved.

* * *

Toward the end of Volume One and the beginning of Volume Two: the world scene has changed radically. In 1961, the Berlin Wall is built, fortified, and made to last 'forever.' In 1962, the Cuban Missile Crisis looms suddenly, and is quickly averted. In 1963, President Kennedy is assassinated. In 1964, USA involvement in the Vietnam War begins to escalate; Ian Smith becomes premier of Southern Rhodesia (not yet Zimbabwe); and Martin Luther King receives the Nobel Peace Prize.

The Beatles come to prominence at this time. Barbra Streisand is singing about *People Who Need People.* Peter, Paul, and Mary have caught the world's attention with *If I Had A Hammer,* and *Blowin' in the Wind.* A strange wind is scattering the seeds of new ideas around the world. It is a time when the first 'flower children' will soon begin to move restlessly across the land, in search of a counterculture. Madonna House is growing rapidly, with many new members. Hordes of visitors will eventually come to Combermere, hungering for answers. Tents will have to be put up on the lawn to 'house' them, bedrolls to 'sleep' them.

As for the Roman Catholic Church, something is definitely blowing in the wind. Its windows have been thrown open, and fresh air is flowing along its corridors.

Pope John XXIII had summoned some 2500 prelates to the Vatican for an ecumenical council in October 1962, just before his eighty-first birthday. A man thought to be naive and simple and old, a 'caretaker' pope whose name was expected to be forgotten by history, had surprised the world. More properly, *the Holy Spirit* surprised us all.

Catherine's response to the opening of Vatican II was to reveal a Russian word that the West has never heard before: *poustinia* (a 'desert'). "If all those people are getting together to renew the Church, we must pray for them. Now in my country, this is what we do...." Eventually, she will write a book on this topic which becomes a spiritual 'best seller.'

Catherine always reads a lot: books and magazines in two or three languages. She often travels a lot: giving lectures in one place, going to meetings in another, visiting the fieldhouses for a 'hands-on' experience of mission activity. In the early 1960s, at the request of bishops, she begins to send mission teams to foreign lands. She notices how the Peace Corps operates. Night and day, the training of committed, dedicated lay apostles concerns her. She is asked to provide a six-weeks' orientation program for young men and women who have been accepted by other Catholic groups for overseas missions. She does so, as volunteers are sent to her, for ten years.

During the 1960s, color television becomes popular in North America; an old black-and-white set is given to Madonna House. The broadcasting station is eighty miles away, but the snowy screen brings in recognizable images — scenes of war, violence, racism. These images crowd across the doorstep of Catherine's mind, push their way into her heart, and sear her memory.

* * *

Towards the end of Volume Two: Catherine has seen all the ravages of the Vietnam War. As for spiritual warfare, in the battle for souls, her heart has been torn in two at the viii

sight of so many priests and nuns abandoning their
commitments and leaving their 'ministries.' She weeps
continually for 'the little ones' who are being led astray,
seduced by strange new ideas about life and love.

By the middle of 1973, the Vietnam war is over (so far
as the USA is concerned), though Asian troops will
continue to fight there for another two years. Almost a
decade has gone by since the Ecumenical Council
published all its official statements, but a ferment continues
in the Church-at-large as the various recommendations are
discussed, clarified, implemented. By this time Madonna
House has become an organized and accepted group, but it
has yet to learn how to function without Catherine's
presence.

She continues to teach, to challenge, to commiserate.
In the late 1960s, she begins to withdraw from the day-to-
day running of the Apostolate, so that others in her family
may develop the art of leadership. In the early 1970s, she
unveils another Russian word, *sobornost* (unity of mind
and heart), and makes it the centerpiece for a new post-
Vatican II Constitution of Madonna House.

In the fall of 1972, Catherine visits the land where
Jesus once walked. In October 1973, Arab-Israeli fighting
breaks out there, in the Yom Kippur War. In November
1973, confronted with the request to write a Yuletide
message for the general public, Catherine remembers what
the Holy Land was like during her visit. And what it is like
now. She writes an unusual Christmas poem, a strong
antidote to the traditional 'sweet baby Jesus' sentiments
that her readers are imbibing from secular newspapers. The
poem is a bombshell. There is, almost, a whiff of napalm in
the air.

To her own followers, however, her Christmas
message that year is one of joy. She knows how much
they have been buffeted by the winds of change, how
patiently they have carried the burden of the world's
miseries. And they must find the strength to continue

carrying that load, without faltering, without failing. Catherine tries to succor them.

* * *

As Volume Three begins: The Watergate trials have been bannered across the front page of every newspaper during 1972, 1973, 1974. Like a mournful dirge, voices everywhere are echoing that heartfelt song of Barbra Streisand, as little people everywhere reach out to comfort one another. Martin Luther King has been laid to rest. Bobby Kennedy, and John F. Kennedy, and Pope John XXIII are gone. The honor of the US presidency is in question. *The Age of Heroes* is past.

The world has begun to move into *The Age of Ecology.* Since April 1970, 'Earth Day' has become an annual celebration. Leakey has recently found a human skull in northern Kenya that is thought to be over two million years old. A Stone Age tribe called the Tasadays has been discovered living in caves in the southern Philippines. Human habitation is everywhere. Even the moon's surface has felt the imprint of an earthling's foot. And people, who need people, begin to draw closer together — looking for warmth, seeking faith, needing Christ even more than warmth.

The Editors

x

CONTENTS

SPIRITUAL DIRECTORS

January 13, 1964

Dearly Beloved,

It seems that we have to clarify the question of spiritual directors once more, so let us briefly review what we already know about spiritual directors.

I am sure there isn't a member of Madonna House who doesn't realize that the life of perfection, to which we are called in this Apostolate, demands a *total* dedication. To live out this dedication under the counsels of poverty, chastity, and obedience, we must have a spiritual director. The waters of life are turbulent and dangerous, and Satan loves to place pitfalls along the way. Definitely we need a guide.

We are generally familiar with the procedure of obtaining a spiritual director. First, we must pray very earnestly to God before choosing one. It is a very important relationship that we are entering into with Christ the Priest, and we must turn to him to direct us to the right person. He may do this by giving us a certain spiritual attraction to some priest. Perhaps it is through a sermon, a retreat, or a spiritual truth expressed by this priest that went straight to our heart. These can be indications that God is directing us to him.

Once we have found the priest, we must enter into a very childlike relationship to him. We must love him as we love God – supernaturally. We must trust him completely. We must obey him implicitly. Otherwise, we wouldn't need a spiritual director. If we try to get around him in the thousand ways that human beings try to get around even God, we will encourage Satan to trap us. One does not do such things to God.

These rules apply to everyone, both in and out of the

Apostolate. And we as lay apostles should encourage those with whom we work and serve to have spiritual directors. I repeat, not to have a spiritual director is to be a foolish person, one who is guideless in a great, utterly unknown wilderness.

Also, for someone to take a spiritual director who is thoroughly unfamiliar with the Apostolate – and I stress the word thoroughly – this, too, is acting in a foolish and unintelligent way.

I once had a spiritual director, a Discalced Carmelite, who was thoroughly familiar with Friendship House. But six months after I moved to Combermere he refused to direct me, and rightly so. He said he was utterly unfamiliar with the new accent that our Apostolate had taken, so he could not advise me in this new context. This is a very important point to remember. It doesn't apply to lay people in general, but only to lay apostolates.

A priest is familiar with single life in the world. He has been a layman himself and has socialized with women before he became a priest. He is thoroughly familiar with married life, and usually he is pretty familiar with the religious life of monks and nuns. But, unless a given apostolate is his apostolate, he would not be that familiar with it. If a wife comes to him, complaining about her husband, and he suspects that she is biased, all he has to do is to ask her to bring her husband in. He can talk to the husband privately or in front of her, as he wishes, and get both sides of the picture.

But if you choose a priest who doesn't know Madonna House, or knows it only superficially, you put him behind the eight ball, and yourself behind the twenty ball! Many priests are not *prepared* to do spiritual direction according to the Madonna House point of view, and they will say so if you ask them.

You can seek out a priest who is unfamiliar with Madonna House and spin him any kind of yarn that you wish. You can seek from him friendship, compassion, and merciful understanding. But your spiritual life will not progress; in fact it will regress. Any priest in his right mind will understand this.

True, according to the rules of the Church, you are

free to choose anyone as your spiritual director. The directorate of Madonna House does not impinge on your freedom. But if you remember the reason for having a spiritual director, it becomes obvious, both in the natural and supernatural order, that since we are blessed by our own priests who know us in the Apostolate, and other local priests who are very familiar with our Apostolate, you can and should go to these priests.

Intelligence, I repeat, guides your choice. You want to go to God, don't you? You desire rapid spiritual progress, don't you? That means choosing a priest who *knows* our Apostolate.

The majority of you, because you come here to be trained in the Apostolate, usually choose one of our Madonna House priests. Then you go to the missions. Because you find it difficult to write and to express yourselves, because there is a lapse between your letters and the answers of your spiritual director, you easily get discouraged.

This should not happen. You are approaching this whole matter of direction-by-mail in too natural a fashion. You are depressed; your emotions get the better of you; you have a 'real' problem, so you think. I spoil you a little too (God forgive me!) by answering your letters right away and at great length.

Your relations by mail with a spiritual director, however, are quite different from your relations to me. I know you love your spiritual directors, but you do not trust enough. Write without any worries; you are writing about your soul. The priests have the grace to read between the lines. Don't worry about your manner of expression, your grammar, or anything like that. Trust God fully. He will see that the priest clearly understands the poorest letter.

If you do not receive an immediate letter, remember that God may not give an answer for a long time either ... sometimes not until you meet him face to face. Sometimes an answer will come very slowly. This is God's way of clarifying the doubts that you might have. The answer may not make sense to you at this moment, but will make sense if you meditate upon it.

The silence of the spiritual director may mean that he

is teaching you patience; that he is teaching you how to grow in trust and obedience; that he is allowing the problem, which he understands very well, to work itself out in you; that he is praying about it. In fact, the reasons for delay can be myriad, all beautifully hidden from you to make you grow in faith and trust. Do you begin to see what I mean?

So when you go to a spiritual director in Madonna House, you have to *love, trust, and obey.* Continue to be his spiritual directee, no matter how far away God might send you. That would be the sensible, the supernatural thing to do *if you really want to become saints and live the spirit of Madonna House perfectly.*

Now, I want to discuss with you some reasons why you could sever connections with your spiritual director and seek another. I must admit that there are a few reasons for doing this. The first, of course, is if he tries to induce you to sin. This is an almost inconceivable idea; but it is one that may happen, because the Church has been entrusted to human beings and not to angels. If such a thing should occur, it is self-evident that you cannot possibly continue to be directed by such a person, even though he is a priest.

Another reason would be: if you begin to realize that, though there is no sinful situation at the moment, there might occur a situation which could be considered 'an occasion of sin.' Now don't immediately jump to the conclusion that this occasion of sin means a sin against purity, or that it is necessarily connected with sex. This can happen, of course, if too great an intimacy or natural friendship develops. Normally it doesn't, for the priest usually sees to it that the relationship is kept in bounds, even if you might not. I presume that the members of Madonna House, especially the women, are aware of this and are always very watchful.

Other situations may arise. One of these happened to me, and this example may help you. I had a very good spiritual director, a secular priest, and everything went along fine for a few months. Then I noticed that, for some reason or another, he began to ask *me* my advice on *his* spiritual life. At first I thought I was mistaken and allowed a few more months to pass. But then it became evident that the situation was continuing, and I was becoming his involuntary spiritual director! Our roles were being reversed.

Because this was becoming an 'occasion of sin' for me – the sin of pride – (nothing to do with sex, whatsoever), I severed the relationship. It would have been easy for me to have convinced myself to continue because he was paying me a great compliment. "The man supposedly knows my soul," so my thoughts might have run, "and he thinks that I am good enough to advise him. Hum! I must be pretty great!" But I saw the danger in time. Because I loved, trusted, and obeyed the man, I told him why I was severing the relationship; he understood and agreed.

Some moral theology books give another reason for severing relationships with a spiritual director: the cessation of communications because of conflict. Personally, I cannot fathom this possibility. To me this is unclear. I am not a moral theologian, but I look at it with the simplicity of faith.

Let us presume that your spiritual director does not go along with an idea that you think is totally in accord with the Gospel, and your communications break down. You are thoroughly persuaded that you should go to the right, and he thinks that you should go to the left. Here is where your trust and obedience should prevail. Without question you go to the left. If God wanted you to go to the right, he would (in due time) show your director that this is so. Meanwhile, you will earn untold merits and win many souls for Christ by your obedience.

A story is told of Sister Josefa, a holy Sacred Heart nun who is up for canonization (she died in 1923, so she is our contemporary). Christ appeared to her and told her to go to the chapel at recreation time. She was very obedient and revealed this to her superior, as she should have done, for that sort of phenomenon must be known to the superiors as well as to the spiritual directors.

Her mother superior said she was very sorry, but they would be having a sewing bee on the children's uniforms, so she could not go to the chapel. Without a word, Sister Josefa went to the bee. Later she met Christ in a corridor. He smiled and told her, "Had you come to the chapel against the will of your superior, I would have not have been there."

How much more is he 'not there' when our wills and ideas clash with him in the priest to whom we have prayerfully entrusted our souls!

If communications have broken down between us and our spiritual director, it behooves us to examine ourselves – not our spiritual director. Read the lives of the great saints and you will see that they obeyed spiritual directors who seemed to be bereft of any intelligence, but out of that obedience God brought tremendous results for themselves and the world around them. So I personally don't 'buy' the excuse for severing relations with a spiritual director because of a conflict.

If things become so impossible that you can neither eat nor sleep, however, then you have one last resort before severing your relations with a spiritual director, and that is to go to another priest, someone known for his wisdom and sanctity (it should be a priest whom you have never met). When you have found this person, you should talk with him personally. If he is too far away, write the full details of your situation. Be as objective as you can about your spiritual director, but then accept the decision of this priest as final.

Under no circumstances should you go to a priest whom you know through the Apostolate, or whom you knew before you came to Madonna House. He is already disposed in your favor. You want God's answer, purified of any human factor. What is at stake is your immortal soul. That should be worth everything to you!

I once had that temptation. My spiritual director was pretty harsh with me and had put me in a corner which I did not like. I wanted other advice and, in my loneliness and self-pity, I sought out a Dominican priest whom I knew well. I knew that he loved me very much and thought that I was a pretty saintly Catholic woman. "He," I said to myself, "will surely understand the situation." So to him I went.

When I presented my case to him, he rose from his chair, got a bottle of holy water, and blessed me with it. Then he read a short exorcism over me to chase Satan away from my soul. He told me in no uncertain terms not to be such a damn fool and wreck my whole spiritual life by separating myself from my spiritual director; that I should go ahead and do what he told me – period! Then he gave me a cup of coffee. Now that's a sensible man!

At spiritual reading one day, I presented the gist of this letter. Father Briere pretty much confirmed what I said and added a few words of wisdom. What he said was very simple: you pray for a spiritual director, for someone you judge to be competent and interested in you. Then you love, trust, and obey him, for he is Christ for you.

Father Bob Pelton contributed a very profound thought too. He said that competency is self-evident. The priest is trained for spiritual direction, has the grace of the sacrament of priesthood, and is obviously interested in the salvation and sanctity of souls.

Besides this, you must enter into the mystery of the Incarnation. A priest is not chosen for his personality, his intelligence, his deep knowledge of theology, or for any other such traits. He is chosen because he is the incarnation of Christ in this special moment of spiritual direction. Fundamentally, you must pray for faith because you are face to face with a mystery of our faith. This mystery cannot be probed by reason, but must be accepted by faith.

One question came up in the discussion: "What is the difference between counseling and spiritual direction?" It is a good question because our priests, out of kindness, do both. Because of this confusion, our priests have now adopted a new technique. When they counsel you, they preface their counseling by saying, "I speak to you now, not as a spiritual director, but as a friend and counselor in the natural order." When that part of the interview is over, and the spiritual part arises, they say, "Now listen, this is your spiritual director talking." Actually, no priest should do much counseling; it confuses the directee. But, because there is no one else to do it, priests do counsel. Now you know the difference, and that is good.

Lovingly yours in Mary,

8

THE NATURE OF MEN

January 25, 1964

Dearly Beloved,

A false and dangerous notion exists among the men and women of the Apostolate. It concerns relationships which have a seemingly spiritual motivation. Sometimes the person involved in a relationship with someone of the opposite sex *believes* that the motivation is spiritual (and that may be so, especially at the beginning). The only thing that can be said about such a person is that he or she is very innocent – or very ignorant! – first, of oneself; secondly, of human nature; and thirdly, of the devil and his power.

Because Madonna House puts great stress on receiving everyone as Christ, or perhaps because this subject has not been discussed as fully as it should have been, the members of Madonna House may not have been alerted to the dangers that arise between men and women.

Let us be very clear when we speak, for instance, of men. We mean not only laymen; we mean also seminarians, priests, and religious brothers. It often happens that women get the idea they can solve the problems of men who come to Madonna House.

This is dangerous. Actually, I could end this letter right now by simply giving a rule – a fundamental, axiomatic rule – and bluntly state that no single woman of any age can help any man, be he married or single. But that, I think, would not be sufficient; so let's go into the depths of the matter.

Our friend, Sister Mary Andrew Hartmann,* once explained very clearly why this is a psychological impossibility. She described a man's growth in general,

* A professor of psychology who taught in the graduate school at the University of Ottawa. She gave courses in 'developmental psychology' at Madonna House.

and his sexual growth in particular. She explained that, at the age of eighteen months, a child of any sex recognizes the difference between the sexes. The male child knows that there is a being who is gentle, kind, and loving, who caters to his needs. At eighteen months, he knows that this person is different from the other adult who fills his life and who represents authority, law, strength, and security.

As an aside, Sister mentioned that, at her clinic, she finds great damage done to babies two or three years old by the very fact that today the baby has difficulty in separating the sexes. Not only does the woman wear pants (physically), but often the woman in North American civilization is the figure of law, authority, strength, and security *without* the corresponding warmth and tenderness. The child, therefore, is confused. Instead of having a mother and a father, he has two fathers. The man can never be for the child the nursing female figure that the mother is. Bereft of the mother figure, his personality is already warped and sick at the age of two or three.

She went on to say that between the ages of three to six (if all is normal up to then), the child will begin to be jealous of his father; he wants his mother for himself. He wants to be the center of her interest, and he will compete for the attention of his mother. If the father pays great attention to him during this particular stage – plays with him, takes him for hikes and so forth – this infantile jealousy will soon change to great admiration and imitation of his father, and a normal balance will be restored.

Between the ages of six and nine, the male child separates himself from his mother and attaches himself not only to the father but to the gang. Now he still loves his mother very much, but he doesn't want any signs of affection from her. We all know *that* stage in a boy.

From the ages of nine to twelve, he enters what is usually the calmest period of his life. He has now established good relations with his father and mother and with the other boys. This is the time when he will accept girls and play with them. Sex is dormant, and he considers women as a weaker counterpart of himself.

From the age of twelve to twenty-one or so, he

enters the turbulent stage of the male. Because of his anatomy, he becomes cognizant of sex. It bothers him very much. His organs grow, and he becomes very aware of them. He is unable to bridge the gap between himself and the other sex, however. This is particularly true between the ages of twelve and sixteen. It is a painful period in the development and growth of the male. Already the signs of his maleness are apparent. He fully realizes the difference between the male and the female, and not only anatomically. He is deeply attracted to the opposite sex, and his habits change. We all know one sign: when he begins to care much more about his appearance.

If all goes well and there is a good background in his home (psychologically speaking), plus a religious upbringing that has fully taught him to distinguish right from wrong, he will quite easily arrive at the stage when he is mature enough to marry.

Next comes a very important point for us in the Apostolate. Sister Mary Andrew showed very clearly how young men approach this marriageable stage. She showed us also how sex works in a man, according to his nature.

1. **Selectivity:** When a man is ready to marry, he consciously or unconsciously 'selects.' He might have a large group of female acquaintances and friends, but suddenly his eyes, as it were, are open to just one person in their midst. Or he might enter a room and come upon a sea of female faces, but he will see only one; and the rest are as if they didn't exist. This is wonderful *for marriage*. Nature has made it this way. But all of us, especially women, must recognize *that this selectivity in the man is a natural built-in tendency.*

What does this mean for the Apostolate? It simply means that if any male – be he a member of the community, visitor, seminarian, priest, brother, married man, or whatever – selects one person to tell his troubles to, to walk with and talk with, or even just to be with in a group and addresses all his comments to this one person, the women of the Apostolate must sit up and take notice. For this is the start of a dangerous situation which the man may not realize and neither does the woman. It is nature's way of leading toward sexual union with the selected one. Danger signals are all around, and must be recognized as such. The woman must be aware of it immediately and remove herself from this situation at once.

She must never, under any condition, imagine that she can 'help' this particular male. No matter how innocent or spiritual the situation, the man's built-in sexual pattern, created by Mother Nature, is already at work in the depths of his unconscious. (Few men realize these things at the time!)

2. **Protectiveness:** The second built-in preparation by Mother Nature is the male's tremendous desire to protect the one he has selected. His whole maleness is aroused. This, of course, is wonderful *for marriage,* for the husband must protect his wife and children.

How does this relate to a woman of Madonna House? Flattered by being selected, intellectually unaware of the dangers inherent in this selectivity, filled with illusions that she can 'help' this person, she begins to bask in the protectiveness of this newly-acquired friend. Or, as she sees it in all simplicity, it is a 'person to be helped for Christ.'

The nature of woman, as Sister Mary Andrew described it scientifically and psychologically, is *passive, dependent, in need of strength and protection.* You can see for yourself that a young woman of Madonna House, struggling with the loneliness that is inherent in all life and in all vocations (but, at times, very acute in the vocation to a life of perfection), unconsciously surrenders to what is natural and normal for her – *the protectiveness of the male.*

What has become an unconscious illusion that she can help *him* now continues in reverse. His protectiveness, his deep interest in her, still without any outward signs of what one calls 'men-women relations,' calls from her passivity and confidences. *Now* she has a *person* with whom she can talk, and to whom she can impart, still perhaps unconsciously, much more than what she had originally planned to do. Her idea was to listen, console, to talk about God and the things of God – in a word, I repeat again and again, somehow to 'help' this man solve his problems and find God. But now she is telling him *her* problems, *her* difficulties, *her* needs.

You can see for yourself where this leads. At this stage, in the case of married people, seminarians, priests, or religious brothers, the tragedy is already half begun. In the case of single lay people, one can foresee (without using too much imagination) the forthcoming misery and tragedy.

If any of these people are psychologically disturbed (and many people today are), then danger is at hand. None of us are psychologists or psychiatrists. Can you realize the effects of these unconscious mechanisms (built-in by nature) which are already at work and then compounded by psychological problems? Well, anything can happen! A priest can leave the priesthood; a seminarian can leave his seminary; a brother can desert his religious vocation; a married man can leave his wife. Over and above these vocational problems, tragic situations such as suicide and scandal can occur. No matter which way you look at it, no good whatsoever is effected. There can only be harm, tragedy, temptation, confusion – all works of Satan.

3. **Selectivity combined with Protectiveness:** These two natural steps which lead men and women to marriage now cause the male to engage in certain actions. He will desire to touch, to hold, to look at the object of his selectivity and protectiveness. These gestures occur in two parts. First, a looking gently, touching the hand, maybe patting the head and so forth. They are seemingly innocent gestures, but they are always precursors of sexual desire. It is only a matter of time and opportunity when the bonfire of sex will burst forth and burn sky-high. That desire to possess fully will first be expressed in a passionate embrace.

Again, I draw the attention of the female staff never to overlook these beginning stages: selectivity and protectiveness. They will inevitably lead to the third stage when the damage will be done.

Sister Mary Andrew explained that the above steps are normal for people called to the married life. Each of them is good and, if properly handled, will lead to marriage and be consummated there.

Sister then returned to the childhood and adolescent years of the male. She reviewed the fact that, generally speaking, the male child and the adolescent love only themselves. This is especially true of the infant from birth to school age. From school age on, the boy does not yet love the other – his school chums or the members of his gang and so forth. He is still in the infant stage; *he loves those who cater to his needs and pleasures*. It is still a form of self-love.

Love-of-the-Other begins to develop in adolescence. We see that in many young people who become interested in racial issues, in the poor, and so on. This love is still amorphous, however, and not very well defined. It is only when the selection of the opposite sex occurs that *true love of another comes forth in all of its vitality*. Now the man doesn't matter to himself, *she* does. He truly loves her enough to 'lay down his life' for her!

The same process takes place in the female child. She, too, reaches the moment when she loves the other, and is ready to 'lay down her life' for him. After marriage, their love matures greatly. The small stream becomes a river flowing into the sea of children. Now, both of them would lay down their lives for the children.

As men and women mature in matrimony, their love begins to flow out into the community. You see them becoming interested in other people's children. The father often becomes a Boy Scout leader; the mother may help with the Girl Guides. They also become interested in community improvements. Still, their love for these latter will be somewhat limited.

Their first concern must be for their family, and only secondarily for the community, the nation, or international concerns. (Nowadays, many families even go to mission lands.) Beautiful and immense as this marvelous vocation of marriage is, it is still only one aspect of the Love-who-is-a-Person, for it is from God that all love flows.

As Christians, we are capable of Universal Love. We are capable of opening our hearts, totally and completely, to our neighbor. Who is this neighbor? It is the world, composed of innumerable individuals who are in need. This universal love begins with *falling in love with Christ* and, for his sake, loving all people in the person of one's neighbor ... and 'neighbor' means whoever comes to the door.

This universal love leads some men and women to forego the founding of their own families and to engage in strengthening the whole family of humanity to whom Christ is wedded, and to do so for his sake, and for humanity's sake. These men and women are ready to lay their lives down for *anyone*. They have channeled all of their natural and supernatural powers – sex and everything else – into this immense, universal river of love.

Instead of founding one family, they have given themselves to the family of humanity. In order to seal their universal Christ-like love, their wedding with God, they have bound themselves by promises of poverty, obedience, and chastity. In this way they are utterly free. This is the foundation of the life of religious, of secular institutes, and of thousands of lay people who have taken private vows.

Having presented this immense and wondrous picture of love, Sister then went on to say, very powerfully and truthfully, that – contrary to the common notion – *genital sexual expression is not essential to the full blossoming of human life*. This truth cuts across the conscious, subconscious, and unconscious ideology of some Catholics. We believe secretly (we would not acknowledge it, perhaps) that all unmarried people are probably frustrated, and that sex and marriage would cure their frustrations. The fact that three out of five marriages on the North American continent fail doesn't seem to deter us from these false notions.

No, sexual union is not necessary to the full development of a human personality. The love of men and women has a thousand ways of fulfilling itself. The greatest, of course, is the way that Christ showed us in the call of the rich young man. But many other people, for a greater cause, do not marry either. Some communists forego marriage to be more dedicated. So do scientists, artists, pagan philosophers, ascetics, and holy men. Endless is the stream of men and women who have renounced sex and the founding of families for what they saw as a greater good.

Now we in Madonna House have been called to this *universal love*. We have entered into it with our eyes wide open. We have been given a good preparation for it. At no time did anyone hide from us the pain of the cross. We responded to God's call voluntarily and sincerely.

It behooves us, then, to *know our natures* and to take care not to upset the delicate balance of our lives and that of our Apostolate. So I would like to summarize what I have been discussing in this letter:

Men of the Apostolate

If you are drawn to selecting one person from among the opposite sex in the Apostolate, recognize what is happening. Stop right there! Discuss the matter with your spiritual director. Be alert! Pray! Fast! Be watchful! Natural danger is stalking you. Satan is seeking to use this chink for his own plans.

If you feel protective toward anyone of the opposite sex, you have already gone through one stage. Now the danger is real. Now your rhythms are at work. Be frank and very watchful; pray and fast much. Satan has put a wedge into the chink.

Exactly the same applies to people outside of the Apostolate. You will be going to the missions. You will have to work with the opposite sex – teenagers, young adults, middle-aged matrons. Follow the same rule exactly. Be watchful for the same signs. (This also applies to women who must deal with men.)

Never, never think that you can help a woman. If any female seeks your advice, tell her honestly and simply that you cannot help her, and hand her over to the nearest woman in your community. Or let the priest handle those situations.

Women of the Apostolate

Because you are more inclined by nature to be 'helpful,' all of you women of Madonna House must be alert. *Never, never even try to help a male staff member, or a man outside of the community, be he a priest, seminarian, religious brother or layperson.* It is impossible that you can be of any help to him. It will inevitably lead to tragedy.

Never, under any circumstance, correspond with any member of the male sex on the pretext of 'helping him out.' Letters are dangerous because we are more uninhibited in letters. Also, they are written proofs of your relations with this person. Suppose the person you are trying to 'help' is psychologically unbalanced, or becomes vengeful when the chips are down, and you have to withdraw your friendship and support. Imagine if those letters were brought out publicly – as they well might be! How many interpretations can be made of the written word, especially words carelessly written?

I know of a woman who was sentenced to life imprisonment because she wanted very much to 'help' a married man. She was utterly innocent of any infidelity to her husband or of any sexual relations with the other woman's husband. But she was foolish; she wrote letters. When the wife of the man was found murdered, the letters were found, and she was condemned on the evidence of those letters for a murder which she never committed! Eleven years later the true murderer confessed, and she was released.

I leave to your imagination how utterly foolish, how completely dangerous, letters may be. This is especially true in the case of priests. You mean well. You try to help. You write. The priest suffers an accident, dies, or becomes ill. The pastor, the police, or some strangers get hold of your letters. Are they letters that any stranger can read? You 'meant well' but maybe you expressed yourself too freely, and now the fat is in the fire!

To sum up these two points:

(1) Never imagine, in any way, that you can help a member of the opposite sex, whoever he may be. Refer him to priests, or to other men, or to much older women. Under no condition carry on a

correspondence with men, whoever they may be. Just don't get involved!

(2) Watch for the feeling of *being protected* and of *being selected*. Women will always respond to the selectivity of men, even if ever so slightly. So never make a confidant of any male in the houses of the Apostolate. By this I mean long conversations, even in public. At no time go for a walk, either on the city streets or in the countryside, with any man whatsoever – even if he is old enough to be your grandfather. Even if he is a bishop, a cardinal, or the pope.

While we were discussing these things, one of the most saintly, holy, innocent members of Madonna House exclaimed at one point: "Gee, I'm glad to hear that! Last summer a young priest kept asking me to take a walk, and I quite naturally went without thinking anything of it. Nothing exceptional transpired, except that he was telling me about his problems, and I didn't know what to do about them. I ask myself now, why did he want to walk alone with me when there were plenty of chairs on the lawn where we could have talked. I also ask myself, why did he want to discuss *his* problems with me who know so little of life." This person has seen the light, and I hope you all will.

So the answer is very simple. Relationships between men and women of the Apostolate must be holy and honest, embracing everybody, never selecting a single person for special confidence. *Do not try to 'help' the opposite sex, and never be alone with them.*

Lovingly yours in Mary,

18

OPENNESS

January 28, 1964

Dearly Beloved,

Again and again, in letters and discussions, I am asked to explain what *openness* is. It seems that this little word creates many difficulties. Yet it is such a simple and clear word.

We understand very well what we mean when someone says: Mrs. Jones held an *open* house last Saturday on the occasion of the Silver Jubilee of her son, Father Jones. It simply means that the private house of Mrs. Jones was *open* to all who wished to come.

We are quite clear when we say that a contemplative order held an *open* house on the occasion of the blessing of the premises by a bishop. It means to us that the hidden (and to us strange) environment of contemplative men or women was available to public viewing on this day.

We speak of people who are *open*. We can read on their faces whatever they think and feel, whereas others are more closed and no one ever knows what they think. We speak with warmth in our voices of places that are *open to all in need*. They admit the poor, the pilgrims, anyone − irrespective of race, color, or creed.

In all these cases, the word *open* or *openness* conveys something positive, something pleasant, something warm and friendly, something that we somehow associate (consciously or subconsciously) with a loving and caring attitude.

Well, we are right. The heart of Christ was *opened* with a lance, and the Church was born on Calvary. Brilliant or ignorant, all of us Christians understand the symbolic thrust of this lance into the heart of God. To all of us it means that God loved us so much that he allowed his heart to be opened in this painful and brutal manner, so that we might find shelter there.

So *openness* must have its roots in love, or it isn't *openness*. We must open ourselves for others to come in and see all the secret chambers of our being. We must open the house of our minds, souls, and hearts to the gaze and investigation and appraisal of others.

But the main topic I would like to discuss with you today is the openness of the members of Madonna House to their spiritual directors, to their superiors, and to one another. We begin with the premise that Christian openness *deals exclusively with oneself and not others.*

Let us see how this truth relates to each of the people mentioned above, for there are many different types of openness:

With Your Spiritual Director

Openness with a spiritual director must be utterly complete, without trying to hide a single corner of ourselves – souls, hearts, minds, or bodies. How can I be 'closed' to my spiritual director? There are endless ways which our corrupt human nature has devised. Let us discuss a few.

We can present a biased, one-sided picture of a situation. There are devious ways in which women, especially, can do this. We can color everything the way we wish. It will not be the whole truth, though it may appear to be.

For instance, a person can begin by saying that she has a problem with 'obedience' because her Department Head asked her to do something stupid. Under the skillful questions of her spiritual director, it develops that the greater problem is not with 'obedience' but with *charity!* Openness with a spiritual director means stating the facts truthfully and relying on his judgment.

When discussing another personality with a spiritual director, *openness* demands that you ask that person to be present (if the matter is grave) so that the other can hear the accusation. If you are in the missions, that part of your letter to your spiritual director which deals with the specific accusations of anyone in your house should be read by the accused person, so that this person might have a chance to write to your spiritual director his or her side of the question. This would be openness.

Do not attempt to handle by yourself even the smallest temptation, considering it too picayune, too unimportant to bring to his attention. Verbally, or in writing if need be, state every little temptation. If you have a director you must be utterly open. Not the tiniest corner of your soul, mind, or heart should be neglected. One grain of sand can stop huge machinery from working. A temptation that is insignificant today can ruin your vocation tomorrow, just because you used your judgment wrongly and were closed to your spiritual director.

If the tragic moment arrives (and it may) when you feel 'out of tune' with your spiritual director, that is a moment of grave danger. This is the time to be so utterly open and receptive that you go to him and state this situation in plain, brief sentences.

You must also be entirely open to accept his judgment and his conclusions. If you are open only in the presentation of your problem and closed to its solution through this holy man, you are only half open ... and that means closed!

This is a very important part of openness and one of the hardest. Note that it always relates to *you* and not to the director. You are not asking the director to open his mind, soul, and heart to you. That is his business. As a general principle you must always be open to others, but others need not necessarily be open to you.

So to clarify: when you have problems with a spiritual director, *you tell him what your problem is, not what you think is wrong with him.* There is a vast difference between the two approaches.

With Your Director General

What is openness with a Director General? It is the same openness that has been discussed in all of the previous pages, but it basically concerns *the outer forum.* The priests, men, and women of the Apostolate may (if they wish) open part of their souls to their respective Director General, especially in that area of their behavior which affects others.

Every act has a moral significance. If one's inner

problems begin to affect the common good, then of course the Directors have a right to ask the person to discuss these problems more deeply. Your openness, however, should forestall their having to ask. You yourself should be ready to be open as every Christian should be.

You need to be open for your own spiritual and apostolic growth as well as the growth of the common good. Unless there is openness among the members and all of their superiors, direction is impossible, and the common good suffers.

I needn't point out how many times some tragic problem has exploded in my face and rocked Madonna House, simply because the members were not as open to me as they should have been. Again and again we have had to 'pick up the pieces' because of this lack of openness.

Why do you think that I give you the obedience of writing me twice a month? It is to make it easier for you to be open with me. It is because I love you and want you to be open in every way, and because I want you especially to grow in wisdom and grace. This is why I desire passionately that you be open with me.

Here again, I draw your attention to what openness is. It begins and ends with the words *I* and *me*. You are open about yourself; you are not discussing others. You state only the facts about the others, never being judgmental about their intentions or their ways of thinking and doing things. If you have difficulty with another, you simply state the bare facts of that difficulty. Leave the rest to God and to your directors. But about yourself you tell the fullness of truth without shame or reticence.

With Your 'Superiors'

The same principle applies to local directors and department heads. At no time do you tell them what you think is wrong with *them*. That's not openness; that is criticism. If you feel you have a just cause, go to them and state it directly, but include in so many words: "I'm sorry, but I was a little upset about your order yesterday. Please tell me what is wrong with *me* that I feel this way."

If it's 'a matter of conscience' that relates to your

local director or a department head, examine *yourself* first. Write or speak to your spiritual director, stating the facts about the other person and the facts, emotions, and reactions about yourself; wait and be open for an answer.

If the matter concerns both inner and outer forum, then write to your spiritual director (or speak to him if you are here) as well as to your director general.

With Your 'Equals'

With your peers, you may choose many different forms of openness. There is the ordinary openness of loving and friendly people, banded together in an Apostolate tending toward perfection. What kind of openness is this? Again it pertains to *you* and only to *you!* You are quite free (and it would be a good idea and in keeping with openness) to tell your brothers and sisters all that it is needful for them to know about you. You can tell them of your background, your family, your education, your skills and interests.

But you *cannot* ask openness from them, nor can you probe them to find out from them anything which they do not wish to reveal! We pray that each and every one of you may come to the openness that I am describing in this letter, for this is the spirit of Madonna House. But always keep in mind: *openness is always about yourself, and not about the other.*

It is not necessary – in the so-called name of 'openness' – to tell your brothers and sisters the problems of your family, such as that your father is an alcoholic or that your mother is in a state institution. Here again we come into a delicate field. Remember that openness is about *you* yourself. You don't have to discuss your parents, ancestors, or siblings.

The 'confidential discussion' of someone else's problem is as far removed from true openness as hell is from heaven. This kind of openness (whose other name is *gossip*) is a sin against the loyalty you should have to Madonna House and to Christian love. One doesn't gossip about, nor open the sores of, confidential problems of the Apostolate. This is like probing the wounds of Christ with dirty fingers. And, I repeat, it is as far removed from real openness as hell is from heaven.

There *is* an openness you can exercise toward another, in order to help that person. In the case of emotional problems, we find that it helps the young ones who come to Madonna House when one of the seniors quite casually says, "Oh yes, I had that headache when I first came. It's of emotional origin, and I can tell you how I dealt with it." This type of openness is based on Christian love, compassion, and empathy.

Under extraordinary circumstances, out of pure charity, when someone is beside themselves with grief (say, about a family member or situation), you might interject that you understand the problem because you have had similar experiences. You say enough to console the person, but you needn't give away any details.

With Other People

Spiritual directors, director generals, local directors, heads of departments, and directors of training – all these are 'superiors' of Madonna House. You must understand that superiors are persons 'set apart' by the very nature of their office. They must lead and teach constantly, both by word and example. Thus, they have to teach about openness as well. Their openness is somewhat different from yours, however, though it is similar in many ways.

How should they be open? Well, in the same way that you must be open. As Thomas Merton says, "They must be humbly open about their shortcomings and their personal difficulties with you." I am as open as a director general could possibly be. If my spiritual director permitted me, I would make a general confession to you – and I mean a confession of *all* my sins.

I certainly do not try to hide my shortcomings or difficulties, and I do not hesitate to apologize when I am wrong. In all my books and articles, I have opened my soul, heart, and mind to you. Soon you will get the *History of the Apostolate.** It has been one of the most difficult things for me to write, but – in obedience to my spiritual director – I have had to be utterly open with you in this history.

This is the type of openness that your directorate and your superiors must have with you. And this is the way that *you must be* when you become a superior. But God help any superior who has the wrong kind of openness ... one that develops out of his or her personal 'needs' or one that puts the problems of superiors on the not-yet-strong-enough shoulders of the young! It behooves superiors to keep much to themselves.

To conclude: I don't know if I have clarified openness for you. The essence of it is that one talks about oneself and not about the others. So it is completely *'off base'* for two members to discuss what is wrong with a third person; whereas, to discuss one's own shortcomings is to be *on the beam* – Christ's beam.

Likewise, someone telling a 'superior' what is wrong with him or her is *way off base* and not in keeping with the spirit of our Apostolate. If there is really something wrong, you have the ways I've described for dealing with the matter.

Lovingly yours in Mary,

THE FRAGILE VIRTUE OF CHASTITY

February 21, 1964

Dearly Beloved,

My letter on men and women in the Apostolate evidently made you think and clarified for you this area of our lives. Even if it might be repetitious, I want to state once more that this letter was based on scientific facts as presented by Sister Mary Andrew, a doctor of psychology.

Its main purpose was, especially, to make the men of the Apostolate (but the women as well) realize that the physical makeup of a man 'tends to union' with a woman long before he is aware of it. In other words, it means that the natural bodily rhythms of a man are 'ahead of' his conscious self. This is a fact little known to the average layman, and one to remember. These rhythms begin with *selection,* continue into *protectiveness,* and then reach the 'conscious stage' of wishing to be close to the person he likes.

People under a promise of chastity should be aware of this, and *should not indulge in selectivity or in the protectiveness of a person of the opposite sex.* The women of the Apostolate, realizing this, must remove themselves from such subconscious selectivity and protection, thereby helping men not to be tempted against the virtue of chastity.

But this doesn't mean that a man should *not* protect every woman in the Apostolate. This is part of his being a man! But note the difference: his protectiveness must be directed to all.

The call to chastity, however, means much more than this. Stop for a minute and prayerfully meditate on the meaning of our chastity. Do this especially before the Blessed Sacrament. You will see once more how the immense wisdom of God never leaves his Church, his Mystical Body, in times of trials and difficulties, but always answers her needs.

Consider our world today. Reams have been written and are still being written about sexual morality. Classical Rome at its decline does not seem to have been as decadent as today's so-called Christian Civilization has become. Even the people of what we consider 'backward countries' are simply horrified at the moral decline of Europe, England, and the North American continent. There is more morality and an obedience to moral laws in pagan countries than in the so-called Christian ones.

The worship of sex and of 'the body beautiful' has reached proportions of idolatry. The allied vices of drunkenness, drug addiction, juvenile delinquency, illegitimacy, and emotional disorders have risen to epidemic proportions. It is a sad state of affairs that we behold.

Gently, Christ bends down to his Church in distress and calls forth some of its members (already in the thousands) to a new apostolate – a remedy for this idolatry. He has called into being various forms of the lay apostolate. He obviously wants to show chaste dedicated youth to a world that is drunk with immorality and self-indulgence. He wants them to live this dedication to chastity right in the marketplaces of the world.

There is an interesting dimension to this call of Christ. Have you noticed that he often calls very attractive men and women? Again his wisdom shines, for if the members of such apostolates were only the unattractive, the world would not take notice of them. God is wise; he chooses the best as ambassadors of his beloved virtue of chastity.

So, each one of you, my dearly beloved, has been chosen to manifest that virtue in the marketplace. This virtue is so much needed to counteract the idolatry of sex in our day and age. *What a responsibility! What a glorious task!* I hope that you are beginning to see that this promise of chastity is vitally important to the Apostolate, and brings souls back to a sense of balance in a world drunk with sex.

You are good. You love God. I feel certain that you desire to serve him in this beautiful and chaste way. But you are young and inexperienced. You might be innocent as doves, but you are not yet 'as wise as serpents.' So I write these letters to clarify, to warn, and to encourage.

I have already written to you that, under no circumstances, should young men and women imagine that they can be of any help to their own age group. But to the women of the Apostolate, I add this warning: you cannot be of help to *any man* no matter what his age or his state in life. This is beyond your competence. You have no graces from God to do so. You must not even try, for it might be an occasion of sin or, even worse, an occasion of scandal.

We hear of the influence that our members have on married people, teenagers, seminarians, and priests. It is a power that comes to them from God and their own cooperation with his grace, and it flows from their promise of chastity. Parents have found us wonderful examples for their children. Seminarians take heart when they hear Madonna House mentioned. And all seem to say, "If they can be chaste, so can we."

Chastity is a fragile virtue; it must be guarded. Many depend upon some of you for moral support. But suppose one of our members spent a long time with a member of the opposite sex, sitting in a kitchen somewhere, drinking coffee. Maybe they are talking about God and the things of God. You and I know that there isn't a shadow of impurity in that meeting. But what do other people see? Perhaps, because of your past faithfulness, they have found that they can fight temptations to adultery or fornication. Suddenly, their 'lifeline' seems to snap because they question *your* chastity. Can you imagine their disappointment? You would be responsible for their doubts.

We of the Apostolate must be especially aware of what our chastity means to the world today. What a beacon of light we are supposed to be! Yes, the love and wisdom of God has bent with tenderness over the world and has called us to show the face of chastity in the marketplace. Chastity is one of the jewels in that crown of virtues which the world needs.

So, dearly beloved in Christ, knowing your innocence and purity of heart, knowing that you do not want to convey these false impressions to others, I implore you to be watchful, to think seriously and deeply whenever you are dealing with a member of the opposite sex. Try never to be alone with him or her in a separate room or even in a place filled with people. Never allow a shadow of disappointment to enter the hearts of those who watch, and to whom your indiscreet action may be the last straw for one who is tempted.

God love you! I do.

Lovingly yours in Mary,

Cathman

BOREDOM AND SOCIAL AMENITIES

February 24, 1964

Dearly Beloved,

Today I would like to discuss boredom and good manners. There are some among us who, occasionally or for long periods, feel a sense of boredom. Do you know what boredom is? It is a kind of *death* in a human being.

It means that people have let their interior resources dry up and have reached a sort of coma that is akin to death. It means their motivation is at an absolutely low ebb. Boredom is a forerunner of many emotional problems, even mental breakdowns. It may lead to alcoholism, or to drug addiction, in a desperate effort to escape that sense of uselessness and failure.

In his youth, a man dreams that he will achieve 'great

things.' Then he gets a job on a production line where, for eight hours a day, he keeps putting a bolt into a hole. He never sees the completion of his work. He begins to get bored. He feels he isn't contributing anything to anybody. He is just a cog in a machine.

It will become worse in our computerized society. A person will just sit before a panel and push buttons. Our industrialized highly-technological society creates this monotony. It is understandable that anybody would be bored under such conditions.

But when *nurses* become bored with their job, when *teachers* become bored with their work, when *priests* get bored with being a priest – or when a member of Madonna House is bored with being a lay apostle! – then the breath of Satan is upon that person. His or her motivation has 'fallen asleep,' has gone comatose.

And what is (or should be) the chief motivation of nurses and teachers and priests and lay apostles? Love ... love of humanity, at least. Love for a cause, and dedication to it! For Christians, the love of God as well. For us, then, boredom spells danger. Grave danger.

I ask you, how can I be bored with writing personal letters to each of you day in and day out when I love you? How can I be bored teaching the shining truths of God, even to the half-listening ears of youth? It just isn't possible. When you are in love with God, it is *impossible* to be bored! Those of us who have become bored have either ceased to love or are in danger of ceasing to be *in love*. This would be a first step to a breakup of the family.

Granted, we do live in routine. We get up at a certain time; we eat at a certain time; we pray at a certain time; when we work, we work in a sort of routine. There are always the same things to do, whether in Combermere or Timbuktu, and that becomes monotonous.

Being human, we try to escape this monotony of 'things' through withdrawal into our private selves. We desire some kind of change from dealing constantly with 'other people,' whether the public at large or our own family members. These breaks are provided by retreats, days of recollection, holidays, and by other means.

But that *boredom* should enter the mind, heart, and soul of a member of Madonna House? That is hard for me to imagine, unless he or she is beset with temptations, unless Satan is present and whispering his weird half-truths.

How is it possible to be bored when we believe the marvelous words of St. Paul that *we can make up what is wanting* in the sufferings of Christ. In his infinite mercy, God calls us through grace to become *co-redeemers* of the world with him! Do you realize this, dearly beloved ... that you are co-redeemers with Christ? He has given you this immense power. So this seemingly grayish routine of ours isn't gray at all, but resplendent with light. At least it is in our power to make it so.

How does this work in our daily lives? If my secretary, sitting here typing letters, 'offers up' the tiring task of hitting those keys hour after hour under my dictation, then she is co-redeeming the world with Christ. The cooks in our fieldhouses, working with scraps and donations each day to make the 'eternal stew,' can bring joy and hope to others throughout the world, if they have a mind to. The men – getting up for early-morning chores, performing ordinary routine jobs, driving cars and trucks, cleaning light fixtures, repairing and maintaining our buildings – can save souls from the jaws of hell!

How in the name of the All-Holy can one become bored with this typing, this meat-cutting, this potato-peeling, this repairing and cleaning, with all the other routine jobs, if one knows in faith that *everything helps to redeem the world* and to render glory to God!

Stop for a moment and think of a member of Madonna House 'being bored'! Isn't it incomprehensible? In the light of what I have just written, the answer should stare you in the face. This person has allowed his or her love of God and of others to sink into a coma. The remedy for this affliction is prayer, fasting, spiritual reading, retreats, days of recollection, and the examination of our consciences. For boredom spells danger to the soul. Satan is there!

The Social Amenities

Now I want to speak of ordinary social manners. They include posture, ways of sitting, ways of eating, certain niceties such as men opening the doors for women, carrying their parcels and so on. In Madonna House, our previous education or so-called 'class background' does not matter at all. Scripture says that God is not a respecter of persons; but we *do* place great value on charity.

You may not know which fork to use for salad, but charity makes it very simple. Without false shame, you simply acknowledge that you don't know and ask someone for help. If you have been accustomed to eating with your knife, you'll soon desist because you will see that no one else does. You will realize that putting your knife in your mouth makes everyone tense, because you might cut yourself. And it just isn't charitable to make people tense.

Posture is an important part of the Apostolate. A saint is one who teaches by the way he sits, the way he stands, the way he walks. Let that be a lesson for you. Consider how a saint would sit, stand, or walk; then do likewise. Again, charity demands that you assume a posture that doesn't offend others.

Besides these good manners, charity consists in being concerned about the others around you. It is not good manners to engage in an argumentative discussion, and you know what I mean when I say 'argument.' I don't mean a dialogue, in which you can learn from others by exchanging ideas politely, charitably, and peacefully. By argumentative, I mean that you hold onto your own ideas no matter what. The discussion becomes heated, unpleasant, and it is uncharitable.

Politeness and good social manners really stem from love. Your concern should be for the other person. So please note this, for this is a very important part of the Apostolate. *Being concerned for others should be for you like breathing.*

Can you imagine Our Lady, like a lump, sitting with her two elbows on the table and taking no part in the conversation? Can you? I can't. Doesn't the Gospel give you a tremendous picture of the graciousness, gentleness, and good manners of Christ? And I am sure that Mary was like him. In spirit, go to Nazareth! Then act in our houses as if you were in the presence of Jesus, Mary, and Joseph, and you will automatically be a gentleman or a gentle woman.

> Love in Christ, the Gentleman – and in Our Lady, the Gentle Woman,

ON BEING MISJUDGED

February 27,1964

Dearly Beloved,

I have had several people write to me about problems of general interest, so I will answer them in this letter. They concern *justifications, misunderstandings,* and *free time.*

About Justifications
Again and again I have stressed the fact that we must not justify ourselves. This attitude is substantiated by Scripture, especially by Christ's silence during his passion. I agree with you that it is a bit difficult to know when to justify oneself and when to keep silence when corrected. It is especially difficult if one greatly desires (as we all should) to strive for perfection.

Let us look up the word *justify* in the dictionary. It

says: To show, to be just, to vindicate, to defend; also to make right and just, to adjust or fit, to make exact. Synonyms for this word are *absolve, acquit, approve, authorize, clear, defend.*

The dictionary goes on to state: "There might sometimes be excuses which can *not* be justified, for that which *can* be justified does not need an excuse." Let us look at this sentence and see how many things will become clear, especially in the light of the phrase, *that which can be justified does not need to be excused.*

Such an attitude fosters a peaceful, loving approach to life. For example, your local director (or anyone for that matter) accuses you of failing to 'live out' your vocation. This might be true. So you thank them and say that you will try to do better, for you know that every Christian can always do better. Until we die, we can always improve.

On the other hand, this accusation might *not* be true. You are trying your best at the moment, and that is all that anyone can do. In that sense, you are not a bad member of Madonna House, but you will *become* a bad one if you start to justify yourself.

Though the accusation might be unjust, you will have great merit if you simply remain silent. God is working in the other person's soul as well, and eventually the person will either apologize to you or, if this isn't done, you will grow in grace and sanctity. You will be more Christlike than you have ever been before.

Another example: You have been told to take charge of some event in a house. There will be a party or some affair at which there will be priests and lay people, and you are put in charge of it all. You are also preparing dinner for the family.

You do all of this with a happy heart, believing that you are managing it all very well. When everything is over and the director of the house returns, you report in a nice way, satisfied that you have managed so many things at once. But *you appear to stress the fact that you have managed the kitchen well.* The director gets the mistaken idea that you were occupied in the kitchen to the neglect of the guests and reprimands you.

Trustingly, like a child, you explain again how it was,

not with the intention of justifying yourself (for there is nothing to justify; it is a misunderstanding). You say that evidently you expressed yourself poorly, for in your heart the kitchen didn't matter, you were just glad that all went well. Remember, this is an explanation, not a justification, because there was nothing to justify or excuse; all *did* go well.

Be simple about these matters. When your director doesn't understand you, then you make yourself clear. But suppose she *still* doesn't understand you. Well, here you rejoice! Now you think of the Eighth Beatitude. It becomes almost a false accusation. Of course, that depends on her intention. She might be positive in her own mind that she understands you rightly, but you could care less about the outcome.

You have made the effort to explain a semantic difficulty, and you rest on that. You win graces; and eventually, in God's good time, the director will see the matter as it really was, so all will eventually be well.

If you are accused of doing something that you didn't do, then you have two choices, spiritually speaking: (1) you can simply state the truth, which again is not justification in the exact sense of the word, but a statement of what really happened, or (2) you can remain silent and 'take the gaff.' This latter is considered heroic in the spiritual life and is very commendable.

You see how hard it is to answer these questions because we are dealing with intangibles. You are not trying to justify yourself; you are merely straightening out a misconception. If it concerns you alone, however, you might take the high road of heroism and be silent.

To justify oneself *wrongly* would be something like this: I come into the kitchen and find a messy table, knives lying around that should be put away, etc. I 'blow my top' at the person in charge of the kitchen. If she starts giving me long excuses that she told the girls to do it, that the men came in and messed it up, and so forth and so on, that is a wrong justification of oneself. Because she is the person in charge, *she is responsible* to see that the mess is cleaned up, *no matter who did it or what happened.*

To give you an example from real life: I was in Ottawa, in the midst of founding the Friendship House there, when I got a long-distance call from Toronto. The secretary of the Cardinal wanted me to come to his office immediately. Naturally, I went at once. In the meantime I found out that one of our volunteers (a woman who had been highly recommended to us by a well-known monsignor) had gone berserk. She had gotten drunk, gathered up a lot of beer bottles, went over to the Polish rectory, and smashed its windows.

I was in Ottawa; I had nothing to do with the situation. The person in charge of the Toronto House was the one officially responsible, but I knew better than to say so to the Cardinal. He wiped the floor with me, and rightly so, because *I was the highest authority* in Friendship House and should *bear the brunt of responsibility*.

I took it unflinchingly. When he was finished, I quietly handed him the Monsignor's letter of recommendation so that, without defending myself, the situation would be made 'right and just.' The Cardinal apologized, but he needn't have. I was responsible, so I was the one who had to 'take the gaff.'

So when you are unjustly accused, say the name of Jesus and consider in your heart: "Will my answer make things 'right and just'? Am I the only one accused, and do I wish to be heroic and silent?" Then act accordingly.

Since *justify* also means *to defend,* you must always defend *the other person* if there is occasion to do so. If some member of the family falsely accuses another of something they haven't done, and you know the true situation, then it is your duty to speak up.

I know that I haven't done a very good job of explaining this, but it is a difficult business. The key lies in your intention, but at no time should it worry or upset you. You should always be in perfect peace about it. It's *the lack of peace* that can damage souls.

About Misunderstandings
The dictionary defines *misunderstanding* as: to understand wrongly, to fail to understand, to disagree.

Here we enter the realm of psychology rather than that of theology.

Consider that misunderstandings mean to *understand wrongly, or fail to understand.* Why do we fail to understand? Mostly it is because we hear what we want to hear and see what we want to see. Our powers of perception are very often limited by our emotional state. Semiconsciously or unconsciously, we select what we want to see and hear. Most misunderstandings arise because of this.

In addition, we 'project' ourselves. I had an example of this one morning at a meeting of the department heads. One member had been slowing down on the job and I suggested that, since we all love her, we work together to help her to speed up.

There was a moment of silence; none of the seniors seemed to think well of my suggestion. We had a little discussion, nothing big, but it became apparent that none of the seniors wanted to 'move in' on the staff worker because they all had, at one time or another, slowed down under emotional stress themselves.

They were all sitting there, projecting themselves *as if* they were that person. They were reacting to my suggestion, not as *she* would react (that was an unknown quantity) but as they would react *if they were she.* We clarified the matter speedily, but here was the beginning of many misunderstandings, had it not been clarified.

Emotional reactions are at the bottom of most misunderstandings in the Apostolate. Of course, there is also the desire to be well thought of, to put one's own point across, to have everyone's approval. And sometimes we use wrong words to express our ideas, and we end up with people misunderstanding what we've said. Because of that, our ideas are not clearly shared.

One important reason why we often misunderstand each other (and it should be constantly fought against!) is an emotional dislike of one person for another. As you know, there is a big difference between *like* and *love.* Here, our emotional prejudices must give way to caritas.

About the Use of Free Time

Now, let us talk about charity in connection with free time. Suppose that you have an hour or two off, and you are faced with the following possibilities:

(1) You know that your local director needs help in some way or another.

(2) You know that one or more of the other people in your house are in need of some help. For example, the demands of hospitality in a given house is keeping a one member away from her job, which you know is urgent; perhaps you could take her place for a while.

(3) You, however, are interested in using your free time to do something for the gift shop or to beautify the house.

(4) Perhaps you feel that you should do some correspondence; a friend in trouble wants to hear from you; your mother has been waiting for a letter from you; a young nephew has been writing to you about his problems.

You make a choice and, let us say, you are on your way to do some copper work for the gift shop. Another member of Madonna House meets you; knowing that you have some free time, she asks you to translate a Latin hymn. You finish that, and someone else asks you to look up some symbols for him.

What are the proper order of charity in this example? Frankly, there is no one who can tell you this. This is where your free will has to make its *own* decision.

If I were asked to give an order of charity, however, I would say that:

(1) Hospitality to guests should take precedence over everything else.

(2) The local director's needs must be met, if they are genuine and urgent.

(3) The needs of the other members who might ask me to do this or that must be carefully examined; and perhaps I would say that I was very sorry, but that I had an important letter to write (letters to parents and immediate relatives would be very important).

(4) The gift shop would be the next step.

(5) Other things would come after these.

But I wouldn't be at all worried if I did not follow this sequence, because the free time which belongs to me by the grace of God and his mercy is at his disposal. So no matter what I do, if I have the intention of loving, then I have done the right thing.

I hope this clarifies the matter for those who have asked me. If not, let me hear from you.

Lovingly yours in the Lord of Wisdom,

LOYALTY AND LETTERS

March 6, 1964

Dearly Beloved,

Life in Madonna House goes something like this. First, you come to Combermere as a 'working guest' to participate in our life. If you become interested in joining our family, you stay here a while to soak up the life more fully. When you're accepted as an Applicant, you are given some courses in our history and spirituality.

If it seems to be your vocation, you become a Staff Worker and take promises of poverty, chastity, and obedience for one year. You renew your promises periodically until, after eight or ten years, you make a lifetime commitment.

During your training time here, you will meet all types of people – bishops, priests, seminarians, missionaries, lay people, married and single, young and old, VIP's and humble folk. You may encounter the atheist and the agnostic, the dedicated and the fallen-away. They will be Catholic, Protestant, Jewish, Orthodox, and unorthodox individuals. And they will come from many countries and cultures, for Madonna House is a crossroads of the world, a place where the four winds meet.

Because it's the nature of our Apostolate to be so open and available, visitors of all types may happen to talk to one member of the Apostolate more than to anyone else. Perhaps they will get to know one of you better than they know the others. That makes them feel 'in,' especially if they know several of you well. That's understandable, for those who come to us are usually predisposed to like us. That's why they come.

They also come for information about the Apostolate. They do not always differentiate your status here; they do not know whether you are a long-term guest, a fledgling member, or a seasoned mission-hand. Usually they bunch you all together as part and parcel of this lovable whole that is Madonna House.

I don't want to offend you, but just to state the obvious truth: if they had met you, young and inexperienced as you are, *outside* of Madonna House, it might be that they would not pay any attention to you. You can't imagine a bishop casually meeting one or two young people, becoming specifically interested in them, remembering them with a view to having further dealings with them. This is outside the scope of a bishop's normal relationship with the laity.

If, by chance, you visited the homes of some families who come to Cana Colony,* you wouldn't expect that – after a few visits like that – you'd find yourself being invited to address the Christian Family Movement. No one would think you were qualified to do that.

But if you are thought to be a *member* of the Madonna House Apostolate, then bishops and priests, nuns

---

*A week-long vacation camp in a nearby county, run by Madonna House during the summer months, for families with children.

and seminarians, single and married people would listen with interest and respect to your opinions, *especially on the Apostolate, its foundations and goals.*

You will find that, if you go to a mission house where there are very few Madonna House members, where there is a homey atmosphere, where it's easy for people to get to know you individually, all of the above will be enhanced.

I'm sure that people will like you for yourself, because you are a likeable person. But do not make the mistake of thinking that this is the only reason why people are kind and interested and inquiring. You are important to them *because you are a member of an Apostolate – a whole with which they totally identify you.*

Should you leave the Apostolate (or be transferred from one fieldhouse to another), their reactions will be different. If you try to keep in contact with people whom you met through Madonna House, you will find out that – in the long run – people keep their allegiance to the Apostolate, not to the individual.

Though they might like you and sympathize with you, your relationship with them will eventually come to an end. After all, they were attracted to you in the first place because you sold what you possessed, took up your cross, and followed Christ in a rugged lay-apostolic way. And should you choose not to continue on that path....

Be that as it may, you have to get it into your lovely heads that you have made these friends, not as an individual in your own right, but as a member of an Apostolate. Whatever you write to those friends you have made through the Apostolate is a reflection, not only on you personally, but on the Apostolate as well.

Now, let's take the case of a member who has been in one mission house and has made many friends. She is then transferred to another house. Let us presume, for sake of an example, that this person is not happy about it (humanly speaking) but she obeys anyway. During the slow stage of readjustment, she goes through all kinds of emotional upsets. She lacks the desire to express them to her spiritual director and her superiors. So she proceeds to write about her emotional states and reactions to those acquainted with the Apostolate whom she considers personal friends.

What is the reaction of those friends outside of the Apostolate? As an individual staff member, you may not know their reactions, but we of the directorate do. These people write to us, or they simply go to the local director of the former mission house. They bring your letters along, and discuss them.

They wonder why you do not seem as dedicated as they thought you were. Or else they demand 'explanations' and want to know why you are being so shabbily treated. They comment that *now* they are getting the real 'low-down' on the Apostolate – a look behind the scenes.

Whatever their reaction might be, this sort of thing does not do the Apostolate any good, nor you any good. So please do not use the friends whom you made in the Apostolate to 'blow your stack' and give vent to your emotional problems, difficulties, or black moods. That would be both discourteous and uncharitable.

Do not 'gossip' with them about the private affairs of Madonna House. Such letters would be disloyal to the Apostolate (which means to God). Pray over it, and be very careful not to harm God's works, for this is one thing that arouses God's just anger. And who wants to enter the awesome anger of God?

Elsewhere, I have written to you about The Alms of Words* and how they must be thoughtfully, graciously ('with grace'), given to those in need. This applies to words on paper as much as to verbal conversations. People are desperately hungry and thirsty for your love and friendship; *do not deny it to them.* But remember, these gifts are from God! You are but a channel for his mercies.

Lovingly yours in Jesus Christ
Our Lord,

*Letter of October 1, 1962. (*Dearly Beloved,* Vol. 1, page 275)

SEEDS OF LOVE AND FORGIVENESS

July 2, 1964

Dearly Beloved,

Recently I received several letters from one of our members in the Far East. Her letters made me stop and think. She raises some profound missionary questions. One concerns the whole missionary apostolate to the Moslems; the other concerns adaptation to the East. Here are my answers:

Yes, I understand exactly what you are sensing. You feel that there is an impenetrable wall around Islam; and deep down inside, hidden somewhere beyond the sight of human beings − and perhaps unknown to the Moslems themselves − there is a fundamental coldness, a cruelty, a certain pride that (according to Mohammed) shouldn't be there, but nevertheless is.

True, they have a missionary spirit. They are zealous, loyal, true to their religion. They believe in God; they revere Mary. They consider Christ a great prophet. The roots of our faith grow from the same biblical soil. Judaism, Christianity, and Islam all have a common father in Abraham, and the Bible is revered by both. In a sense, the Old Testament is the mother of the Koran, as it is the mother of the New Testament.

But one thing seems absent: caritas. The Moslems believe in the sword, in conquest. Their history, their subconscious, their spiritual dreams are filled with the greatness of Islam. They often take to force, whereas the Hindu is gentle and peace-loving and seems to understand caritas better. Strangely enough, the Moslem knows how to value the fruits of caritas − hospitality, almsgiving, and love (at least for his Moslem brother).

I would say that Islam is still in the process of development, as far as religion is concerned, much as the

Jews were for thousands of years. The Jews expected the Messiah; but Islam, when the Messiah came, acknowledged him only as a prophet, so they are marching over a longer road.

For them, the beginning of Christianity will have to be the belief that God has come – has been incarnated among us – that the real messiah has come to them, even though their belief in Mohammed has blotted out his image. Yet they believe also in Allah, the true God. In centuries to come, there will be changes, but note the words I use: in centuries to come.

This means that we who have been so strangely called to divine history are little signposts of the truth that God has come. That makes our little seed of belief that Jesus is God even smaller than a mustard seed.

Yes, there is this to consider and meditate upon, but as far as you are concerned, there is more. In your case, that more is a very special grace from God. You are called to exemplify in your person, hiddenly but vividly, Christ's great commandment: Love thy neighbor as thyself. In a few cases, like that of your good self, the Lord asks us to go higher and to love our enemies!

Moslems have been the enemies of your people; they have made martyrs of your people for generations. For centuries your people have harbored, in their unconscious and conscious life, a great fear and an emotional hatred for them.

You are asked now to till the soil of these Moslem souls and to plant the tiny seeds of love. The furrow that you are beginning will be long; and you will not realize how long, until you see God face to face. That furrow will extend for generations. Members of Madonna House will, in turn, plant seeds of their lives in the mission which you are pioneering.

That is what I see without even visiting your house. This is what my intuition tells me about you and the Moslems. Strangely, I rejoice that this is so! That one of my spiritual daughters is so clearly called by the Lord to love her enemies. You will do this simply by being among them and witnessing to the fact that Jesus is not only a great prophet, but that he is Allah himself! They will come to see that Allah is One-in-Three and Three-in-One.

Look at your vocation and your mission in this world with the eyes of God. It is already resplendent in glory, in proportion to your perseverance and your understanding. You have been called to a tremendous task. I envy you with holy envy.

This member of Madonna House also wrote that she had met a nun who had lived in India for a long time and whose Order still had no vocations. She was often confronted by religious and laity (and even by the police!) with this one question: "How long have you been in the country, and how many vocations do you have?" Invariably, she had to answer that she had been in India for twelve years but, as far as any native vocations were concerned, there were none. Her Order was replenished from the West.

That nun didn't mind the personal humiliation she experienced or the reflection which seemed to be cast upon her Order. What worried her was that the whole Roman Catholic Church was not adapting to India. She knew there would be many vocations if this adaptation were made.

One reason for the lack of vocations, she said, is that her Order strives to be a very modern and active one, though it does have a contemplative side. The nun went on to say that *the active life has never impressed the East.* Gandhi, among others, was tremendously impressed by a Trappist monastery which he had seen in Africa.

Another problem the nun mentioned was the fallacy of sending native vocations to Europe or North America for training. Those who were sent did not persevere because the cultural gap was too great. I agree fully with that nun. Yet I feel that our Apostolate must be active, and we must also be contemplatives.

How do I reconcile these two in our Eastern missions? Very simply. All of us in Madonna House must be 'contemplative' in the sense that I try to express in my writings. Perhaps this type of contemplation has a Russian accent; nevertheless, it blends with the rest of the East, for we Russians are predominately people of the East ... particularly in the religious sense.

Over and above the fact that all of us must become contemplative, we should in future times have a truly Eastern-type, quiet, hidden, inactive community or group.

This is how I visualize it: Someday we may have a social center someplace in the Far East. And next to it, living poorly and humbly (yet not quite in the destitution of those around them), there will be a group of people who will pray and do penance.

They will earn their living at handicrafts, so dearly beloved by the East, and be as hidden as Charles de Foucauld was in his Sahara Desert, as the Russian saints were in their forest poustinias. Yet hospitality and availability – such as these others had – will be shown to those who come to talk to our staff about God and the things of God.

Yes, dimly but clearly do I foresee this. Someday it will take place, for the 'soul' of Madonna House is open to new ideas, and to traditional ideas in new settings, using them flexibly and pliantly always to speak of God. It remembers that charity, hospitality, and availability remain its foundation stones, but it knows there are a thousand ways to 'cry the Gospel' with one's life.

These are my answers, written for you and for posterity. I hope it helps to enlarge your 'vision of the whole.'

Lovingly yours in Mary,

THOUGHTS ABOUT MISSIONS

July 16, 1964

Dearly Beloved,

I would like to discuss the essence and spirit of missions, especially those in foreign lands. Today, the whole world can be considered mission territory. All places are mission territory, even our own hearts, souls, and minds, and those of our neighbors.

I must confess that this letter was spearheaded by one of our members in the foreign missions. She is very open, has great love and trust in God and in the directorate of Madonna House, and constantly reports everything that happens. She has many problems, but the gist of them is her struggle with adaptation.

This last word must be taken in a very broad sense. There is the adaptation to a new culture which includes food, habits of thinking and speaking, climate, and a new language. But to all lay apostles in foreign missions (as this team is) other forms of adjustment constantly present themselves: adaptation to the ways of thinking and acting of the apostolate itself, as presented by bishops, priests, and religious.

There is the adaptation to the constant stream of lay people who come to the foreign missions — the trained and the untrained, the totally dedicated and the temporarily dedicated. Some come in search of God; they really desire to work in a mission apostolate, and are qualified to do so. Some are in search of adventure as well. A few are emotionally disturbed people, who drift across the apostolic horizon of the missions as shadows which disturb and complicate life.

A wise and experienced priest once told me: "Every newcomer in the mission field will face an older missionary (or many of them), each of whom will want to turn the newcomer into 'an image of himself'! Do not allow this to happen to you or to any of your spiritual children. Teach them to form and shape themselves into an 'image of God' that is faithful to the constitutions and spirituality of Madonna House. That's what God wants."

Therefore, you have to prepare yourself maturely, as an adult, to face a barrage of opinions and ideas with which older missionaries may assault you. It takes a great deal of maturity – emotional, intellectual, and spiritual – to be able to listen peacefully to the image of yourself, as presented by the bishop of a given missionary diocese or by the priests and religious, not to mention the many volunteers who come and go. And in the mind of the average villager, there are the lingering impressions made by those drifting or dedicated lay people who lived there before you came.

Yes, it takes maturity. It also takes intelligence, peace of heart, an ability to listen, an ability to answer lovingly but firmly. Gently, you can point out that these are wonderful insights, that it is extremely kind of the person or persons to enlighten your team with these marvelous ideas. You are thankful for their advice.

Listening to all of these opinions can be confusing, however, and they should be reported to me and to our directorate. Those in distant missions should remember that, no matter how far they are geographically removed from our center in Combermere, they can find guidance, help, and protection at the other end of a postage stamp. And a directorate that is pledged to stand behind them unto death.

So our members everywhere must be very simple and just say that these ideas and clarifications will be reported to the directors of Madonna House, that they themselves can only be a listening post because the final decision must be made in Combermere. If that is done, then peace of heart and mind and soul will abide, not only in the local director, but in the whole team. Remember that the directors in Combermere exist to take responsibility for such decisions, and they will not compromise with the spirituality and Constitutions of our Apostolate.

It is also to be remembered that the organization of a mandate and its acceptance require two parties: the head of the diocese and the Madonna House directors in

Combermere. The directorate prayerfully considers the mandate offered by a bishop for a team in his mission area, and discusses it with him. When 'the chips are down' and all the advice and suggestions have been taken into consideration, the mandate will be accepted or refused. It will certainly be rejected if it does not conform to the spirit of the Apostolate.

The duty of the local director and the other members in the missions (or anywhere else) is to report and to keep the directorate fully aware of every idea they receive. Then, and then alone, can the decision be a good one. This doesn't mean that the local directors and their staff do not help to shape these decisions. Love and trust is a two-way affair, and the directors in Combermere try to listen – not only with their ears and mind but with their whole being – to every opinion, suggestion, advice, or clarification they are given. So let the hearts of local directors and their staff be at peace, for the truths that we hold are, in a manner of speaking, self-evident.

There is only one thing that can really disrupt a mission, and that is *a lack of charity* among its members. To me the success of a mission is never in its works, in its wondrous ability to learn new techniques, in its intellectual growth. It rests – first, foremost, and last – in the love that the members of a team have for one another. For this I pray now and always.

Lovingly yours in Mary,

HIS GIFTS FOR YOU

December 9, 1964

Dearly Beloved,

This exciting year of 1964 brings us once again to the celebration of the Birthday of Christ. More and more deeply I feel my utter poverty before God and you, my beloved children in him. I cannot even bring you my heart because you already possess it, as does he. I have given it totally to him long ago, but he allows me to share it with you.

So what shall I bring you on the holy night of his coming? I must turn to him and beg him to fill my empty hands with his gifts for you. In his tenderness and compassion, he hears my prayer, so here are my gifts for you, dearly beloved. They come from his hands through mine.

I give you *joy* – the immense joy that he alone can give, and that I hope will fill your hearts from now on until you meet him! And I offer you this joy in the beautiful chalice of his *peace,* which no one can take away from you. Cherish them both. Like a glowing flame in a burnished lantern, they will light your way in the thousand darknesses that his love will guide you through.

I give you *a lance,* gold-tipped like the crown that the Magi offered him, to open your hearts to him in everyone whom you meet. Then you can possess him constantly in your neighbor.

I give you *myrrh,* that bitter herb so sweet to those who fully accept it, for it is the symbol of a soul in love with God, who wants to share his whole life of joy, of peace, of suffering.

I give you *frankincense.* The frankincense that you will become when you accept all the other gifts that I have mentioned. It will make you and your life one of burning before the Lord. May it burn so well and so fragrantly that you will set the world on fire with your burning.

Finally – because of his goodness, compassion and love – he allows me to give you *himself,* a Child. By holding him even for the space of a few seconds, you will become childlike. Remember that the door to heaven is only as big as a child.

Before you is the world. A world of strife, pain, love, and hate. A world in turmoil. I know, however, that the gifts he has given me to 'pass on' to you will give you power to overcome the world. So I close this tiny gift-filled letter with an immense alleluia of joy and gladness that we are one in his Mother before his crib in Bethlehem – one in our vocation, one in our love, one in our gratitude, one in our joy.

Lovingly yours in Christ the Child,

Catherine

VOCATION WITHOUT COMPROMISE

December 29, 1964

Dearly Beloved,

I've been reading the letters and diaries of a particular staff worker, meditating on all she has said ... and all she hasn't said. There are moments in everyone's life when words do not come easily. The heart is so filled with emotion, and there is a deep realization of the joy, the light, the mercy and goodness of God. Time must elapse before an attempt is made to put one's thoughts on paper, to express to another human being even a tenth part of what is in the heart.

Father Callahan and Father Briere thought my letter to this person should be shared with all the staff. Read it aloud, discuss it in your various houses, and see if it pinpoints for you the essence of our life. The question of "What is the vocation of Madonna House?" occasionally raises its head in the soul of the staff. This might help to solve it.

It is eminently fitting that we should be reading your diary during Christmas week because you lead us to Bethlehem. You lead us straight up the narrow path to the very essence of Christmas – God taking the form of a servant. For by going where you have gone, living the way you do (probably without realizing it yourself), you are not so much identifying yourself with the people who surround you as you are with Christ himself.

This is what I call *identification with the Lord*. This identification is a hidden thing and not clear to the one who thus identifies himself. It is a mysterious thing, for one who makes this identification *enters into the mystery* of the Incarnation. He can enter into it only by the grace of God. Man by himself cannot do this.

Strangely enough it does not consist of poverty, of rats in the eaves, of mad dogs outside, or mad men singing. It does not consist in trying to carry water on one's hips. It does not consist in drinking putrid water when the good well is broken. Nor does it consist in eating food that upsets one's stomach, or in spending hours visiting people whose language is only half understood.

No. What happens is a *mysterious* thing because it is a mystery worked in a soul by God himself. It is the mystery of dying to self, through the others, for love of him. It begins with compassion, tinged with many emotions, salted with implementation, spiced with determination, and crowned with witnessing. No matter how you feel, you are there. That is what witnessing is. If you never opened your mouth, never taught a moral lesson, never did anything but just remained there the way that you are, you would fulfill the great commandment to love God through your neighbor.

Yes, all those things lead to that identification. They lead to union with God in the manger – to union with his weakness, poverty and dependency. He alone can take hold of you and make you one with him. Perhaps you do not realize that this is happening. But it *is* clear to us who read what you write.

So keep forgetting yourself totally. Keep dying to yourself. Keep entering the purity of your vocation, without compromise, without seeking anything for yourself. Face reality in its absolute 'nakedness' ... its rats and mice, its dust and dirt, the toilets and showers to which you must carry pails of water, the constant presence of an alien people, with alien tongues and alien ways. This is the straight, direct path of our vocation that will lead to the heart of God himself.

This annihilation-of-self, this surrendering of all one's needs to the others – including one's emotional, intellectual, and even spiritual needs (it is not easy to pray constantly in a foreign language) – will help you to rise to great sanctity, if you persevere.

This is what I call facing the reality of our vocation. This is what I call 'seeking the Absolute' ... seeking God the Father through Our Lady, who is the door to Christ the Way. This is what I call living our vocation. You have begun, by the grace of God, to do so. You will stumble, you will falter, you will fall. But don't stay down. Don't compromise. Keep cooperating with those tremendous graces that God has given to you.

Of course your stay in that small village was fruitful! There is no need to give me any results or 'reasons why.' Things that really matter in the Apostolate show no results; they have no other 'reason' than love. There *are* results from your stay, but it is not given to you to see them. That, too, is part of our vocation – often not seeing any results for years. We must always remember that we are tillers of the soil, the ones who plow it and make ready for the Sower.

He, and he alone, will harvest it. He will use us as grains of wheat to be sown into the field we have prepared, for "a grain of wheat must die before it bears fruit."

Your stay in the village, dear heart, is not only a grace that has taught you much. It is a grace for the whole Apostolate. No, you are not a hermit. It is a natural reluctance – that of finding it hard to go out to people so alien from ourselves. It is part of "taking heaven by violence" as heaven must be taken – through violence to oneself.

I would like to know why you think that going back to the big city and to the other members of the team means "giving them pain." Is that a true statement? It could be that they give *you* pain! Are you afraid of that? You know, it is more difficult to serve one's fellow staff members in the Apostolate than to 'serve the poor.' It is easier to embrace the stranger than to love one's own family, with whom one is so deeply involved by a thousand ties, to whom one comes as a servant-giver of so many things. I want you to meditate on that.

The family is a community. The parish is a community. The world is a community. And community living polishes our sharp edges; it is God's way to sanctity. Living in a village is a little different. Ten years from now when you are fluent in the language, when your identification is more complete, the village may become your community and your crucifixion. You see, the bond of community is *caritas*.* Caritas is death to self. It is annihilation and non-being. We exist in and for each other. You are protecting something that you call your 'personality.' This has to be shattered, and it gets shattered with the other team members more than in a village.

No, I don't get the picture that you are 'in a muddle.' I see that you are in the hands of God, and that he is shaping you for himself. And I pray that you will be soft clay in those hands.

Yes, I agree with you that you haven't the sense to

---

*Latin for the highest type of 'love' and esteem that one person can have for another.

know when to 'call it quits.' This comes from youth's eagerness to seek new experiences and adventures. It is normal, but not prudent. You are slowly beginning to see that, when the time of glamor is past, the community of the village also bites more deeply.

The bell has rung for dinner, and I must stop. The next installment will come soon, my love. Keep up the good work. Happy, Holy New Year to you.

Lovingly yours in Mary,

CLARIFYING OUR SPIRIT

January 11, 1965

Dearly Beloved,

We will imagine that I am in your house, sitting with you in some cozy place, and lovingly and gently discussing some of the things common to all the staff. We have only one goal – to clarify the spirit of Madonna House and to make a little smoother for you the steep and narrow path that leads always upward to God. Let's look at a number of points.

Facing Life Directly

First, I would like to discuss your growth patterns. Sister Mary Andrew noticed that we, loving you as we do, fuss too much over you. She feels that this twenty-four-hour-a-day access to myself and the priests – coming to us with every little emotional and physical problem – stymies your spiritual and emotional maturity.

She also put her finger on one problem that we are cognizant of: that after you leave the training center for the missions, and you don't have your spiritual director to go to with every little problem, you go through some hard times *unnecessarily* – the more so because many of you have had problems with your parents in terms of rejection.

During your years at Combermere, you were accepted, loved, given much attention by a mother figure (myself) and by a father figure (one of our priests). Because of this, you suffer unnecessary hardships when these are removed. If you were to leave the Madonna House Apostolate entirely, you would carry quite easily your moods, depressions, elations, and their physical effects. You did this before coming to Madonna House, knowing that *life is life* and that if you did not appear in your office or place of employment you wouldn't last long there.

This does not mean that, if you have a real problem, you shouldn't go to your department head and talk it over. But three-fourths of the time, you should be able to handle the hostilities, depressions, and irritations that are normally carried by human beings who serve in *any* capacity: married or single, in the Apostolate or out of it.

One rule to be observed as much as possible is that you should speak to your spiritual director exclusively about the state of your soul, not about your emotions. For priests and lay directors of any kind, Sister Mary Andrew laid down the following rule, which she said should be unshakable: no person in charge should speak to anybody for more than thirty minutes.

If there is cause to suspect some constant but not-too-serious emotional problem, no unqualified person (which includes most of us!) should deal with it. Instead, proper medical advice should be sought among psychologists and psychiatrists. Sister wants us all to begin what she calls *direct living* ... which means 'facing life as it is,' just as you would in any other type of vocation.

The Feminine Mystique

Now we must consider some other very important points for lay apostles, especially for women. As we grow and expand, we will have to face the fact that our loneliness and our needs may lead us to concentrate a little too much on one priest or another. And sometimes the needs within a priest, who is also a man and who is lonely, may become a danger point for us. Because we are women, we might 'imagine' that we have somehow become emotionally involved with a priest; and this will make us feel exceedingly guilty, miserable, and upset.

In certain parts of the world, because of the shortage of clergy, bishops are often under pressure to accept for Sunday work (or for temporary parish duty), priests who have recently come from places where they had been sent for emotional help. You know that priests, being human, can sometimes become alcoholics, neurotics, or even psychotics; and it is possible that some of us will be exposed to these priests.

There should be a clear understanding within ourselves of who we are and who those priests are. At all times we should remember that we are women and they are men (even though priests). We must behave accordingly, and not expose ourselves to any emotional involvements. We must always be watchful about this.

If we find that we are getting emotionally involved with a priest, let us stop this nonsense at once! It mostly happens because we have fallen into a daydreaming situation in which we allow our imaginations to run amuck; and this leads exactly nowhere. Obviously, any Catholic woman who becomes emotionally involved with a priest will harm both herself and him. She will feel guilty and miserable. He may be damaged tremendously. And let us never forget that it is sinful.

At the same time let us not become too worried about these emotional moods that come and go in our feminine mystique. Let us not *exaggerate ourselves to ourselves.* Here I want to stress very much the quality of a woman's imagination which magnifies many relationships, including that of herself and priests. Often this is done where there is really nothing to worry about. It is part of our feminine human-nature to be imaginative and emotional; we react to everything and everyone with the heart. Knowing this, let us also use our good intelligence to clarify a situation and to laugh at ourselves.

But while laughing let us also be very serious and remember our tremendous responsibility before God, all peoples, the priests, and the Apostolate. We must always be careful for, incredible as it seems, we hold in our simple feminine human hands not only our own souls but the soul of another ... and the fate of an Apostolate! Obviously, the responsibility is immense.

At the same time we must realize what a joyful and wonderful place Madonna House is for priests. One of the great works of the lay apostolate is this unity, this drawing unto itself of priests, and offering them a joyful paternity (young or old as they may be). We offer them a loving sisterhood and brotherhood, and a filial love to boot. We can and should be a spiritual family for them, a place where they can relax and be themselves – their natural, beautiful, spiritual selves. They won't be if there are undercurrents of any kind regarding those emotional involvements, which exist mostly in our imagination. Once more, these priests will have to remove themselves from close association with us and reenter the hard and lonely road that they had walked before the lay apostolate appeared on the scene.

Let us be true Catholics in regard to our priests. Let us use plain common sense, and caritas. We train you well in Madonna House, and we expect you to grow in wisdom and grace during this youthful phase of our Apostolate because, with the *aggiornamento,** our family will obviously increase and bring lay apostles and priests ever more closely together.

The Friendship of Letters

Now I want to talk to you about your letters. The reason why I ask you to write me twice a month is to establish a basis of loving friendship. I also hope that you will eventually become mature enough to look at me as a real friend who loves you very deeply. True, I am a spiritual

*Italian for 'updating' – a catchword of the 1960s referring to the efforts of the Vatican II Council to 'renew' the Church.

mother also; but, above all, I am a friend, a sister in the Apostolate who is interested in you. I am interested in your spiritual life, in what you think and feel inside your soul, especially as it pertains to the Apostolate and its outer forum. For spiritual life always spills over into daily life, or else it isn't spiritual life.

It is in *this* part of your personality that I am vitally interested. Your work and the news of the house interest me too; but, above all, these letters are important to me because they build a bridge of love and friendship between us.

True, I am the director general, and hence to most of you I am a figure of authority; and most of your neuroses are connected with figures of authority. Resistance to authority figures, however, is what most of the psychologists are trying to 'break' with insight and knowledge. Your relation to me as director general comes into play on many levels, but let it never interfere with our love and friendship for one another. As Cardinal Suenens said in addressing the nuns of the United States:

> If you look deeply into your religious community, you will soon see that most of your problems stem from the fact that you have deviated, in one way or another, from the spirit of your community *as given to you by your foundress.*

> Go back to your foundress, then, and you will find out that this 'aggiornamento' of Pope John's (which is so painful to you) was already evident in her life and writings, because she herself received her mandate from God.

Not setting myself up as any 'big shot,' I must nevertheless remind you that I am the foundress of this Apostolate and that God gives me what theologians call 'special lights' concerning its spirit. He has never failed me when I had to come forth to the hierarchy, to priests, to religious, and to lay people – especially to my spiritual family – in the application of that spirit to new situations and to the new demands of history, cultures, places, and times.

I have one treasure that I passionately desire to share with you. It is the 'spirit of Madonna House' which you have promised to love, cherish, and obey, and to make your whole life. You have dedicated yourself to promulgate it in the world. Therefore, you should understand that my tremendous love for you passionately desires to share this 'spirit' with you.

I repeat, it is my only wealth and it is not mine; it is entrusted to me by God. You should make full use of these, my living years, for I am sixty-four, and there aren't many of them left.*

You are going to carry the flame of that 'spirit,' so this is the time to see to it that you know how to light that flame, and that you know the components of the torch from which that flame comes forth. That is why I bade you under 'holy obedience' (which I use so rarely) to write me twice a month. I want us to build that bridge of friendship, understanding, love, and sharing; for the one thing we all have in common is the spirit of Madonna House.

For some reason, mostly emotional, you are afraid to write to me; not all of you, but some of you. It irks you to have to write to me twice a month. You do not understand the yearning of my heart to hear from you. You do not understand that this 'obedience' given to you is but another proof of my love for you. It is my constant hope that, as you write to me and I write back to you, you will get to know me a little more. (I need your love, too.)

Eventually, you will not be afraid of me. Then, instead of writing to seek my approval, you will write to me as a friend and sister and, if you wish, as a spiritual mother; but especially as one who wants to know you more only to love you better.

Personality Problems

Finally, I would like to tackle the difficult and thorny problem of 'personality clashes' which now and again rears its ugly head in one or another of our mission houses. Here I feel really stymied because this situation involves two levels: the emotional and the spiritual.

Let us say, for the sake of argument, that such problems exist in a small house where there are only two

*Catherine was actually 68 when she wrote these lines; she died in her 90th year.

female workers and a director. Several things happen on the emotional level. Both staff workers, consciously or unconsciously, may seek (on a childish level) the approval of the director. One of them might feel very insecure upon the arrival of a new person, or even in the presence of one who came with her at the same time.

In order to find favor (unconsciously, I repeat) from the director, one person might constantly show how much *more* she knows, how much *better* she is at such-and-such than the newcomer. This establishes a spirit of competition which is very hard on a mission house. The second person, feeling utterly rejected and unneeded, becomes confused. And she begins to get terribly hostile toward the director and the other staff member.

In a house where there are many members, other personality problems can develop on the same emotional level. One or two members may be so immature, or act so immaturely that, under the guise of rechecking about an 'obedience,' they beat the life out of a local director or another member by asking for permissions and clarifications in areas where they should obviously take responsibility and make *their own* decisions.

Or two members may clash for one emotional reason or another, and begin to use the arsenal of subtle weapons that are available to people dedicated to charity. They use 'humor' to put their point across, and unconsciously (or semiconsciously) they express their hostility toward one another. Or else they indulge in 'questions' so phrased that it puts the other person on the spot. Or they try to 'hog the limelight' or else withdraw completely from the community.

Sister Mary Andrew says that these destructive emotional tricks can be dastardly effective, and should never be used. Any normal neurotic (which we all are!) has full control of herself or himself and doesn't need to stoop to such shenanigans.

But now comes the spiritual level. Here charity should rise above all situations, and the local director – with kindness but firmness – should vigorously present the situation to the members concerned. Mutual charity should take over and solve this crisis. Those who feel rejected must accept the seeming disapproval of the other, knowing that the rejection is not real but emotional. Those doing the rejection should learn to restrain their destructive passions. They must do violence to themselves, for "heaven is taken by violence" to oneself. They must stop rejecting their brothers and sisters in the Apostolate.

Sister Mary Andrew emphatically stated that the intelligence of neurotics is not impaired at all; they *fully* understand the difference between good and evil. What they have to realize is that they cannot give way to their infantile and childish impulses just because they are in a spiritual family, a protective environment.

If they were in the world, it would be too dangerous. The world would reject them as unfit, and so they wouldn't act that way. If they did, they couldn't keep a job or continue their studies; and if they were married, it would create hell for their families. So they would try to use all their insights, will power, faith, and grace to control these situations.

I have raised many questions, shared with you some of my worries, and now I appeal to your friendship, love, and understanding. I beg you to look carefully at your childish reactions and unnecessary emotional tensions. I beg you to accept the fact that *life is a conflict* between the pleasure principle and the pain principle, and that our duties at Madonna House – just like any other place in the world – will always present those conflicts.

Let our prayer for 1965 be this: "Lord, do not allow the darkness in my psyche and my soul to affect the light of my neighbor." As Sister Mary Andrew says: "Let us carry our neuroses with a smile. God will do the rest."

Lovingly yours in Christ,

62

AUTHORITY AND OBEDIENCE

February 17, 1965

Dearly Beloved,

The peace of the Lord to you all! Upon my return from the Caribbean, I found quite a few letters that discussed obedience, and very intelligently too. These came from various houses.

In one letter was a very interesting sentence that I took to my heart and meditated upon: "Catherine, you really leave yourself wide open by allowing free discussion on this matter of obedience; you must trust God very much and have a deep faith in him, as well as a tremendous trust in your staff."

I understood what this person wanted to say. Authority – as the Church understood it in the past (or should I say misunderstood it?) – had faith and trust in God perhaps, but it didn't seem to have trust in the people. In the old days, there was little room for discussion on this subject. Yet I must admit that, even in the very early days of our Apostolate, I wondered a bit about this question.

Instinctively, and because of the wonderful parents and upbringing that I had, I have never felt any fear or hostility towards authority. On the contrary, I always thought that authority *trusted* me. I wasn't entirely sure of that in Canada and America, but I always gave them the benefit of the doubt.

Because of this background, from the early days of Friendship House and Madonna House, I always accepted the vertical line of the Church's authority: from the pope to bishop to superior. And so I have always tried to let 'the reins of authority' rest lightly on everyone in the Apostolate.

The department heads are aware of this. Once the period of their training was over, I seldom interfered in the running of their department. They can testify to this. That is because I trusted them, had faith in them; and I still have that faith.

The same is true with the local directors. On the whole, they are tremendously free to do anything they really want to do. In important things they check with us here, but we seldom contradict their plans; though, of course, we can and do use the authority that is ours. I hope it is always for the common good of the Apostolate.

Because I love every member of Madonna House, I am open to them and trust them. I must confess that sometimes some of them let me down. Perhaps I should say "let the Apostolate down" now and then. But the quality of trust – its very essence – consists of trusting again and again and *again!*, for the giving of trust must eventually bring forth trust in return.

I must confirm again that I love you all very deeply and I have faith and trust in the God-who-brought-you-here, and whose graces continue to work on you constantly. I know that the Holy Spirit will eventually penetrate those areas of mistrust that you still have ... toward myself, the directorate in general, toward all in authority. Because of your North American culture and your emotional problems, many of you don't yet know how to love authority figures. I understand your difficulties.

This trust of mine and of the directorate in you does not mean that we will not correct, or that we will not officially invoke the virtue of 'holy obedience' when occasion arises. It will occur in serious matters, such as your being sent to a mission, and your writing twice a month to me.

I stand ready to be utterly open to you (and I am sure that the whole directorate does too) because we ask *you* to be open to *us*. Truth can never hurt anybody, even if at times it is a narrow truth – a truth that lacks experience, a truth not well-expressed because of youth or of faulty thinking. Nevertheless, it has to be expressed; that is why we allow such discussions.

But we expect you to understand that we have to speak the truth in its fullness. You understand with your intellect that we have more experience than you, and possess a special grace from God to present the truths of the

Apostolate. While this exchange of truth may be painful to either side, as long as it remains *truth!* that pain is good. For it is based on a profound respect for the integrity of each individual. This respect must be present on both sides.

It also presumes that you fully understand the word *freedom*. In order to clarify that word I quote from a recent magazine article, "The Church and Freedom" by Mr. Donald Gray, published in the *Catholic Mind,* February 1965.

> Persons are unique, and each person possesses his own unique vocation, which must be welcomed and respected by the community. But this is only one side of the story. A vocation is always a ministry, i.e., a service to others in the community. Hence, while the community must allow the individual the freedom to be himself in achieving his own unique vocation, the individual in turn must possess *a sense of responsibility* toward others, which means concretely that he must 'give himself' to the other members of the community precisely through his vocation-ministry, whether this be lived out in the classroom, the office, the home, or the monastery.

> The Pope, who holds a unique position of authority within the institutional structures of the Church, signs himself as 'the Servant of the servants of God.' This is the complex reality of Christian freedom, which is never merely a freedom *from,* but rather, more positively, a freedom *for* – a freedom to be oneself by being *for others*. Freedom divorced from responsibility becomes 'unfreedom' (to use Hans Kung's expression) and makes it thoroughly impossible for the person to achieve authentic personhood, or to put it less technically, personal maturity.

In the light of that sentence a member of Madonna House wrote me – "Catherine, you really leave yourself wide open by allowing free discussion on this matter of obedience; you must trust God very much and have a deep faith in him, as well as a tremendous trust in your staff" – you begin to see that our trust in you is very great indeed.

Because of your youth and inexperience in life – and in certain cases, a lack of theological knowledge – I am not yet sure you have reached this tremendous understanding of freedom which is quoted. It is true that, even with your lack of maturity and knowledge, I trust you deeply and I love you deeply; and I do so because I have faith in the Lord who brought you here. Nevertheless, I ask you to think deeply about this quotation. It is very important to each of you, to all of you, to the entire Apostolate.

We Have Come to Serve

So much for openness, trust, freedom of discussion, and freedom-in-general within the Apostolate. Now let us talk about *service*. I have always taken my general idea of authority from the words of Christ, "I have come to serve." Service and love and trust are to me the basis of authority. A basic factor of authority and its exercise is the deep realization of faith that, of myself, I have no authority in the Apostolate. It is Christ alone who has the authority; and I must constantly remember that. I must never forget that my lips, my mind, my words, and all the rest of me are but instruments of his. It is through them that he expresses his authority in our Apostolate.

My deep sorrow is that my personality traits and my weaknesses often stand between you and him. I humbly beg your prayers that I may conquer these obstacles which often get in the way of your seeing Christ in me. On the other hand, I also beg you to remember that I haven't chosen this position of authority; Christ has chosen me for it, and he knew what a weak instrument he placed there. Since he in his mercy bears with me, cannot you in your mercy bear with me also?

I firmly believe that authority is open to correction. If there is something you do not understand, something you feel is justly wrong, you should not hesitate – through fear, human respect, or any other emotion or idea – to present it to me. Because of the grace of state, I have to answer your correction. At times I seem to justify myself, but this is done only for the sake of clarification. If I feel that your correction is valid, I will thank you for it with deep gratitude and apologize for whatever I have left undone or have done wrongly.

To some of you who read this letter, it will appear as 'just so many words' that any Christian, especially a Catholic director of a lay apostolate, is bound to express. Some of you may think these words have no substance. Is there nothing I can do to persuade you that they are truly my convictions, and that I will act on them? All I can do is pray that you will understand fully what I have to say, that you become mature enough to do so. More than that I cannot do ... except to write these words so that you, and others to come, will someday really believe them.

I have a concept of authority; I also have a concept of obedience. First and foremost, I consider that this virtue must be utterly and freely given. Secondly, it must be given with a mature realization as to *why* it is given. Thirdly, the person pledging obedience must know that this pledge is primarily to God, but he uses human instruments for its implementation. Some of these instruments will be likable, some unlikable; but they are his choice. Fourthly, each person pledging that obedience must realize that he or she must obey as Christ did. He was obedient to his Father even unto death, for the salvation of mankind and the restoration of the world.

I consider that what the Church officially calls 'subjects' and I call 'members of the Apostolate' must love and obey their directors. Christ's commandment tells us that we must love one another. Such love implies that one *trust the untrustworthy*. When a director general is elected by all of the members eligible to vote, they choose someone because they trust him or her. It should be easier to trust a person whom one has elected in trust.

I believe also that all members of Madonna House should love their directors because they see before their eyes Christ's passion which lies in the directors' responsibility to the staff, to the Apostolate, to those whom they serve. The members must show their love by being Veronicas and Simons to their directors.

Finally, I believe that all our staff, by the time they become members of Madonna House, should know the difference between *like* and *love*. The former is of the emotions and is not important. The latter is of reason (illuminated by faith) and of the will; and it is the primary commandment of God.

These are my basic beliefs and ideas about authority and obedience. I have many more ideas which I hope to share with you sometime. But I thought I would share these, especially with the person who wrote me that lovely and beautiful sentence. It warmed my heart.

Affectionately yours in Mary,

OUR COMMITMENT IS TO CHRIST

February 24, 1965

Dearly Beloved,

I would like to share a recent letter which has given me much joy. I can see that the person is honestly and sincerely writing about our discussion on obedience. Here is her letter:

We were very interested in the discussions that were held at Madonna House about an article on obedience.* We read and discussed it also. We were somewhat surprised that the essence of your discussions seemed to revolve around the idea that this new style of obedience now gives us an opportunity to 'get things off our chest.' You seemed

* "Together in Obedience" *Envoy* magazine (late 1964?)

to take it from a very personal angle. We in the field concentrated more on the idea of *community,* so our discussions took a different turn.

The article struck us as a marvellous statement about community living. Obedience* conveys the idea of *listening* to one another and to the directorate, who in turn must be the *Master Listeners* who can sort out what is important from what is merely poignant.

We saw from this article that obedience is a result of a 'commitment to community' and that our individual commitment is necessary to the essential ordering of our community life. It is *because* we are committed to Madonna House (to God's Spirit in it) that we are obliged to speak openly in matters pertinent to the life of the community.

We should reverently listen to one another, with open hearts and minds, as we decide how to implement the decisions that come from those in authority (who have first listened to what we have had to say). Our promise of obedience doesn't give us the right to 'spout off' about things. Rather, it obliges us to consult our hearts carefully and, if we think we have an insight on something, to share it openly.

This seems to rule out a 'blind obedience' that requires us to do something in a certain way even though we think it should be done differently. Instead of acting blindly, we move *in faith,* understanding that we do not have 'the vision of the whole' as do those who are in charge of many more things and have greater 'vision' than we do.

Another insight that struck us was how we misuse one of your favorite phrases: *folding the wings of the intellect.* The article made it clear that we shouldn't say to ourselves: I don't see it this way and *therefore* I must be wrong; now I must 'fold the wings of my intellect' and be obedient! If we think that way, we will then proceed to cram our ideas down inside us (and the emotions that go with this sort of thing) and try to squash them. That would be wrong. What we should do is look at the matter realistically, face the fact

*Its Latin root 'obeo + audio' means 'I go forth and I listen.'

that we may have differing attitudes about the subject, call to mind our obedience, and proceed to obey freely.

The old school seems to have taught us that we must be 'of the same mind' as our directors. I think this terminology is bad; the idea is almost the same, but it should be put differently. It's almost impossible for a whole group of people to think the same way about many things. To try to force oneself to think in the same way as others isn't really a good thing to do. We are all different, and we see things differently. True, we are all 'of one mind' in that we are trying to go to God together and to take along with us as many people as we can; but we still are individuals.

To summarize my thoughts:

(1) Our 'commitment to community' must come first.

(2) This is followed by the realization that, with so many of us living and working together, it is necessary to have a Master Listener. Someone has to draw all of our ideas together and present them in the way that is best for our community.

(3) Our promise of obedience is twofold: we agree to follow the directives of the Master Listener, and we are obliged to contribute our thoughts and ideas to that person.

(4) 'Speaking up' is not the same thing as 'spouting off.' I don't believe that the article even hinted at such a thing.

In many ways, Catherine, though some of our terms may have been obscure and communication made difficult, I think you have been very much a Master Listener, and I'm deeply grateful to you for letting us discuss an article of this sort. This, in itself, shows a great openness on your part.

Perhaps the letters from others will give you a better picture of the way our discussion and ideas flowed. In any case, I hope the members of Madonna House can hear our ideas on the subject. I know that I still have a long way to go to maturity and that we still have our difficulties here; but I believe that the insights we discovered in this article may help our brothers and sisters.

Some of the younger people like myself are still in the throes of adolescence and have difficulties with authority. I can readily see how this article could give the impression that 'here is a chance to speak up!' I think there is much more in this article than meets the eye and that it deserves more consideration. Much love in Our Lady of Combermere ...

My Answer to This Letter

It was a joy to get your letter. I'm surprised that you were surprised by our discussion on obedience here at Combermere, but I begin to understand that many in our missions also think of Madonna House as 'another mission house.' They forget that this is our *main training center.*

In a training center, there are teachers and leaders who train, and – obviously – they have to clarify their ideas on how this aggiornamento, including a new or enlarged concept of obedience, is going to work when it is applied to the reality of training.

But the majority of people here are still in training and it is understandable that they have to 'get things off their chest.' That is not a bad idea either; it is easier to fill an empty room than a cluttered one.

In Madonna House we have always concentrated on 'community' living. We prefer to use an old word, however, a Scriptural word: the family. We speak of the family of God, or of the family of Madonna House. A family is a little church, really. All virtues – including obedience – are to be practiced in a community, a family, a group setting. It is difficult (nay, impossible!) to practice obedience as a hermit, unless one is called to such a life by God and is endowed with extraordinary graces to know his will. Obedience is a social virtue, a group virtue. Someone must command and someone must obey. That takes at least two!

You said that 'commitment to community' comes first. I think it better to say that obedience is the result of a 'commitment to *God* for the good of the community.' We obey out of love for Christ and in imitation of his redemptive action. He was obedient unto death to the will of his Father. So our commitment of obedience is to Christ, first.

By the mystery of the most holy will of God we are allowed to suffer with Christ. We are allowed to "make up what is wanting" in his sufferings (though nothing is really wanting, hence the mystery). This means that obedience to God must pass *through the sieve of humanity;* it must be subject to other human beings, each according to his or her particular vocation. In our case, it is through the community (or family) of Madonna House.

Be sure that you understand this distinction. Otherwise, you will be like the communists; they listen and obey a community for natural reasons, for humanitarian reasons, for any kind of a reason, but not from a Christian impetus.

I'm sorry you know so little about the term 'folding the wings of your intellect.' There is a whole literature that has been written on the subject. It is called 'mystical' literature. Too literal an acceptance of a word or phrase sometimes blurs its meaning.

Let me explain: When I give you an obedience to go and take a course somewhere, you can come and talk it over with me, in keeping with all laws both human and divine. You can state the reasons why you think that this assignment is beyond your capacity. If I am a good superior, I will explain to you *why* I am sending you. I will tell you that, as an objective observer, I see your talents more deeply than you do and wish to foster them in this way.

Intellectually, you may or may not see my point of view; but, because you have made a commitment to God (and I am the channel through which you have made this commitment), you make an act of faith, love, and trust – both in him and in me as his channel. You 'fold the wings of your intellect' and say *Fiat!**

This is a mystery of faith. It is best exemplified in Our Lady, who spoke up and expressed her bewilderment to the angel, "How can this happen since I am a virgin?" When given an explanation, she folded the wings of her intellect and entered the *realm of faith.* Because a woman folded the wings of her intellect and, with an utterly complete and

*Latin phrase for 'let it be done.'

flaming faith, said a 'fiat', Christ became incarnate. Mary's 'fiat' was an act of great Christian maturity and a complete openness to God's grace. It takes some grace and maturity on our part to understand the depths of this.

You keep speaking of 'commitment to community.' It makes me think of the many communist rallies I have attended. They always talked about 'commitment,' 'surrender,' 'dedication to the community of mankind.' Remember that your commitment is to Christ, *and him alone,* even though this commitment is expressed through a specific community.

Lovingly yours in Mary,

[signature]

HUMILITY AND LEARNING SITUATIONS

March 11, 1965

Dearly Beloved,

During Lent I have been doing what one of my prayer books says we should do: "Let it not be vain for you to rise early before it is light, for the Lord has promised a crown to those who watch." I do 'rise before the light' these days. It seems my awakening is from the Lord, for my mind is filled with thoughts of him and of everyone in the Apostolate. It seems that this is the time which the Lord gives me to meditate upon the problems of the Apostolate, and to really answer your letters. This letter, therefore, brings to you one of the points which have occupied several of my 'night watches.'

Learning How to Learn

I have been thinking about why it is that the majority of the people in the Apostolate resent being put into learning situations. Why is that we do not wish to learn from 'the university of life'? For life is God's novitiate for the Christian until his death. I've been wondering why so few of us in this university of life, this novitiate of God, wish to be learners ... and still less, to be teachers. I must admit, however, that we often prefer to teach rather than to learn, even though we are ignorant of life because of our youthfulness and inexperience. Teaching appears to have a higher status in our limited vision.

It seems that no one, in the Apostolate or out of it, objects to learning in an atmosphere and in surroundings that are officially designated for that purpose, such as schools or universities or evening classes. We feel the same about handicrafts in any place where they are officially taught. We don't object to taking dancing lessons or music appreciation courses. We don't mind listening to someone tell us about the Great Books of the world. Oh no! We accept all these without hostility – in fact with much pride. They become 'conversation pieces' because we believe we are somehow rising in stature or in status.

But to learn from a local director the office procedure of a particular fieldhouse, we resent somehow. We resent it especially if we can type or do shorthand already (even if we are poor at it). We become filled with hostility; we want to argue with the director about it all. We want to be 'right' even though we don't know much about filing methods or other aspects of office work.

At first we resent being learners in the kitchen, in the laundry, in any department of our training center. Then we resent being learners when we are asked to apply the Madonna House spirit to a new mission. Later on, we resent being learners after we have been in one mission house for a time and are transferred to a house where a different application of the Madonna House spirit is required.

We do not accept humbly (and intelligently) a very simple fact in the natural order: that every new experience, be it very little or very big, is a growth in the knowledge of life itself. It enlarges our intellectual, spiritual, and emotional vision. It means that we are becoming more and more fully developed, more 'rounded out' in our personalities. It means that we are maturing in every way.

Many of the emotional hostilities, most of the intellectual blocking, much of the psychosomatic symptoms in our bodies still clearly 'shows up' – through our behavior, in our speech, and by the letters we write. Our responses indicate that we refuse this *wondrous* and *exciting* state of being learners. It shows that we don't understand 'what life is all about' ... namely, that life-unto-death is a learning process!

Arguments versus Quarrels

This refusal to be a learner shows up in the many questions about 'training' that are written to me. One question that often comes to my desk is this: "What is the difference between arguing and discussing?" Let us refer to the dictionary to begin with. The dictionary states: *discuss* – to 'argue' for and against; to reason upon; to debate. Again the dictionary states: *argument* – a reasoned 'discussion' offered for and against something; a course of reasoning by the use of evidence or demonstration.

In other words, they seem to be the same thing. But then the dictionary refers us to an entirely different word, *altercation*. So we go to that word and read: Angry controversy, wrangling, baiting, disputation, dissension, disturbance, fracas, quarrel. And there are many other words which the dictionary suggests, such as contentions and controversies.

At this point we start to perceive the difference between a 'reasoned' and an 'unreasonable' discussion, and we wonder how we might improve the ways in which we communicate. Whenever we have conflicts of opinion or of ideas, they should never degenerate into outer impatience. Our conversations should always remain elevated in style, intelligent in content, and filled with good sense. When an 'argument' or 'discussion' lacks these qualities, then the right word to use is *altercation* or (more informally) *quarrel*. On the surface it may continue to appear as an intelligent conversation, but in essence we are 'picking a quarrel' with someone.

This word for quarrel – *altercation* – is not one we use very often, but the dictionary insists on showing us that entry and refers to it as the opposite of a 'reasoned argument.' You can see then, just from a dry official book, how great the semantic difference is.

Unless our argument or discussion has an intelligent content and is being carried out objectively (not subjectively), with reasoned statements and a willingness to concede that we might be wrong, then we aren't really having either a 'discussion' or an 'argument' in the dictionary sense of the word. We are simply being quarrelsome.

In a quarrel, we tend to 'dig our heels in.' We want to be 'right' even if it means being downright stupid. Our words, sentences, or expressions are not helping anyone learn something new, or to grow intellectually, spiritually, and humanly. On the contrary, they are being used by us to put our point across, vent our anger, and verbalize our frustrations, but not to arrive at a peaceful and intelligent solution.

The Give-and-Take of Life

For the sake of clarification, let me repeat myself. In the majority of situations between members and local directors, or between members and members, your letters to me do not indicate that you have had a reasoned argument or intelligent discussion. I have usually found that you were engaged in an altercation! Mostly, this was because you did not want to be a learner. You wanted to be an equal or a teacher; you wanted some 'status' other than your present one.

To me, this spells out an emotional fear. Those who dig in their heels during any argument or discussion, those who need 'always' to be right, are insecure or rigid persons. They cannot 'roll with the punches' of life; they have no intellectual pliancy. They are afraid to move, afraid to change from a familiar to an unfamiliar situation. Fear is part of their insecurity. No matter in what place they work – kitchen, laundry, office, wherever – they will have to learn new ideas, new techniques. And they fear anything that is 'new.'

But for healthy living – emotional, intellectual, and physical – there *must* be a give-and-take! If there is a rigidity of opinion, if there is a need to be always right and never to 'give in' to the other during a discussion or exchange of ideas, then something needs to change. Otherwise, there is the grave danger of remaining unopen to life, of remaining immature and 'set' in one familiar pattern of life.

As the years go by, life and society will demand growth from such persons, and they will not be able to respond. That will be a great personal tragedy for each of them. It is worth noting, as you will find on Sister Mary Andrew's tapes, that people in their latter years often suffer from ulcers, heart conditions, high blood pressure, etc. The stress of that 'inability to respond to change' helps to cause these things.

Yes, we must expose ourselves to learning, and remain learners in 'the school of life' until we die. God, the greatest of teachers, still has patience with us. He gives us the time we need to grow into what he really wants us to be, namely, saints. And hand in hand with our willingness to be 'pupils in the school of life and love of God' goes an openness of heart and mind, and an ability to seek and receive all that life sends us. Along with that goes humility, true humility of heart that fully accepts its state of being a creature, a pupil, and a learner. In a word, this is the path to sanctity.

I hope my 'night watch' meditation has helped to clarify this pressing question of yours. My next letter will be about *personality,* a subject that seems especially to bother you in this new aggiornamento times. To conclude: What I have said above really means that you want to be involved in God, in people, and in life, and that you don't want to be as living corpses.

Love,

ON LIBERATING ONE'S TRUE PERSONALITY

March 12, 1965

Dearly Beloved,

I promised in my last letter to talk to you about personality. So let's go back to the dictionary and see what it has to say about this word: *personality* – that which constitutes a person; that which distinguishes and characterizes a person; that which pertains to character.

We look at the word *character,* and we see that it means many things, but fundamentally, the dictionary calls it the qualities that distinguish one individual from another. The dictionary relates all this to the word *person,* which it defines as 'a human being with a special character, appearance, and condition.'

Just as you have to define words via the dictionary, so you have to define – for yourself first and then for others – what the words 'your personality' mean. You speak of 'your personality' being crushed, maimed, imprisoned, and not allowed to grow. Before you make such a statement, may I ask you if you understand the *character* of your own personality? I would say that you haven't an idea of what 'your personality' is!

The reason for this is that you suffer, as do many others today, from an inability to see yourself 'as you are.' Your idea of 'your personality' is predominately formed by seeing your reflection in the eyes of others. Unfortunately, our civilization judges people by their conformity to the existing standards (which are very superficial) and by the outward production in their field of work. Because of two World Wars and a major economic depression, the family has been nearly destroyed, and most people today have not known the kind of love that is *the food of personality development.*

This has begotten in you a non-acceptance of yourself;

it has kept you from developing the *right* kind of self-love. What is this 'personality' of yours that is supposedly being crushed, raped, or twisted at one time or another by 'someone in authority'? You do not know; you cannot know. Since you do not accept yourself, you are unable to have a clear idea of your own personality.

If you stop for a moment and reflect on the matter, you will slowly come to the conclusion that – far from damaging your personality or in any way retarding its growth – the Madonna House directors and teachers are engaged in the gigantic task of developing your *true* personality.

In doing this, we must deal with a host of emotions that fill every one of you and stunt this 'true personality.' You come to us emotionally wounded. These wounds have been inflicted upon you by various factors in your heredity and environment. Perhaps your parents (or others) have loved you in a 'wrong' way. But you must realize that, by their concern and according to their lights, they certainly did *the best they knew how* for you!

So you come to Madonna House, wounded. You are not alone in this personal misfortune. Alas, you are but one of millions. You all know that the tremendous surge of recent history, which began in 1914 and goes on even today, has wounded people and made them neurotic in various degrees. You are one of the millions who have experienced its swift technological changes, its wars, revolutions, threat of atomic destruction, insecurity, and uprootedness. But you are very lucky; you have been brought by God to a place called Madonna House, which is dedicated to the Restoration of the World.

This restoration begins with *you!* It would be foolish for the Apostolate to try to restore the world en masse. We must begin to restore it person by person by person, and continue to restore it that way. The Gospel of Love, the witness of faith that liberates mankind, is preached and given to one human being by another human being. It is not something that can be given in any other way. It is a person-to-person relationship.

So, God has chosen you for this vocation. And, in his mercy, his own mandate to me includes the clear understanding that the first persons to be restored in our Apostolate must be its members! This is what Friendship House and Madonna House have attempted to do from their very beginnings.

I've always been conscious of this aspect of God in his mandate to me, because our Apostolate is meant to be an apostolate of love. Our crosses testify to it. They are engraved with the words *Caritas* (love) and *Pax* (peace). We love, to bring God's peace to the persons we meet. We serve, to restore them through Christ and his love, so that he can give them his peace.

Grace works on nature, however. We cannot draw from a well of young people who are *not* wounded! This is because those who come to us are called by God; and it is to them that he has given this vocation – the wounded ones. True, some he brings only for a while; they are the very wounded, the very sick. He brings them so that we may lead them to the natural means of healing that he has established in the world – doctors, psychologists, and psychiatrists. But these are rare and extreme cases.

The others, most of them, are first restored by the simple process of loving them. Then they are healed by academic courses, by scientific knowledge such as Sister Mary Andrew gives, and by the counseling of priests. Further secular studies may also lead to a personal restoration.

What is it that we are trying to heal and restore? Your true personality – the depths of which we who are directly involved in your spiritual, emotional, and academic formation can easily and objectively perceive. I myself see tremendous potential in each one of you, but I am confronted with the fact that you reject yourself, and consequently you do not love yourself. Therefore, you do not see this great potential of your own personality. So I and all of the directorate strive to liberate and develop your personality (which has such tremendous potential!) so that you, in turn, can fulfill your vocation to restore others.

How do we do this? First and foremost, Madonna House is by the grace of God a family. Many of you are unused to family life, so have formed no roots in it. Here in Combermere, you learn the give and take, the loving relationships, the opening up to each other that takes place in the atmosphere of a family. This is the best place to learn to know yourself and to lose your feelings of inadequacy, of insecurity, all those the fears and hostilities which form the wounds of so many people today.

Next, you are given new ideas about manual labor and the use of the body. You are introduced to 'the theology of labor' and its creative possibilities. Your true personality begins to emerge through these exciting (though sometimes painful) opportunities which are recognized by psychiatrists and theologians as being therapeutic as well as freeing.

I need not point out to you that rich people, in order to develop their personalities, pay a very high fee at special sanitariums to do manual work such as we do here. Dr. Stern, the renowned psychiatrist, was telling us recently that a new sanitarium has been established in the United States, to which women from suburbia go to be cured. The cure consists of allowing them to live in the same quarters as they do at home, but having them spend their days in another building which costs thousands of dollars.

Dr. Stern told us that this building has antiques of all kinds. There are stoves and wooden laundry tubs. There is no plumbing and water is carried by pail from a well outside. In a word, it turns back the pages of time to pioneer days in the United States.

These well-to-do suburbanites, who have had nervous breakdowns and who often needed psychiatry (partly because of the thousands of gadgets that they have and the leisure time that they do not know what to do with), pay hundreds of dollars a week to spend their days working as their ancestors did. Often in three months they are cured.

I need not go into the fact that the Benedictines and other religious orders have developed a theology of manual labor which stresses the sanctity of work, its psychological value, its liberating value: and, of course, they connect it all with the fact that Christ chose manual labor as part of his redemptive life.

Through your physical labors, you develop your personality in a series of learning experiences. You become proficient in some particular work such as cooking, sewing, ironing, or cleaning. All of this liberates you, makes you whole. And the more learning situations that you can *conquer and make your own,* the more free your personality becomes to grow and to develop to its fullness.

Madonna House also offers you something I have always wanted you to have – that many-faceted thing called handicrafts! Many of you have already experienced the joy of this creativeness. It is one of the key tools in liberating your personality, for creativeness is a built-in need in every person. You realize how much these activities have done much for the growth of your personality; they have released many of the potentials which you were not aware of, but which we recognized within you.

Academic training at Madonna House develops your mind. Anthropology, for instance, makes you realize your kinship with the past and helps to clarify many reasons for your actions. It lets you gain a proper perspective on all human life. It liberates your potential and your personality. Your other courses in psychology, theology, and the study of scripture and liturgy help greatly to bring out your potential.

For those of you who have been wounded more deeply than others, Madonna House gives time and opportunity to consult psychiatrists and psychologists who can heal your wounds and make you free. Some of you have other little wounds which have spilled over into the social fabric of the Apostolate. For these, you have required special training such as speech therapy and various other helps. You have been given catechetical instruction and business courses. You learn about diction, vocabulary, and other 'shaping sciences' too numerous to mention.

Madonna House has always encouraged travel, for it is one of the best ways to meet other cultures and other people. It helps you to learn about history, mores, languages; to realize how different the various cultures are; and to recognize that those differences are beautiful – to be accepted and not feared.

If you were to count all the hours that the directorate has spent with you individually, and the volume of letters dealing with problems begotten by emotional wounds, you will realize that, far from stifling your personality, we have tried to make it grow and grow and grow. And we will continue to do so, so as to bring out the immense potential that each of you possesses.

Consider the freedom of discussion that exists in Madonna House concerning spiritual topics. Consider the many explanations and clarifications you have received, collectively and individually, on the whole gamut of living. I think that you will withdraw many of the points you tend to bring up about the development of your true personality.

I haven't yet mentioned the fieldhouses which bring you into contact with the most visible ills of society across the world. Through newsletters from those houses, personal letters among yourselves, and day-to-day contact with those we serve, a whole new world is opened to each of you. It liberates your personality where it most needs liberating, namely, in your dealings with other people.

Nor have I said a word about the main liberating influence. I haven't mentioned how surrounded you are by the love of others, beginning with your directors, your spiritual advisors, your fellow staff members, and all the teachers who constantly give you so much. Sound, trusting relationships with your family members will help unlock your hidden potential.

From where I sit (and I speak in grave humility), I do not think there is an apostolate in the world where so much attention, so much love and concern, go into liberating one's personality. Nor do I know of another place where the hidden potential of an individual is so lovingly considered and so much is done to develop it. It is time, I think, for you to work at 'direct living,' and to clarify what is meant by 'personality.'

Lovingly yours in Mary,

SIMPLICITY

March 17, 1965

Dearly Beloved,

Today I want to write about *simplicity*. (No! Don't throw the piano at me!) The dictionary defines the word as 'the state of being that is simple,' correlates it with the word *innocence,* and refers us to the word *simple.* When we look up this last word, the dictionary proceeds to give a series of definitions: Consisting of one thing; single; uncombined; not complex or complicated; easy. Without embellishment; plain; unadorned. Free from affection; sincere; artless. Of humble rank. (So much for the definition of a secular dictionary.)

The word *simplicity* says 'to be simple.' The word *innocence* is opposed to sophistication, to complexity. The word *simple* continues this definition by saying that it is free from affectation, that it is sincere and humble, and has nothing added (it is otherwise pure). The definition very positively states that 'being simple' consists of 'being single of mind or affection or interest; being plain, unadorned, without embellishment.'

The moment we apply all these words to the spiritual life, we get an interesting picture. It shows a person who is single-minded, whose mind goes to the essence of things without embellishment, curlicues, and complicatedness. It conjures up a person who is innocent of guile, who is truthful and direct, who – psychologically speaking – *lives directly.* (Remember, Sister Mary Andrew says that this 'living directly' is a sign of maturity.) Each of these images presents to us a pleasing, peace-creating picture; and any one of us would be delighted to live with a person who has this type of simplicity.

Now, what is 'holy' simplicity? The definition that comes forth is "the state of mind and soul that is totally occupied by God." The colloquial word for holy simplicity would be *childlikeness* and would bring us immediately to the Gospel: "Unless you become like children [single-minded, uncombined, uncomplicated, humble, trusting] you shall not enter the kingdom of heaven!" Or words to that effect.

Now you see how important a dictionary is. Now, perhaps, you understand one of our major goals in the Apostolate. 'To be simple' means being emotionally or psychologically simple, in the right sense of the word. It does not mean being naive or foolishly ignorant. It also means that intellectual simplicity should blend with this psychological simplicity, and be practiced in a way that would help us become spiritually simple – or childlike – as Christ wants us to be.

Now, I'm not going to write much more about this. It's up to you to have a discussion among yourselves on it. Get all kinds of dictionaries. Research them thoroughly. Develop a positive explanation for the word *simplicity,* and give its significance for everyday living. If you want to consult a Catholic dictionary, look up 'the prayer of simplicity.'

Simplicity is a term that is vitally important nowadays, because people are so complex, so filled with fears and inhibitions, so fragmented. They need to become recollected within themselves, above all in the type of simplicity that goes to the essence of things.

I would deeply appreciate if you wrote me your findings on this important word, and we will take it from there. Let's have a dialogue – a discussion, too (in the right sense of the word).

Lovingly yours in Mary,

RED LIKE ME

March 19, 1965

Dearly Beloved,

I've just had a letter from one of our staff who's involved in the foundation of a Metis Association. She writes that they are 'running into rough waters.' Something happened when I read her letter. I lay awake at night, seeing a fragile birchbark canoe fighting rough waters. Images filled my mind and heart, and I just had to get them down on paper.

This is not really a Staff Letter as such. (And yet it is.) It is an Open Letter to the native peoples of North America. For you in the Apostolate, it will be a record of my innermost feelings and beliefs about the tragic plight of those peoples – their society, their culture, their lives.

There was a white man, a writer, who recently wrote a best seller under the title of *Black Like Me.** In order to write the truth, he altered the color of his skin for a while and entered the Negro world as a Negro, hence the title. Previous to his alteration of skin pigmentation, he had studied all that a white man could study about the Negro world. But, when he entered it like one of them, all of his previous research paled into insignificance. He became part of a tragic world he never even dreamt existed.

I read the book. I read it and asked myself the pertinent question: "Is it necessary to alter the pigmentation of one's skin and perhaps even have some plastic surgery on one's face, to *identify* with one's brother?" I grant that it might help. Nevertheless, I think that what is more necessary than any physical alteration is a complete rebirth of one's soul!

One must truly ' break one's heart' as it were, break it

*By John Howard Griffin, published by Houghton Mifflin, 1961.

wide open. Yes, wide open to let one's brother in – to let Christ in –whether that brother in Christ be Negro, Indian, Chinese, White, or whatever race or color he might be. To achieve this deep, inward change and to break one's heart completely open is a harder job than just changing the pigmentation of one's skin. It means changing oneself completely.

It is a change that demands faith and love; but it demands even more, for it also demands death – death to self. That self which stands between us and the Love who is a person, who is God, and whom we must *encounter* in our brothers and sisters of all hues, and whom we must *love* in them. Yes, love him in them, as we love them in him, if we want to have the right to call ourselves Christians.

I have lived in the Harlems of my life (New York, Chicago, etc.) for close to ten years. I know that during that time my love, my compassion, my empathy – in fact all of me such as I was and such as I am – were and still are *identified* with the Negro. It seemed natural, inescapable. I do not know nor can I tell anyone how this happened. Perhaps it happened because I've been taught that *God is Love*. Perhaps it happened because I love God passionately in all peoples, and that this loving him in everyone has brought me closer to him in a strange and inexpressible union.

I have had only fleeting and seemingly casual visits with Indians, usually when visiting our mission houses dedicated to them. Yet I identify myself with my Indian brothers and sisters ... totally, completely, utterly! What do I mean by this?

Here I am at the headquarters of our Madonna House Apostolate, located in the small village of Combermere, in the depths of rural Ontario. The nearest Indian is about forty miles away at Golden Lake. I have nothing to do with that reservation there, either socially or physically or apostolically. And yet I live on a reservation. I live on every Indian reservation across Canada and the United States. I am part of the Indian family that lives in a little shack, in a prefabricated house, in a tent made out of branches and pines, or in just an ordinary canvas tent.

My body knows the heat of the day and its cold. It

knows the lack of water. My bare feet can feel the dust of the Arizona desert as I trudge across the well-known, well-worn paths that my ancestors made and that I use now. I wince at the sight of 'white man's grub.' True, I am accustomed to it now, but from somewhere within me, from some ancestral memory, my mouth can still taste the savor of caribou, buffalo, wild fowl, and deer that our men and women prepared so joyously.

I am 'one.' I am all of the Indian children who, by the decree of a paternalistic government, are torn away from the great love that Indian mothers and fathers have for their children and are placed in mission boarding schools in so many places of our land. I am one with those Indian high school youth who, in the Yukon and Northwest Territories, are placed in palatial hostels built by the same paternalistic government. I am 'integrated' with white students in the local public or religious high school, with white children who accept us and yet don't accept us.

Yes, I am that Indian youth and the palatial hostel that is supposed to be my home-away-from-home is to me a prison from which I cannot escape. It is here that I feel, without knowing that I feel it, such a total loss of my own identity that I seem to live in an unreal world that borders on the schizophrenic. I feel that I am going mad. Hostilities I never knew before are taking hold of me like chained-up wild beasts. Although I might seem 'a stoic Indian youth' to others, I cry in the night with memories of a forgotten past – a past where we knew freedom, bravery, courage, and self-sufficiency.

Yes, I, Catherine de Hueck Doherty, sitting at my desk in this busy apostolic headquarters of Madonna House in deep rural Ontario, *I am that Indian youth!* That Indian youth who finally has graduated from the white man's high school. That Indian youth who finally has learned those white man's words which have so little meaning ... cow, apple, oranges, farm. For me, as for a child of the Canadian tundra, they are only strange pictures about a foreign land. Many of these words are still a mystery to me, symbolically speaking, as unnatural in my mouth as French irregular verbs.

I know so many things about wild beasts and birds. I

have learned about plants and berries, about preparing animal skins and the use of them. I know so many things and I would like to tell the white man about them. I would like to learn about them in the books the white man writes, but he won't let me. I must learn about things I have never seen, touched, or smelled.

Yes, I am all those Indian high school graduates. Alienated from even the life on my own reservation and not integrated into the dominant white life of Canada and the United States, I am these youth, the youth of the twilight zone. My life is spent in a fog and a mist – the fog and mist of not knowing where I belong.

The white man's government has given me all this useful knowledge, aims to send me out into this white world, and earnestly tries to do so. But the people, the white people who elected that government and whose taxes supplied this education of mine, *they segregate me in their hearts* before I can even take a step into that world. And this segregation spills over in so many ways. They refuse to accept me as a human being like themselves. They reject me as their brother. What hurts even more is that they reject me even as a member of their Church! Oh, they may tolerate my physical presence, but in so many other ways they reject me. Yes, even though I might be of their own Christian faith – the faith in which Christ taught us that 'all men are brothers.'

Sitting here in Madonna House, I have identified myself completely with all of these youth. I now ask myself the question: "Who am I? Where do I belong?" The answer comes from some hellish depth. It may be the depths of my own inward hell or of the hell outside of me, I don't know. But the answer is clear and unmistakable and comes to me loudly: "You? You belong nowhere!"

I hear tell of refugees, of victims of the wars and revolutions, of the people who are without a country. I understand their sufferings. But today I find myself identifying with those Indian men, those Indian women, those Indian youth who silently cry: "You white people have taken away from us our country too. We are without a homeland, like the refugees of today. But you have done even greater harm to us: You have taken away our *identity.* You have brought us to a tragic crossroad and we do not know which path to take. We ask, 'Who are we and where do we belong?' And the answer comes back that we do not belong anywhere, that we are no one. We are *No-Body!*''

Yes, a strange thing happens to me at Madonna House when, with a flaming love, I identify myself with my brothers and sisters, the Indians. I feel hope dying within me. I feel the fingers of a strange death squeezing my heart, and that touch changes me into some sort of 'living dead' ... for that is what becomes of people without hope.

I, like my Indian brothers and sisters, can read. I have read of my people, of their religious faith, their bravery and their courage. From my readings I know they survived under conditions that few other men could have survived. I gather impressions of a wonderful civilization, an Indian civilization that extends across the American continent even unto the lands of Mexico. I hear in my heart the songs that my people have sung in the freedom of their forests, plains, and mountains. I remember their reverence for nature and all living things.

I remember other things too – the cruelty and wars and other dark things that went with that civilization, as they do with all civilizations. But the good in my people's history outweighs the bad. We seem to have killed for 'good reasons' ... in defense of our hunting grounds, out of extreme hunger, etc. We did not kill senselessly.

What has become of me and my people now? Identifying with the Indian, I ask myself that question. The answer is that we have been reduced to the anonymity of people who live by the handouts of a paternalistic government. Hope has been taken away from us and hopelessness has been given to us with 'treaty money' and all the rest of it. An infinite apathy has taken hold and, deep inside of us, a question rhythmically repeats itself as if to the accompaniment of drums that are no more. This question becomes a song, a dirge in our soul: What's the use...? What's the use...? What's the use of striving, of reaching out for a better world?

Yes, I, in this corner of rural Ontario, feel like the Indian! I feel so demoralized that I cannot even formulate a hope, a dream. I am like one stricken blind. I am like one from whom healing has been taken away. Wordlessly, I cry out to the Lord from the depths. I cry out to the One who cured the blind man, who gave healing to the deaf one, who loosened the tongue of the mute. But even the Lord to whom I cry out from my depths is hidden for me, as he is hidden for so many Negroes, because the Christians who render him lip service have not incarnated his Gospel of love in their lives.

From where I stand, in the depths of this apathy, it is hard to see the face of God. Those 'lip-service Christians' are still in the majority and they speak so well at meetings and conferences about Indians, Eskimos, and Negroes. But when we ring their doorbells in response to all the jobs they advertise, these same Christians close those doors gently but firmly against us. It is easy for them to do so, for they have never really opened the doors of their hearts to us!

This is what I feel with my Indian brothers and sisters, as I so strangely identify with them without painting my flesh red or changing the shape of my face.

And all that I have said about the Indians includes the Metis also. I feel the pain that they must feel, for if the full-blooded Indian has been relegated to that twilight world we all know about but do not want to face, what happens to the Metis? Who are they, these Metis? By blood and inheritance they belong to both races, White and Indian, but they are not accepted by either. They have another cross to bear: not being a full-blooded Indians, they have been rejected by that same paternalistic government and have been left to fend for themselves.

Am I 'red like an Indian'? No, I am a white-skinned blue-eyed blonde. But my soul and heart and I are 'one'. The whole of me is one with my Metis and Indian brothers and sisters. One in love!

That means in an identification which is total – complete as only love can make it.

Oh, Indian and Metis brothers and sisters of mine! I have nothing to give you, for I possess neither gold nor

silver. But I offer you the inn of my heart, the bread of my
love, and the wine of my identification with you. That is all
I have to give you, for that is all I have.

Lovingly yours in Mary,

A SIGN OF LOVE

March 22, 1965

Dearly Beloved,

In a recent letter to you, I spoke of being simple and
single-minded and, as so often happens, one thought led to
another. It came to me that this 'being of a single purpose'
is what God meant for all Christians. He made us,
individually; but not to act as individuals only. He wanted
all of us, together, to be 'of a single purpose.' So he made
the Church; and he made it as a *Sign of Love*.

I wrote an article about this for *Restoration*, but I
thought I would incorporate it into a Staff Letter:

At the Vatican Council, the role of the 'Church in the
World' was discussed and is still being discussed by the
Fathers of the Church. These men certainly are illuminated
by the light of the Holy Spirit, whatever their personal
talents or weaknesses as human beings may be.

Yet, strange as this may seem, I feel that lay people –
who are members of his Mystical Body, who are part of
the 'People of God' – may also contribute something to

the clarification of this role of the 'Church in the World.' Small and insignificant as any one of us may be, or brilliant and occupying high government positions as some of us are, I think that all of us can contribute. That is because the Holy Spirit abides in us too; and he illuminates us according to his own measure and our needs.

As I write this, I am filled with strange reactions and emotions. I find myself hesitant to put on paper (or even to articulate within myself) the thoughts that come to me in the quiet hours of the night, for these are the hours when I can meditate best on God and his truths. Why am I so hesitant to allow thoughts on such a weighty subject as the 'Church in the World' to shape themselves within my mind, much less put them on paper? Perhaps it is because I belong to the generation that has been trained to leave such thoughts to the clergy and hierarchy.

Yet I know – as I knew thirty-five years ago, when I began the Apostolate of Friendship House and Madonna House – that this was not enough. Even then, the stirring of these thoughts possessed me. It is true that I could not articulate them correctly then; I could not put them on paper either. But I had to do *something* because those thoughts were clamoring to be released from within me. As I look back today, I ask myself if I define the word 'thoughts' well. Perhaps they were graces of the Holy Spirit that I mistook for my own thoughts. Maybe (I hope that I am not presumptuous) ... maybe they were God's thoughts that he put into me. Yes, maybe.

Thirty-five years ago I had to incarnate them, silently but actively, into a life lived according to their prompting. They were stronger than I was. To the people who questioned *why* I had to incarnate those 'thoughts' in such a radical manner – radical for the times of which I speak (1930 and onwards) – I could not explain. I just had to do so.

They were very simple thoughts. I sensed them more than I knew them intellectually. To put it another way ... I 'knew without knowing' and almost against my reason that, when I tried to apply my human intellect to this strange knowledge which I called my 'thoughts,' I was inexorably drawn to one idea: *I must sell all that I possessed!* I had to give my money to the poor, take up my cross, and follow Christ wherever he led. That is all I could express; that is all I could articulate. Asked why I was doing this, pressed from all sides to give an answer to priests and bishops and Christian laity, I had then (even as now, thirty-five years later) only one answer: *because I love!*

Today, meditating on the Council and its tremendous work of defining the role of the 'Church in the World,' I find again this answer relentlessly surging in me as the sea surges onto the beach. It comes upon me again and again, inexorably, invading hidden sandy coves or attacking long stony shores, spending its waves in a relentless clamoring that seems to go on forever and ever. The role of the Church in the World – as I see it (I, a small and unimportant grain of sand on God's beach, battered, perhaps by his grace, relentlessly) – is to be a *Sign of Love.*

I'm not a theologian. Yet it seems to me that the changes in the world have far outstripped the work of theologians. We live in a world that orbits men into space, that discusses cybernetics and automation as facts already accomplished; a world girdled and made 'one' (at least mechanically) by satellites and supersonic planes. Yet it is a fragmented and fragmenting world, where pluralistic views create divergent societies, where communications are faster than sound and sometimes good sense. It is a world where millions of people do not bother with any kind of religion (let alone the Christian religion), where Christians are becoming an ever-diminishing minority and are in the diaspora. In a world like that, theology will take many years to 'catch up' with life's realities.

In the meantime, who will be able to prevent modern man from falling a victim to the myth of Prometheus, from reaching toward that 'deification' which would mean his failure? Who will bring forward the real motives which will enable men to end the cold war, to undertake the works of building one world – that sense of brotherhood which alone will save it from ultimate self-destruction? By what means will this be done?

The answer, it seems to me, is the Church. When it shows its true face to the modern world, when it meets twentieth-century man in the center of his anguished heart and reveals itself to be a *Sign of Love*, then the world will make progress. That is the real need of this present age. But the Church must be 'present' in this world, and this consists in meeting one's fellow man *right where he lives*.

I do not express all of this too clearly because I still have a difficulty in articulating things to myself, but I repeat: What is needed is a *Sign of Love* where the Church meets Man in the fundamental core of his life. This is what God meant for each of us to do. We, the average person, wherever we are, have the mission of 'not being separated from the other.' At the present time, this means participation in all stages of the changes that mankind is passing through. It applies to everything, or so it seems to me: science, technology, existing organizations in the world, *anything* that is trying to meet the needs of people today.

But this demands something tremendous from all of us Christians, especially Catholics. It demands that we abandon our limited outlook which approaches all problems of mankind in terms of a narrow 'ecclesiastical vision.' Am I heretical if it seems to me that, for instance, the problem of Latin America is not a lack of priests but a lack of economic, political, and educational development?

Yes, I feel I am not expressing myself too well; yet these thoughts hammer at me like waves crashing on a beach. Isn't the Church a community of love, and faith, and worship? But how is anyone to find out that it is a community of faith and worship, if no one knows it as a Community of Love? The words of Scripture come back to me: "The blind see, the deaf hear, and the *Good News* is preached to the poor." Wasn't that a definition of the Gospel message that everyone understood? So, it seems to me that the Church must become a Sign of Love *everywhere;* and this means that each member of the Church, individually and collectively, must cooperate with everyone else, with other Christian religions, with all social reforms (even those which might seem to its conservative element as 'revolutionary'). We have to go deeply into the community.

It seems to me that we have to watch out for the temptation to establish God's kingdom by human means –

even social action born of private initiative. (I am speaking of an attitude of mind more than anything else!) We're inclined to build hospitals and schools – our own hospitals, schools, congregations, lay apostolates, etc. (with emphasis on the words 'our own'). Yet as a *Sign of Love* which the Church is in this world, we must embrace everyone. We must not build 'our own' only. We must blend with all the forces of a community of men to effect these immense changes that are demanded of those who love and those who need.

First of all, however, this Sign of Love must begin *with ourselves.* We Christians must love one another! The pagans will be attracted by that, and they will seek to find out 'why.' As the Sign of our Love becomes evident in a concern that spills into every nook and corner of our modern world (as *Pacem in Terris** wants it to), then indeed, we can begin to preach the word with our voices. Because we have first preached it *with our lives* and have broken down all the invisible walls which, in the past, kept us away from being a Sign of Love, now we can *begin to talk!*

When we *all* are a Sign of Love – the whole Church, hierarchical and lay – then people who do not belong to its community of faith and worship will wish to do so, for we will have 'incarnated' the word. Our Sign of Love will be palpable and visible, as the wounds of Christ were to Thomas.

Lovingly yours in Mary,

Catherine

*Social encyclical of Pope John XXIII, 1963.

PERSONAL RENEWAL AND WORLD RESTORATION

March 27, 1965

Dearly Beloved,

I recently received an interesting letter from one of our members. I want to share it with you because it deals with various important ideas. I cannot tell you how happy I am that our members are beginning to ask intelligent questions and bring forth ideas worth discussing and clarifying.

Part of my belief is to answer every question that the members of Madonna House (or anyone else) may ask me. I believe in doing this with simplicity and directness, going right to the essence. If I don't know the answer, I must say so or else seek to find it. As all the members in the field know, I have tried to incarnate this as lovingly and as patiently as possible. To me, no question is too small; no question is too big. I stand ready to repeat the same things over and over, praying all the while to the Holy Spirit to give me an ingenuity of love and patience. I ask him not to let my repetitions become too monotonous, but to give each one a little sparkle of newness.

Because of my tremendous reverence for the individual, I have always resisted the temptation to print up a mimeographed leaflet listing the questions asked by many members, even though they are often the same. That's also why I am so happy about the subtle change in the accent of questions being asked. They deal less with a person's emotions, or problems of individuals, and more and more with ideas. This is truly wonderful!

Incidentally, I want to clarify another point of my philosophy (one can almost say Articles of Faith) which would fit in here. It is the need for 'those in authority' in our Apostolate – at whatever level they may be – to contemplate deeply the definition of *charity* in St. Paul's celebrated hymn. Long before the aggiornamento came, I held this belief as very sacred and tried to act upon it. For myself, I also think it necessary to 'have a lifetime' to meditate on the first sentence of the definition – "Charity is patient" – in order to fully accept it into one's being.

The rest of that definition of St. Paul will grow to maturity within us, provided we incarnate that singular patience he speaks of. In a good translation from the Latin, the word *patience* means *martyrdom* semantically speaking.* It's an interesting point, too, to realize that the 'white' martyrdom of incarnated patience is akin to the 'red' martyrdom of shedding one's blood. Both are a 'seed of faith' in people's souls, and help them grow closer to God.

However, let us go back to the letter I mentioned. ... One of the questions asked by this person is about "achieving a balance between the intramural conditions in Madonna House and what could be called the extramural ones." By intramural ('within the walls') he means the emphasis placed on letters from me that discuss those things which all of our members are interested in – themselves, and their personal problems in relation to other people (to authority, to local directors, to other members, to those whom they serve). By extramural (an area of discussion which he thinks is lacking!) he means a broader involvement in the world of ideas, including social justice, communications, the aggiornamento in its fullness, etc. He goes on to suggest, somewhat timidly, that there's a sense of guilt in his mind about even *asking* that question, and thinks other staff sometimes have the same feeling. It may appear to be a criticism, he suggests, and hence a disloyalty to Madonna House to do so.

Well, I think that is a wrong attitude. There should be neither timidity, nor feelings of guilt, nor a sense of disloyalty about asking an honest question, if it is brought up in an objective manner for the purpose of clarifying either the Apostolate and its role in the world, or the role of a particular member in his or her assigned task. It would be a very poor directorate that wouldn't welcome and try to answer such questions and want to have peaceful

*In other words ... to 'willingly endure pain and discomfort' is in effect to 'witness' to one's beliefs about life.

discussions about them. By 'peaceful' I mean intellectually objective discussions; not altercations, not a venting of hostilities, not a hidden desire to emotionally escape from something or other in the Apostolate. An honest, true, sincere question is never disloyal.

I had to smile as I reviewed this question, for sometimes 'the obvious' is not always obvious to some of us. In point of fact, the writer of this letter has himself been appointed – under 'holy obedience' so to speak – to immerse himself into the larger stream of the Church. His work demands a 'plunging into' that turbulent river of cursillos and communications, into a maelstrom of activity for imparting information and ideas. He constantly deals with people *in* the world and *of* the world. That's his job!

His very position should answer his own question, if he would just stand back and look at himself and what he has been assigned to do. We at Madonna House realize there is a tremendously exciting world "outside of our own intramural discussions." We have deliberately sent him into that extramural world as a leaven, a ferment, a witness there.

Incidentally, it often happens to us human beings that 'the obvious answer' does not come easily to mind. The reason is that we haven't given the problem enough objective thought. We all need to learn the art of stepping back from a situation and taking in a larger view of it.

To give a recent example: we at the training center were discussing an idea which has struck many of the staff so much – 'folding the wings of the intellect.' It was a lively discussion, to say the least! I was being pushed into a corner, from which I hope I rose battered but unbruised; suddenly someone spoke up and 'pointed out the obvious.' The person said, in effect: "Hey, stop this challenging of Catherine's idea. She's not against the use of intelligence and knowledge. She's proving it right now by using all her intellectual powers and her vast knowledge of philosophy, theology, and allied sciences to prove why one should *fold the wings of the intellect' at certain times and use it vigorously at other times.*" It showed me again how we sometimes 'miss the obvious' because we do not think about it long enough and deeply enough.

But back to the letter we are considering. Let me repeat: no one should have any hesitation about asking questions. The person who wrote this letter is *quite right* in saying that there is, across the Apostolate, a type of concentration that appears to be indrawn, pulling back into itself. Yes, the Staff Letters have dealt mostly with intramural matters, with clarifications and discussions about the personal growth of members of Madonna House, about clarifying relations among themselves as staff workers, and rarely (but not too rarely) about their relationships to the people they serve and their place in a given community or neighborhood.

There are many reasons why this has happened. The first is that, by its very nature, by its very mandate given by God to me, Madonna House is dedicated to *the restoration of the world to Christ** via living the Gospels with one's life, doing little things with great love for God and for neighbor. This restoration, this Gospel-preaching through one's life, these doing of little things with great love, is one of the most powerful means of entering the present 'green revolution' of the Church. Green for the color of Pentecost, of spring, of renewal.

We have a proof of this in a newsletter from one of our fieldhouses. Here was a group of people who for years did 'little things with great love.' They answered the telephone many hundreds of times a week, attended what seemed like hopeless meetings, cried out with their voices in the wilderness of housing, interracial justice, labor, questions of minority groups, etc. They spent years of their life seemingly treading water. Suddenly, the fruits of their labors became immense. Their involvement in the wide stream of the Church's thinking and acting, their penetration into our modern, secular, pagan world now stands revealed for all to see.

I remind you of a recent letter from the foreign missions which we shared. Remember the near despair which afflicted our team? It was about doing little things that seemed to have no rhyme or reason. Later, they learned

---

*This phrase, from Ephesians 1:10, became the motto of St. Pius X, the pope who urged 20th century Catholics to involve themselves in the secular world. Madonna House publishes a newspaper called *Restoration*.

by hearsay how some of the native people had been deeply affected by seeing these little things done with so much love. It was a revelation to their souls!

There are other people who at this moment are outstanding in the apostolate of the Church, influencing it tremendously at its very base. The Charles de Foucauld people do not enter into the larger stream of the apostolate (as this letter-writer envisages it). But they have had a tremendous influence on the Council, on Cardinal Lecaro, Cardinal Suenens, a body of French cardinals, and many others. There is also the group of Father Gauthier in Jerusalem. I understand that their presentation on poverty (now published in English under the title *Jesus Christ and The Poor*) affected the Council Fathers more than any other document. Father Gauthier is the head of a priestly lay-apostolate in Jerusalem. This group lives a life of stark poverty and doesn't enter the various apostolates of the Church; instead, its members spend their time as carpenters and servants to the poor. They never 'give' anything away, but simply offer others the work of their hands and their own poverty. Here again, we see that the restoration of the world must begin with *being before God*.

In Europe, reams are being written about Father Monchanin, a holy man who – with the permission of his superior – went alone to India and spent years there perfecting his Sanskrit and his knowledge of the Eastern religions. Then he divested himself of everything he owned and spent close to twenty years living the life of a poor man in India. He dressed in a dark blue robe (in honor of Our Lady), had an open shrine built on some main street in the slum districts of Calcutta, and offered Mass there every morning. The rest of the day he spent in meditation, sitting immobile with his beggar's bowl visible to all passersby. Father Monchanin is dead now, but he became a legend in India. All the great people of India – the monks, the learned ones, the holy ones – made pilgrimages to his place and talked with him about Christianity.

I needn't stress to you the effect that the celebrated Mother Teresa of Calcutta has had in India, as she and her followers pick up the homeless poor from the street and allow them to die in decency, surround by loving care, in a humble native-like hospital. Speaking of myself, I was recently invited to lecture in Chicago. I was introduced to the large audience by a Negro who, as a youth, was one we had served in Friendship House there. What he said might well be repeated here. In essence, he simply stated:

> The Baroness is a woman who pioneered in all that the aggiornamento of Pope John has now brought to us. She pioneered in the storefront apostolate, accepting poverty for love's sake. She also pioneered in interracial justice. At one time her voice was the only one being heard on the subject of interracial justice in America. She pioneered in cooperatives and in labor schools. She made history in the apostolate of communications. She spoke on the lecture platform, on street corners, through the radio, through innumerable articles – in a word, through all the then-known means of communication.

It might be good for the writer of this letter, and all the members of Madonna House, to think about these words. It shows the involvement we have had in a number of large streams of the Church. For 'restoration' means bringing Catholics back to Christ: those who have fallen away, those who are the tepid ones or the ignorant ones. It also means preaching to the pagans and neo-pagans, the atheists and agnostics, or what-have-you. In a word, to *all* people!

This is not done en masse, or to immense groups. It is done *person-to-person*, even at mass rallies or through the mass communications media. Even then, it must be geared to the individual receiving the message because, between the giving of the message and the receiving of it, the Holy Spirit enters in. Each person is unique and irreplaceable and will get out of the message that which he or she can, with the help of the Holy Spirit. There is really no such thing as 'mass conversion' with the rare exception, as happened at Pentecost, when the Holy Spirit specifically desires it. So we might 'take it as read' that this applies to all apostolates within the Church, but especially to the lay apostolate ... and very specially to Madonna House.

Now it stands to reason that the apostle must be *himself* 'restored' before he can give this message to others. It is less than fifteen years since the Madonna House Apostolate was founded. That's not too long a time to be involved in this business of restoring each member to Christ. Factually, some of you have been here only a few years, and may need much more restoration than others. Yet we can see among ourselves the miracle of that complete restoration slowly taking place in some of our members. It is a slow process, that restoration, because it is so thorough. It constantly deals with the mystery of grace.

At the present moment, we are studying psychology with Sister Mary Andrew. But psychology, while it clarifies, also *disturbs*. A lot of clarification is necessary and has to be given as we progress. New friends are coming into the stream of the lay apostolate. Again clarification must be given, but usually it is given to individuals (as I am doing now to the writer of this letter). Not all have reached the spiritual and emotional maturity in which they can ask the larger questions. They are still drawn 'intramurally' into the Apostolate. Only when they have clarified this will they be able to go out to the Apostolate elsewhere. We feel that the individual is very important in Madonna House, for he or she will touch the hearts of the many whom God wants reached through these intramural discussions and clarifications.

I have taken a long time to lay the basic foundations of my answer to this letter, but what is being asked here is very simple. And it can be answered simply: Madonna House Apostolate implicitly follows the statement of Pope Pius XII about Catholic Action, whatever style it may take: *"Nothing is alien to the lay apostolate except sin."*

The directorate of Madonna House is deeply occupied with every new trend, every new accent. It tries to absorb, digest, evaluate, discuss, and clarify them not only on behalf the lay apostolate but for the whole Church. I read a great many magazines every week. We have the latest books on every subject in the library, and we read them. We, the directorate, try to keep aware of all that is happening. As our members mature and grow in grace and wisdom, as they become individually 'restored' to Christ (physically, emotionally, intellectually, creatively, and spiritually), they will be moved – slowly, with deep evaluation of the whole spirit of Madonna House – into the broader streams.

At no time, however, is there any injunction or restraint put upon any member of Madonna House concerning the question of intramural 'versus' extramural activities, Madonna House 'versus' the wide stream of the Church's apostolate. Madonna House is definitely a part of all this (and not a sluggish part, either!).

But first things first. The tragedy of haste and unpreparedness and lack of formation is, at present, the bane of most lay apostolates; and Madonna House stands out (for the time being, at least) as one of the groups to which others come for formation and information.

No, there should be no cleavage between these states of affairs, between intramural and extramural activities! But the first definition of charity in the hymn of St. Paul is still the word *patience* and, in this case, haste would be the opposite of patience. It would be a little strange if half-restored people in our Apostolate would go around trying to restore a sick, bewildered, confused world. No, they must first become unconfused themselves.

Love,

LOYALTY AND FREEDOM OF CONSCIENCE

April 2, 1965

Dearly Beloved,

As you have seen, one member sent me a very interesting letter. Besides his question on the intramural versus extramural activities, he also asked (as many of you have done) the seemingly difficult question about *folding the wings of the intellect*. This is how he words it:

> There is a profound truth in this statement of yours. But it often seems in direct confrontation with the modern man's legitimate desire (and, I think, need) to discover that religion and service of God is *freeing* and is not a prison house. How do we strike a balance? I think that what you're doing on this confrontation and evaluation is tremendous.

> But I think that many in the Apostolate – including myself at times –have overstressed 'loyalty' at the expense of 'honesty.' We feel, I suppose, that to be absolutely honest smacks somehow of disloyalty. We do not yet feel *free* either in the Church or at Madonna House to truly express ourselves. This is 'the' problem – or rather, 'a' problem – for the whole Church, the People of God.

I confess that I was a little confused when I read these words. By no stretch of the imagination did I ever feel that either the Church or Madonna House could ever be a prison! Before I answer the question of 'folding the wings of the intellect,' however, I would like to make a very clear statement regarding *freedom*. As you all know, I have had my share of persecution, rejections of all types, open and underhanded attacks, and much disapproval. There has been very little cooperation, approval, or help from 'people who matter,' people who were supposed to uphold me rather than crucify me.

Yet, throughout these thirty-five years of the Apostolate, and even before, I never felt that I was either a prisoner or in any way 'unfree.' There is so much talk today about 'liberty' and 'freedom of conscience.' Either I live in a fool's paradise and have done so all of my life, or I must be a nitwit and have missed a lot of what's been going on.

I have always been 'free' in matters of conscience. In fact, I reveled in my liberty as a Christian and as a Catholic. I knew my faith. I used my reason, illuminated by that faith, and I stood full square on that freedom and liberty of conscience which belong to the children of God. I never compromised with it! When I had to speak in Roman Catholic circles on interracial justice, during an era that had never heard about it, I spoke openly and took full responsibility for my words. I did so in entire liberty and freedom of conscience, without caring where the chips fell or what happened to me.

In Savannah, Georgia, I was almost lynched. I had known it might happen when I publicly discussed interracial marriage there; but I didn't hesitate to discuss it just because there was a danger of being lynched. Once I respectfully told a bishop that, if he continued to discriminate, I would earnestly pray for his soul because he was likely to end up in hell. You know the story and its sequel. I can't think of a place or a time where I have compromised with my conscience out of a mistaken 'loyalty to the Church' or to its representatives. I am a little confused, therefore, about all of this discussion about *liberty*. I presumed that it was always there, and I have acted on that presumption.

At the same time, however, I also have obeyed without compromise. I will continue to obey 'the powers that be' because, to me, *obedience is not a compromise*. It is an act of love that I give with a free conscience (otherwise, it is not obedience) to the representative of God in anything-but-sin. Let me clarify: If a bishop asked me to compromise a tenet of my faith, one that 'in conscience' I couldn't compromise, I would resign. I would not disobey, but I would resign in obedience to my conscience. I would not be disobeying him, for then I would no longer speak as an official or semiofficial representative of the Church and of an Apostolate. I have done that in the past, when my staff in the States tried to force me about an issue. I simply wouldn't compromise. I resigned from Friendship House, and went to Combermere to start all over again. I cannot imagine anyone feeling 'disloyal' whenever there is a matter of truth involved. The question is: *is a truth involved?* Or not?

I think there is some confusion here because of the action of the devil and also because of historical conditions (after all, the Church is part of the human history and of various popular movements). Heresies such as Jansenism and Puritanism affected Catholic Christians. They were heir to these heresies and to many others. I am not going to enumerate all of them. Some heresies began even in the time of the apostles (circumcision versus non-circumcision). Various heresies have had an effect on the spiritual formation of Catholics throughout the last few centuries, which has resulted in a lot of stresses and strains and tremendous tensions in our psychological makeup.

As a result of this, all Christians (Catholics especially!) became greatly confused ... emotionally, psychiatrically, intellectually. They became frightened sheep in Christian ghettoes. They defended their faith, but they didn't spread it very much. We have been heir to all of this confusion, so much so that we may come to regard simple honesty as a form of disloyalty, even though the Gospel says that *"truth will make you free!"* That is why I think there is this confusion of loyalty versus honesty. There is this unfortunate 'conditioning' of the Christian soul because of these historical factors. Proper use of the intellect should abolish it, however, or at least lessen it.

As far as Madonna House is concerned, I will simply restate it this way: If a question is objective, if an honest clarification is truly sought in any field – spiritual, psychological, or intellectual – then there should never be any fear of disloyalty (or any *other* fear either) in asking that question. It's a matter of speaking in utter simplicity with a view to getting to the essence of truth. If, on the other hand, a given question is loaded with hostility, with emotional disturbances and overtones, if it is asked for any reason other than for getting at the truth, then the question should be reconsidered by the individual. That type of 'speaking up' should not be confused with liberty and freedom of conscience.

I could write a book on such questions. They often come to me through letters, not seeking a true answer to a given problem, but consciously or unconsciously trying to 'get me on their side' of whatever argument they are having with an authority figure or with each other. Sometimes, via such questions, they wish to show me someone else's problem or else they try to rationalize away some truth that they *know* is the truth.

Well, I guess I'll send this letter to you and write another one later on, about 'folding the wings of the intellect.' I got carried away with the strange question that confused me: whether religion in the service of God is freeing or a prison house. Perhaps I reacted this way because I never felt that religion was anything *but* freeing! Never in my whole life have I equated it with a prison.

Love,

ON FOLDING THE WINGS OF THE
INTELLECT

April 8, 1965

Dearly Beloved,

Here we are back again, this time to discuss 'folding
the wings of the intellect.' The phrase seems to arouse
much interest among us, so let us try to clarify it. I guess I
should start again by clarifying what exactly I mean by the
expression.

Before I do this, I want to state that this is a
theological expression taken from the mystics of the Latin
Rite Church. To put it even more simply and plainly, it is *a
concept of faith*. You can find out much more about it, for it
is discussed and clarified in seminaries and among
theologians in that part of sacred studies called mystical
theology.

There are two parts to theology: *ascetical* and
mystical. Ascetical theology deals with man's ascent to
God through the reasoning faculties, the human intellect.
The intellect, of course, does not accomplish this unaided;
God's grace is also present. Man's intellect is illuminated
by faith through the sacrament of Baptism, nourished by
the sacrament of the Holy Eucharist, and helped by all the
other sacraments. Man learns to use his intellect, supported
by that faith, that love, that strength and wisdom which
comes to him from God. This includes the courage to
practice *kenosis* (the 'emptying' of self so as to be filled
with God), the dying to self by the practice of many virtues,
especially charity. Many non-Christians – Aristotle, Plato,
the great leaders or founders of pagan religions – arrived at
similar conclusions through their powers of intellect. These
powers were probably illuminated by God's grace (as all
good is), but not in the fullness of the Christian way.

The second part of theology, called mystical theology,
concentrates on *God's way* of dealing with man. While
ascetical theology has many major divisions (such as

Pastoral, Moral, etc.) mystical theology has no divisions or subdivisions. Though I stress the workings of God in the soul and the need to be open and receptive to those movements of his grace, I repeat constantly that a *true and deep encounter with God* really happens when God acts upon us in the special manner that is *his alone*. Then he gives us a knowledge of himself through the Holy Spirit, a knowledge that is that is *beyond* our intellect, *beyond* our capacity to acquire it. It is a pure grace, a pure gift of love from him to us.

Yes, I have a great desire to foster growth in *all areas* of your life, because I believe in the restoration of the *whole* person through Christ. I try to inculcate this growth constantly, even though many times I am working under difficult circumstances and quite often meet much misunderstanding. What is meant by 'all areas' of your life? This means the intellect and its development. This means creativity and its development. This means emotional and volitional restoration of the whole person, individually and collectively. From the very beginnings of our Apostolate, when it was Friendship House, I offered the staff intellectual subjects. For the record, they include:

1. A course in apologetics, Sheed and Ward style – then called Evidence Guild style.

2. A course in theology given by the Dominicans in New York who, at my request, specially rewrote St. Thomas of Aquinas for people like us who did not have the background necessary to study him. This course was very successful. Even today it is being used, with few changes, by people like Father Wendell in New York and in theology schools for the laity across the United States and is soon coming to Canada. They call this 'Father Donovan's Course' because he was the priest with whom I first worked on it. (Incidentally, I myself took four years of Thomistic Theology from Father Henry Carr, one of the greatest theologians of his time. He is the former superior general of the Basilian Fathers, and a cofounder of the Institute of Medieval Studies along with Jacques Maritain and Etienne Gilson.)

3. A continuing course in liturgy with the top-notch liturgists of the time, such as: Father Godfrey Diekmann, a Benedictine of Collegeville, Minnesota; Dom Virgil Michel of the same Order and place; Dietrich von Hildebrandt, the celebrated German philosopher, whose book *Liturgy and Personality* was written from the lectures at Friendship House; and many other top-notch specialists in liturgy. Incidentally, I was one of the pioneers of the liturgical movement. I remember our early meetings at the so-called liturgical conferences in the middle '30s, when we thought that forty people at a conference was a *crowd!* The members of Friendship House and I were also pioneers in the Vernacular Society. We had to be courageous, intellectually speaking, because everybody belonging to this group was considered suspect by The Powers That Be!

4. We had continual courses in social justice according to the papal encyclicals. In order to teach those, the then existing staff of Friendship House and I took an eight-week course in the celebrated Labor School run by the Jesuits. Previous to that, while we were in Canada, we had the benefit of lectures in Friendship House, in Ottawa and Toronto, by priests who were specialists in those encyclicals.

5. Courses in various parts of the cooperative movement, meaning the Producers Co-op, the Wholesale Co-op, and the Retail Co-op, plus the philosophy behind the whole co-op movement and its social effects.

6. Courses on atheism, and on communism. These were two separate subjects because there are atheists who are not communists. So we had a course that dealt specifically with atheistic communism. The course on communism that we officially had was given by Father Ledit, S.J., who teaches the Royal Mounted Police in Canada and the F.B.I. in the United States. He is a super-specialist. In the United States, we even had ex-communists teaching some of the courses.

7. Courses on interracial justice, as part of the larger issue of social justice in the United States and Canada.

These included Negro history in America and a general survey of the history of slavery in the world, followed by two weeks on minority groups who were not Negroes.

8. Courses in recreation, leadership, and handicrafts were constantly given to members of Friendship House and Madonna House staff.

9. Ecumenism is fashionable now. It was fashionable with me 'way back when.' At the very beginning of our Apostolate, I and my Russian friends – such as Helen Iswolsky, Baroness Taube, Russian priests of all kinds (in and out of communion with Rome, both in Canada and New York) – constantly gave courses on the Eastern churches. Many of our staff were vitally interested in, participated in, and encouraged wherever possible the ecumenical movement with regard to the Eastern Rite churches. We were all very much involved in this.

In addition, I contributed much to the Russian papers about immigration problems in Europe and America. I helped to establish the Orthodox Russian Church in Toronto. (It was not in communion with Rome. I did this with the blessing of Archbishop Neil McNeil, however.) All of this involved many people.

We did not stop with the Eastern Rite. We were involved with both Jews and Protestants, and were all members of the Conference of Jews, Protestants, and Catholics. Through our newspapers – *Social Forum, Friendship House News,* and *Restoration* – the ecumenical movement was and is being stressed, and it will continue to be. I beg you to remember that in this field Friendship House and our staff and myself were again pioneers!

10. Scriptural studies, long before they were the 'in' thing, were given to us both in Friendship House and in Madonna House by such outstanding scholars as Msgr. Doherty, now Bishop Doherty, the president of Seton College. Benedictine priests also helped us in various courses of liturgy and scriptures, way back when.

11. So much for what was, has been, and still is in existence in Madonna House. If you give this list a moment's thought, you will understand why I feel it almost unnecessary to stress to you how our Madonna House training is constantly growing. I now include anthropology, geography, history, and psychology (next September we will begin a course in sociology), to mention but a few.

12. There is need to work on the intellectual restoring of people, especially in that part of the mind which deals with Creativity – the 'fifth psychological need of human beings.' Creativity through handicrafts is virtually sweeping through Madonna House. May I remind you that I have been collecting materials (tools, books, clippings on various handicrafts, etc.) long before there was this interest among you. Speaking frankly, it took a lot of faith and persistence – and 'folding the wings of the intellect' (smile!) – before I made you aware of this tremendous need.

13. There are the many extramural courses which our members are constantly taking: courses in alcoholism (specifically in A.A. techniques), studies at the Coady International Institute in Nova Scotia, and other courses too numerous to mention.

14. Should I mention the utter openness of Madonna House to academic courses? I mean the 'officially academic' ones from universities. For example: Joe Hogan is finishing his B.A. in Oregon, Mary Jean is finishing a postgraduate course in public health, Irene and Ray Gene are taking postgraduate psychiatry. We are ready to continue this sort of thing if the needs of the Apostolate require it.

15. Nor should I fail to discuss the academic, vocational and practical knowledge that all of our members acquire through correspondence courses from accredited universities and other learning centers, such as Albert took at the Volkswagon Institute; and the general knowledge which both male and female members have acquired in auto repairs, beekeeping,

carpentry, cooking, electronics, gardening, and morse code, to name some of them.

16. Nor should I fail to mention the *liberation of the intellect* (that you discuss so much) from the prison of emotions, which Madonna House stands ready to give (and has given) through having our members go to psychologists or psychiatrists. This might be called a medical restoration; nevertheless, during this process of healing, these members acquire that intimate knowledge of their own inner workings which philosophers say is the basis of all knowledge. *Know thyself* is the beginning of wisdom; it gives one the ability to acquire more and more knowledge about the things which pertain to oneself (and that means *everything* – politics, economics, gardening, the whole physical universe, as well as religion and the things of the spirit).

17. Should I remind you that our team in East Pakistan is taking a specialized three-year course, not only in the language of the country (Bengali) but in the history, culture, music, geography, and anthropology of Pakistan and India.

18. Madonna House and Friendship House have continued to sponsor another form of learning (and a deep one at that, for it brings many kinds of knowledge) which is called *traveling*. Not traveling for travel's sake, but for its cultural value, its spiritual value, for the value of opening wider the hearts of those involved, and extending their intellectual horizons. The Pakistan team, for instance, was tremendously grateful for the extra two months of travel in Europe and the Near East, as they slowly wended their way toward the Far East. Those experiences of travel opened their eyes to new possibilities and different lifestyles, greatly helping them to appreciate the far-different cultures of southeast Asia when they arrived there.

I think this suffices to show you my postulate about 'the proper attitude towards the intellect.' I know you are not attacking me, nor am I defending myself. I hate justifying myself even to my own family, but I wanted to put these comments in writing for the sake of the present members of Madonna House and all future generations. To me, this record of accomplishments shouts to any objective observer of my deep personal concern for intellectual knowledge, in fact, for *any type of knowledge* that can restore people fully to God.

May I add that we have only just begun! We are investigating courses in theology, in San Francisco and other places, for some of our members. I have just been in correspondence with *Lumen Vitae* in Brussels about the possibility of sending someone there to learn the latest in catechetical techniques so as to be able to train teachers in the United States and in Canada.

We are preparing ourselves to give a course in sociology in the fall; it's possible that we will get a sociologist from Ottawa University, or else a very good correspondence course from an accredited university. I am investigating language courses also, and Sister Mary Andrew is going to continue to give us lectures in psychology. We are sponsoring weekly seminars on Current Events and encouraging interest in them; they are very successful at the present moment. We continue to do research into drama, and we are evaluating TV programs these days. I am working on trying to find someone to give us a critical intellectual approach to the all-important mass media.

So now you have it in writing! What sometimes escapes you who live here year-round is certainly obvious to the stranger who visits for a week or a month; for we are being besieged by every lay apostolate, and by many many priests, religious, and lay leaders. We have the reputation for having a very open directorate, one which doesn't hesitate to enhance, enlarge, change, abolish, and constantly review the intellectual and non-intellectual approaches to the restoration of the whole person.

I wanted also to go on record that, while I live, I will never give up this vision of 'giving the members of Madonna House the benefit of all possible intellectual and cultural training,' in fact, the whole gamut of whatever is needed to restore 'the whole person' that every Christian should be. And I hope my successors will continue to have this same accent!

Nevertheless, I will never cease to promote, explain, clarify and pray for the establishment of the 'mystical' part of theology which must complement the 'ascetical' part of Madonna House. The higher our members go on the intellectual scale of human and spiritual values, the better they will understand that they will have to *fold the wings of their intellect* and become like little children. They will have to be open of heart, soul, and mind to the Holy Spirit. He alone can lead them (with the help of his beloved spouse, the Blessed Virgin Mary) to a true encounter with Christ and hence to the Father. For this type of knowledge is *beyond* our intellect! Yes, beyond our natural all-too-human intellect. Christ desires this mystical encounter with us, and he demands for it a humble and childlike heart.

Lovingly yours in Mary,

P.S. Incidentally (smile!) it takes a lot of intellect to write this letter.

MY EASTER GIFTS TO YOU

April 12, 1965

Dearly Beloved,

Christ is risen, verily he is risen! Alleluia! Alleluia! On this great Feast for which the whole human race waited these many many years, and which stands out as a luminous and glorious signpost to the final resurrection of all humanity – the final union of creature with Creator in the parousia – I want to give a gift to you, beloved of my heart. But as I examine my stores, I find that my granaries are empty, for I am exceedingly poor. So I give you my emptiness and my poverty.

I look again, and find that I am exceedingly 'rich' because my emptiness has been filled by God, both directly and through all of you. I find that my poverty is bedecked with the splendor of his love, and yours, so I give you my wealth.

I look again and see that the Lord has come as a pilgrim into my soul, bringing me gifts innumerable – gifts of light, gifts of graces, gifts of ideas. I give you his light, his grace; and I share with you the ideas he has sent me. I cannot really *give* them to you, since he has embedded them so deeply into my mind and soul; so all that is left for me is to *share* them with you.

I look again and I see that the Lord has heard the voice of my crying from the depths where I have been for so long. He has heard the voice of my pleading and he has increased my love. And with that love, he has sent me compassion, tenderness, empathy and mercy.

Having given to you what the Lord has given to me, I stand a beggar at your door, a beggar who knows that he will receive again the gifts of the Lord; because it is to the beggars, the poor ones who need the Lord most, that he comes most quickly. He comes to them through others, so on this glorious Feast of the Resurrection, I beg for his gifts from your hands. I am hungry for your love, for your compassion, for your mercy, for your empathy. I wait, as Mary of Magdala did by the tomb in the garden. I know that you will come, laden with your gifts, and that I too will be able to exclaim, "Rabboni!"

This is the feast of Love Incarnate; Love who died for others; Love who rose again to make us one with him. May it be for each of us 'a resurrection from the tomb' of all the things that are not yet God's, so that we might – even now – become one in him. For, as he has told us, the kingdom of God begins in this world.

Christ is risen! Verily he is risen! Alleluia!

Lovingly yours in the
resurrected Lord,

EVERY CHRISTIAN IS A LAY APOSTLE

May 3, 1965

Dearly Beloved,

In a recent letter, a member of Madonna House gave an interesting summary of her thoughts. In doing so she raised a good question: "In discussing points important to us as Christians, i.e., the uniqueness of the human person and the responsibility to live for others, shouldn't we of the Apostolate realize that we must also be lay apostles *in the world* as well as lay Christians in Madonna House? " She went on to say: "Now the two concepts are really the same. But I fear that the neglect of the first point can undermine our understanding of ourselves, both as lay apostles and as a lay apostolate."

This question is both intelligent and timely because she reflects the confused state of Christians, and because we are discussing Catholic Christians of the North American continent today. If you have been following the Catholic Press, it will not come as news to you that all kinds of fine distinctions are being made in an attempt to clarify the concept of 'the lay apostolate' and of 'lay apostles.' It was somewhat the same in previous years; hierarchy, priests, lay people, religious of various types, all of them struggled with the definition of *Catholic Action.**

It is vital for us of Madonna House to have some clear ideas about it all. First of all, please remember that *each and every Christian* is meant to be an apostle, an ambassador, a giver of the Good News; not just a special few 'chosen ones.' Upon receiving the sacrament of Baptism, which incorporates them into the Body of Christ, Christians become members of the People of God. Each and every individual becomes 'one who is sent' to preach that Good News. This is because God loved us first, and because our response of faith – this 'love affair' between God and us – is meant to be 'expressed through others' who are our neighbors.

The sacrament of Confirmation is the sacrament of a mature apostle. It gives each of us courage, zeal, and other gifts of the Holy Spirit. We are made ready to be fearless apostles, ambassadors, givers of the Good News – even at the expense of our lives, if need be.

Every Catholic Christian must preach that Good News of the Gospel, first and foremost, with his life; and then, if he is able to do so, by word of mouth. Each of us Catholics, therefore, should see to it that we know our faith well and are able both to defend it and give it to others whenever we are called upon to do so. We exercise this according to our state in life, the intelligence God has given us, and to the full measure of our talents. None of these must be allowed to lie fallow.

God saw to it that his ambassadors, his apostles, the

---

*The term 'Catholic Action' was modified in its definition and scope quite a number of times between 1905 and 1965.

People of God (both lay and clerical) would be fortified and nourished along the way of their 'crying the Gospel with their lives.' He did this by giving us the sacrament of Penance and of the Holy Eucharist. He also provided for our nourishment by his word in the Scriptures.

This is the foundation of the broad ideal life of every Catholic. The very fact that each lay person is a Christian, a Catholic baptized and confirmed, means that each one (without exception!) is meant to be a 'lay apostle' and should be engaged in the manner just described.

God, however, works constantly for an even deeper sanctification of his Mystical Body, which we are both individually and collectively. This is as it should be, and it is reflected is what St. Paul calls *the diversity of unity*. He said – speaking about lay people, 'saints of the Church' as he calls them – that some of them will be prophets, some will be doctors, some will perform miracles, some will dream dreams. In a word, he pointed out the variety of 'callings' (vocations) that God in his infinite love and mercy planned for all his lay apostles.

Some will remain single, as in the parable of the rich young man, because Christ's words about virginity call them to a dedicated chastity out of love for God. These single people will be asked by God to work in various special apostolates. They will remain single, with or without any vows or promises. They will be part of the world, yet will be totally dedicated to the service of God. Their choice will be a deliberate one, freely and joyously made, done out of their love of God and love of neighbor.

Some lay apostles will get married, and their apostolate will exercise itself (as it should) first to one another as husband and wife. They will lead each other to holiness through their mutual love. They will live out their love day-to-day, letting their lives 'preach the Gospel' to one another. Then to their children; then to the community; then to their country; and finally to the world, according to their state of life and the talents given to them by God.

In the process of their growth in 'the apostolate to the community-at-large,' God may reveal certain plans for them. He may illuminate their intellects with a special grace and lead them to a more specialized type of married apostolate (such as the Christian Family Movement started by Canon Cardijn). If so, they will remain in the stream of the world's life, yet have something special added to them: the help of other married couples. Their work might be a greater leaven in the Mystical Body than that of a single couple, acting alone.

Unmarried individuals, as well as some specially-called married couples, might be given what we realize today are 'temporary vocations' from God. These are temporary commitments to bind the wounds of the Mystical Body and to preach the Gospel in special sectors of the Church. Among these are the Papal Volunteers for Latin America (known as PAVLA) the Agency for International Development (known as AID), and many others of these types. They are usually more specialized than the Catholic Family Movement, the Young Christian Students, the Young Christian Workers, etc. Their members, especially the organizers and leaders of them, often take temporary promises. There are many such specialized apostolates which are constantly arising, adapted to and trying to answer specific needs of our times. But they all are – and always will remain – part of the generalized 'lay apostolate' to which every Christian is called.

It must be clearly understood, I repeat once more, that this call to 'preach the Gospel with your life' and tell the Good News according to one's talents is incumbent on *every* Christian, no matter what his vocation may be. This time I use the word 'vocation' in the sense of 'occupation' – teacher, doctor, lawyer, nurse, auto mechanic, bus driver, etc. *No one is exempt!* This call is for every human being who has reached the use of reason. Canon Cardijn, for example, has an apostolate for school children from Grade One onwards. This type of apostolate is essentially one of 'like-to-like' – teacher witnessing to teacher, student to student, lawyer to lawyer, and so forth.

Finally, the Christian lay apostle may be called by God to an apostolate such as ours which, in its total dedication under promises, does not detract from the lay apostolic state. It simply means that God has chosen a group of lay people to go where they are most needed, and to be helpers of other apostolates of which they form a part. For example, the Grail goes to Brazil to train Brazilian women in the Grail technique. While they are doing it, they are also teaching PAVLA and Peace Corps people there, and assisting in the formation and development of such groups as the Catholic Family Movement, the Legion of Mary, and others.

We of Madonna House play the same role already in Portland, Oregon, where we are assisting many apostolates, taking part in the ecumenical movement, and helping our fellow Christians with such lights as we have. Therefore, there should never be any division in the mind of Madonna House members about being lay people, lay apostles who must enter into the stream of the whole world. *This concept is deeply embedded in the mandate God has given to me.* I started as a lay apostle, and I hope the Apostolate of Madonna House will never compromise with that lay state. At no time do we wish to become 'religious' (in the juridical sense of canon law, which refers to a very clearly stated and special vocation that God gives to some).

I might also point out to you, however, that the concept of religious life is also changing (Deo gratias) and that 'the religious' are beginning to understand that they belong in the world – our world of the laity – but with a special 'religious' accent. Madonna House, nevertheless, does not have that accent; God hasn't given it to us.

I beg you to remember that Madonna House (as an Apostolate) is still in the process of formation. We are very aware of this fact and are constantly seeking to enlarge our entry into the big stream of the world. Do not fear, dearly beloved. We will not leave the world; and the world will not leave us; for we are deeply rooted in it. It is God's world, too, and we must make it our business and concern to be present there. Remember that 'nothing is alien to Madonna House Apostolate, except sin.' Be at peace.

Love,

THE SPIRIT OF NAZARETH

May 18, 1965

Dearly Beloved,

In the poustinia, I have been praying and meditating a great deal about God's mandate to me. I have repeated it ad infinitum. I have explained it this way:

> The spirit of Madonna House is 'the spirit of Nazareth.' It is to be humble and hidden. It is to be poor in earthly goods, having only the necessities. This spirit should lead all belonging to Madonna House to a detachment from one's will, to a detachment of heart – especially from one's possessions, family, friends, and country. This should be done in a manner that will lead one to find all of these in the heart of Christ.

> Madonna House 'preaches the Gospel with its life.' Madonna House does 'little things with a great love' of God and neighbor. Madonna House is a 'family,' like the one in Nazareth – a family of God, hence a community of charity or love. Madonna House believes that it must *be* before the Lord first, and *do* for the Lord next. It bears witness to God in 'the marketplaces' of the world. It 'identifies with' those it serves.

In these few sentences, I tried (simply and in the ordinary language of today) to translate what I consider God's mandate to me. Thus did I write it down when Reverend Doctor John McGrath, our canon lawyer, first asked me to do so. He asked this so that it could be discussed by all of those who wished to bind themselves to that spirit under promises of poverty, chastity, and obedience. Instead of being a group of temporary volunteers, we were becoming a permanent lay organization as Pope Pius XII and Msgr. Montini, his

Secretary of State (who later became Pope Paul VI), had suggested in 1951.

Out of this simple statement grew our Constitution, which is familiar to you all, and upon which all the members of Madonna House agreed. It was voted upon word by word, line by line, idea by idea. In the archives of Madonna House, the whole story of its being created and voted upon lies waiting for anyone who wants to see it.

I was in the poustinia recently, praying to the Lord for a further clarification of this mandate. I was led, in the great silence of God, to meditate upon this explanation which I have just given to you and to try to put it into words that would, perhaps, be more easily understood. I will try to do so now.

(1) Madonna House spirit is the spirit of Nazareth.

(2) Madonna House spirit is that of a family.

(3) Madonna House spirit is that of a family, the Family of Nazareth, which was a community of perfect charity and love.

These three points go together, but let us see what the spirit of Nazareth was. First and foremost, it was of course a spirit of *charity*. Even before Christ's birth, there existed between Mary and Joseph a great and sublime love. These two were already a community of perfect charity.

I believe God arranged that Madonna House, the child of Friendship House, would be a replica of this type of love, this community of charity. Almost from the first day of our foundation, God brought men and women to Madonna House, to live together as Mary and Joseph did ... in perfect and total chastity. (A mixed community of men and women, living a celibate life, was considered most unusual at that time.) We must constantly return to this point and pray over and meditate upon it. Only then can we have a deep understanding of this beautiful mystery, this facet of Nazareth.

There is another facet of Nazareth that I often meditate upon: the pregnancy of Mary. She was already carrying God within her when the Holy Family, that 'community of love' between her and Joseph, was established so miraculously. Each one who comes to Madonna House is 'pregnant with God' in a manner of speaking. Those who aren't simply do not have the vocation to Madonna House, for this 'pregnancy' is a grace from God himself. He gives them a desire for himself. This becomes a 'seed' within them, leading them to the modern-day Nazareth of Mary and Joseph – Madonna House – to dwell there in hiddenness and in humility. He leads them each day to laborious work at little tasks which, if performed with great love, would truly preach his Gospel loudly!

There are many places he could lead them: to the vast deserts of the Contemplative Orders; to the rocky road, beautiful but steep, of Married Life; to the heights of Priestly Life; or to that of the Active Religious Life. He could lead them through all the facets of his own life, as reflected in the various religious orders and lay apostolates of today. All of this is true ... and perhaps each of those called to these various vocations would have to 'go to Nazareth' for a time. But it would not be in the way that the Madonna House mandate indicates. For our Apostolate, Nazareth seems to be a very *permanent* place, spiritually speaking. Even Eddie and I, in our mature years, have been very mysteriously led there to live like Joseph and Mary.

So then, those people whom Christ has chosen to be 'pregnant' with himself are – very specially, very specifically – brought to the Nazareth of Madonna House. They are brought here to give him birth and to allow him to grow to his full stature by living hiddenly, humbly, industriously. They will reside in a village of no importance (as the world knows it), as people of no importance (as the world considers them). In a word, they are brought here by Jesus to live as he lived with Mary and Joseph for many years.

The next point that came to me in my meditation was the extent of the Holy Family's *identification* with the villagers. The Holy Family formed part and parcel of the familiar landscape. They spoke the same language. They had the same status ... or perhaps in some way even a lower one than the other villagers, for the Scriptures say of Christ, "Isn't he just the carpenter's son?" This is also in the Mandate of God to us: that we 'blend with' and 'identify ourselves with' those whom we serve, as much as is humanly possible to do so. Especially with those who live in physical poverty. If, as happens on rare occasions, we are called to serve the 'rich poor' in their needs, then *even more* are we called to bring Nazareth (and all that it stands for) to them. We bring to them a community of love. We bring poverty, simplicity, hard work, and joy.

There is no denying the fact that Mary was a contemplative. First and foremost, *she was always before God*. She lived in his presence, the presence of God the Father. God the Holy Spirit overshadowed her. God the Son was with her, in human flesh! Yet she *worked* for the Lord, too. She worked hard, serving the needs of Jesus and Joseph and many of the villagers, and the pilgrims who passed by, and others. She served by listening and gently advising those in trouble and sorrow, by sharing her food, by general hospitality, and in many other simple and direct ways which today we call the corporal and spiritual 'works of mercy.'

Joseph was also a contemplative. How could he be anything else! He lived with God, and with God's Mother. He was a silent man, a man of deep prayer. Yet one feels sure that he, too, *worked* for the Lord; first by being the provider for his own family, and then surely by assisting his neighbors. He not only did things for them but probably also counseled them 'at the gates of the elders.' In these two quiet human beings, Mary and Joseph, I see so clearly the Madonna House spirit and its techniques.

As for Christ himself, *being* before the face of his Father was his very life – the very essence of it. *Doing* the will of his Father was also the essence of his existence. What a simple answer I find here to the complexity of questions you ask me! God the Father chose these two earthly parents of Christ. Christ accepted them lovingly all of his life, from the cave of Bethlehem through many years of manual labor in a hidden life; and in his ministry, passion, death, and resurrection. He *hastened in all things* to do the will of the Father. Our Madonna House life should be like that – being, doing, hastening – accomplishing *the will of the Father* as revealed by the needs of the Apostolate every given moment of our lives. It seems so simple.

Now we come back to the question of 'how to preach the Gospel with our lives.' Again, we look to the Holy Family for examples. They lived the Law fully and completely; for Christ came to fulfill the Law not to abolish it. But he gave us a New Law, and it is that New Law that we have to live, just as the Holy Family lived the will of the Father in the Old Law – *without compromise!* Whenever we are in doubt about the application of Scripture to our lives, let us read it over slowly, seeking from our priests as well as from our own conscience, the true meaning of a given sentence, statement, or command. Then we must proceed to implement it in our lives, no matter what the cost.

Our poverty should be the poverty of Nazareth, and of the Holy Family. They were artisans. They had enough to live simple and uncomplicated lives. They were not destitute, but they obviously had none of the luxuries of the day. In fact, if they lived in our times, they would likely be eligible for government aid under this new Poverty Bill! But their poverty was *luminous* because all three of them were utterly detached from their own wills and completely attached to the will of God the Father. Here, an endless wealth of meditation presents itself to all of us; parallels for the Madonna House spirit abound.

Nazareth is our model and our spiritual home. Like the Holy Family, we seek to be a community of love, of caritas, of poverty, of detachment from self and self-will. We lead an ordinary life, filled with many monotonous jobs to be done with great love for God and neighbor. Through these little daily tasks, we become 'witnesses' of God. What does that mean? I would define it as follows: "To be a witness does not consist in engaging in propaganda, or even in stirring people up, but in being *a living mystery.* It means to live in such a way that *one's life would not make sense* if God did not exist." That is what I mean when I say that the spirit of Madonna House and its Apostolate is one of 'witnessing' to God before men. In the marketplaces of the world, we must be preachers of the Gospel with our lives as well as (when required) with words. We must be preachers without compromise.

Madonna House, therefore, is a group of people called

by God to give him birth in a particular Nazareth setting, namely, in the modern marketplaces of the world. We are to show him to those who dwell around us, and we do this by how we *live*. All of this sounds so simple, but it presupposes a death to self – a death which we call *kenosis,* an 'emptying' that does violence to oneself. Yet, as Scripture says (Luke 16:16), "Heaven is taken by violence." Therefore, we must learn to exercise a loving and gentle 'violence' towards ourselves – and to do so out of love of God, with whom we want to spend this life and all eternity.

Yet there is a proviso to all that I have written above. I give it to you as it came to me in the poustinia, and as I have known it from the beginning of the Apostolate. The Lord showed it to me gently but vividly. He showed it, not only for myself, but for all those whom he has called to Madonna House to give him birth and allow him to grow to his full stature in them.

This is the proviso, the special accent: For us to live in Nazareth we must, strange as it may seem, *begin with Golgotha* and the tomb! After that, resurrected in him by his grace, we will *journey to Bethlehem* with the knowledge of the resurrected Christ, and *live in Nazareth* in expectation of the Parousia. Having this grace of knowledge, we shall understand how to do God's will perfectly.

Lovingly,

RE-EVALUATION AND STABILITY

June 2, 1965

Dearly Beloved,

Here I come again for a little visit with you. I want to discuss a few topics that have been on my mind, and give you a few answers to your many questions. Some of you still seek a clarification of this perpetually recurring question about our status: "Are we religious? Are we lay? Does a group such as ours have a role to play in our modern times?" So the discussions continue. Well, this is natural.

Changes occur so fast in today's world that we may need to question our role in it and re-evaluate it every ten years. Maybe even a decade is too long a time to wait; at least it will seem so to those between the ages of twenty and thirty. For youth has a compelling need to seriously question *everything* – people, values, authority, even God. In fact, that is part of being young.

After thirty-five years in the Apostolate of hearing constant discussions on endless topics, I am peaceful and untroubled by the latest crop of questions. I listen lovingly, never looking down on anyone just because I have had the experience of years and have, perhaps, led a fuller life than most. I realize more and more that the establishment of communications with youth must come from the older generation. This is because we have had more experience in life; and we should have more understanding, more patience, and more love; for time has allowed us to accumulate a little more of it than youth has had.

On the other hand, however, I cannot help being human. I chuckle to myself occasionally because in thirty-five years I have heard more violent discussions of *what Catholic Action 'really' is* than of any other subject concerning the lay apostolate. I remember a time when we memorized the following definition of Catholic Action, clarified its meaning for our own group, vigorously defended before others – and I guess would have 'died' for it (smile): "Catholic Action is the participation of the laity in the apostolate of the hierarchy. It is *group* action. It is *trained* action. It is *mandated* action (meaning that it is approved by the bishop of a given diocese)." It was not always a well-accepted concept. In fact, one disgruntled priest felt that the definition was better rendered as: the 'interference' of the laity in the apostolate of the hierarchy!

In those days, Friendship House and its members had a difficult time getting out of 'the corner' into which we were pushed by various priests, religious, and lay people. Many of them tried to prove that, of all the groups working in the United States, our work was *not* Catholic Action! I hate to tell you what ingenuity was necessary for our senior members and myself to fight these 'accusations' with peace, love, and intelligence.

Our opponents admitted that we were a group; but they questioned whether we were a *properly mandated* one. I remember so well the days when we were called rebels, anarchists, communists, and what-have-you. That was because we didn't have an official letter posted on the wall, showing that the bishop was allowing us to function there. At best, we might be considered just 'good, ordinary lay people'; but we had no standing whatever in many people's eyes.

As for *properly trained* members who could provide a stable environment for our work, we were faced with an interesting situation among ourselves. People came to Friendship House. People went through Friendship House. They received wonderful on-the-job training that has since proven to be of tremendous value to them. They told me so whenever they came back for a visit: "Catherine, you have no idea how many people bless you for what you have given to them. How many ideas, movements, developments, and other things have come out of the early Friendship House group."

All of this may be true, but few people considered what it did to Friendship House itself. The lack of stability played havoc with the place, and something had to be devised. Those of us who really cared about having some sort of continuity in the Apostolate felt that our 'state of life' would have to be formalized somehow. Eventually, the Lord took care of that. The Holy Spirit inspired Pope Pius XII to take the fourth and 'forgotten' vocation,* that of *the lay life dedicated to God IN THE WORLD,* and to lift it to the stability of Secular Institutes. That stability is most necessary nowadays.

Life in Latin America

To divert for a moment (for this is a rambling letter), one of our priests just returned from South America, having done a thorough survey of the situation of Catholic Action groups down there. After our discussions with him, here are some of the conclusions we came to:

The need for lay apostles is tremendous everywhere. But in order to work in any field, especially in the foreign missions, *training* is necessary. Many groups saw that 'dedication and good will' was not enough; people needed some sort of 'formation.' This lack of training was showing up everywhere; even a year's training was found to be insufficient. The ability of people to live together harmoniously, in charity and peace – people who in one way or another represent the Church – hinges on their receiving a deep *spiritual* formation. I am not referring here to the scriptural, liturgical, catechetical training which is so valuable, but to that *personal* formation known as spiritual direction. This, as yet, is not as available to the laity as it should be.

Some groups have yet to discover the need for continuity and stability. A prime example is that of two nurses assigned to one of the worst slums of Latin America. These nurses worked very well for three years, running their little hospital and dispensary; making home visitations; teaching hygiene, first aid, prenatal and postnatal care, etc. The people in this slum area, for the first time in their history, got fine medical care and received vitamins, powdered milk, and other such necessities.

This lasted three years. When the nurses fulfilled their temporary contract, they returned to the United States. And

*Forgotten by canon law, which recognized only three states of life – priests, religious, and laity. In 1947, the category of Secular Institute was established.

there was no one to replace them! The headquarters of that group either didn't think about such a thing or, more likely, didn't have nurses to send at that time. Whatever the reason may have been, the dispensary closed, and the medical care stopped. So did the milk and the vitamins.

The people were heartbroken and angry. They waited for their government to do something. They said to our visiting priest: "It would have been better for us if those 'Americanas' had never come here. They showed us what life could be like. Now that we know of such a thing, it has been taken away from us. We are in a worse state than before!" That same sort of situation happened at Friendship House in Harlem. I remember our 350 black children looking gloomy and sad because a white volunteer, whom they loved and who had started a program they liked, had later abandoned the project – and the children. She 'faded away' into greater Manhattan, and was never seen again.

As the necessity for training and continuity becomes more evident, Latin American bishops are beginning to request North American groups (such as the Grail, Lay Mission Auxiliaries, Madonna House) and other forms of stable and dedicated lay apostles to go into their countries to teach, direct, console, and support those volunteers (Peace Corps, PAVLA, etc.) who are there only as a temporary commitment, and to provide some sort of continuity at the local level.

Back to North America

But back to the original question that began this whole discussion: "What is our role in this modern world?" First, let's look at our historical development, and some of the actions we engaged in. I remember the times when I had long and heated discussions about what was then called the *Back to the Land* movement. People spoke about 'getting involved' in the rural apostolate. There were accusations leveled at people (such as we were) who were concentrated only in the inner city. I remember all the shouting, the peaceful and unpeaceful pros and cons. I remember youth getting excited, converging on Dorothy Day's Catholic Worker because they were experimenting with this 'Back to the Land' movement and were introducing rural apostolates everywhere. Their followers were donating farms just outside big cities, such as Cleveland and Chicago, or near small towns in Pennsylvania and California. (It was Depression Times back then.) We of Friendship House looked like outcasts because we had our nose stuck in the inner city apostolate. We were told in no uncertain terms that we were very narrow minded! A very holy priest-friend, who was quite radical in those days (as far as clergy went), became very frustrated with me. He asked me when I was going to 'get on the bandwagon' and open a rural apostolate.

I compromised a little. Although I am not of the 'bandwagon' type, I did see the value of having some rural property where we could set up an interracial camp for the kids, and the idea of a Summer School of Catholic Action was slowly forming in my mind. So we got a couple of farms donated; the one in Marathon, Wisconsin, was given to us by Bishop Sheil of Chicago. We began to experiment with that sort of apostolate. Since I knew from personal experience what 'real farming' is like, I had sense enough to rent out most of the acreage to other farmers in the area. For the first years, we kept only a small piece of farmland for ourselves, on which we grew berries, radishes, lettuce, and the like. Whatever we could harvest from the land was taken back to the big city and distributed to the poor in Chicago's southside neighborhood. The property yielded other 'good fruits' too – it got some of the children out of the sweltering city for awhile; and, yes, we did have some interracial Summer Schools.

Years went by. Bishop Smith invited me to found a rural apostolate in Combermere, Ontario. The Depression had passed; we were in the midst of World War II. The face of Catholic Action had changed. 'Back to the Land' movements were failures; so were idealistic farms. We had more discussions about accepting an apostolate to Rural People, without necessarily running a major farm operation ourselves. What I envisioned was a training center at Combermere, where inner-city people could come to learn a diversity of work habits, where present and future members of our Apostolate could be formed.

I called what I saw 'The Vision of the Whole' and I

wrote about it. It was serious business, and we talked about it a great deal. As you know, it was one of the major reasons why I left Friendship House. Its members continued interracial work in the core of big cities, but without my presence. Eddie and I came to Combermere, trusting that the Holy Spirit wanted us here. And so Madonna House was born.

The Rise of Secular Institutes

I have mentioned that all lay apostolates were 'unstable' in the sense that there were no vows or promises whatsoever for its members. These were groups of 'temporary commitments' if you want to call it that, with the exception of a few individuals who might wish to take 'private vows' of poverty, chastity and obedience. After the war, however, a number of lay groups began petitioning Rome for some sort of stability. So in 1947, Pope Pius XII created the category of Secular Institutes.

The Church had seen that a great many lay people wanted to dedicate themselves totally to God and the works of God, and yet desired to 'live out' this commitment as 'laity' – working (as individuals or as small groups) at regular lay occupations in the secular world. By creating this new classification, the Church was honoring the dedication of these lay people. It was giving them support and encouragement by allowing them to take promises (or vows) of poverty, chastity, and obedience ... and by officially recognizing their status as lay people (not monks or nuns).

The Grail, the Lay Missionary Auxiliaries, Opus Dei, and many other groups reexamined their collective consciences. Some tightened their existing constitutions. Others petitioned for Pious Union status (the first step toward Secular Institute standing.) There was a lot of discussion as to whether Madonna House should become a Secular Institute too. Not just from our own members; many clergy, religious, and laity who knew of us felt that we should take this step. There was much probing into our canonical status.

During the first years of our existence here in Combermere, we thought a great deal about it too, and discussed it a lot. And we did petition for and receive the status of a Pious Union; we did not choose, however, to become a Secular Institute. As you can imagine, that didn't sit kindly with some folk. A series of arguments seemed to rage about the correct status for Madonna House, and we were often under discussion. I guess that's because we were fairly well known and had been around for a long time. People had many ideas about us, and we didn't always fulfill their expectations.

Now that the youth of today have discovered the 'inner city' and its problems, many people are telling us that we should get into this type of apostolate. They do not realize that some of our people are already working in the inner city, and with a vengeance! In Portland, Oregon, our staff are deeply immersed in the problems of housing, civil rights, migrant workers, the war on poverty, etc., and have gotten half the city involved in these social issues.

It used to be that parents asked us one type of question, and their offspring another type. But the generation gap is becoming much shorter. Now older children barely finish asking one set of questions and their younger brothers and sisters raise the opposite kind. "Why are you taking promises of poverty, obedience, and chastity – and not 'real' vows? You are not *sufficiently* committed to the Church." ... "Why are you taking promises at all? You are *too* committed to the Church. You are quasi-monks and nuns, and should no longer call yourselves lay apostles." ... "Why are you only a Pious Union and not a Secular Institute? You are not committed *enough*." ... Back and forth the controversy rages. The Old Breed wants it one way; the New Breed (to use Rev. Andrew Greeley's phrase) wants it another way.

I (who am usually categorized as Old Breed by virtue of my chronological age) listen calmly and peacefully to this rush of questions. Then I try my best to communicate my answers, hopefully with patience and love, and with a modicum of wisdom given me by my years. I tell them that there is a *great diversity* of apostolates in the Church, and ours is one of them. Why get all upset, confused, mixed up about the fact that we are different from other groups? Yes, we are lay people. No, we are not a Secular Institute. We think we're OK just as we are.*

Don't let's drag up obscure points that were talked about twenty years ago, when no one except the Pope seemed to be able to define Catholic Action. Those things are not important. What is important is that we are doing God's work, as God and his Church wants us to do; we know that by the mandate a bishop gives us when he invites us into his diocese.

A Constant State of Renewal

I would like to quote from a letter from one of our members. She is younger, and a bit impatient, but she understands the essence of we've been discussing here. Here is what she writes:

> I can't see getting too nervous about the *unsettledness* of anything to do with the Church, since this is part being in the diaspora. If we do stay in a constant state of renewal, there will always be 'elements of change.' That is good and healthy. It will have its own built-in tensions, of course, but they are not necessarily bad ones.
>
> I feel strongly that, while we should listen to people who guide the Church these days and try to absorb whatever they are expressing, it is only *we ourselves* who can effect any changes within our own community. To do this, we have to be totally dedicated to our Apostolate. Not just accepting it with reservations, but accepting *everything* (not blindly, of course, but with our eyes wide open). In other words, a warm-hearted freely-given fully-developed commitment to our life.
>
> What I am trying to say is this: Congar, Kung, and Suenens could all come and spend a whole week talking to us about our Apostolate (presuming that they grasp what our 'inner spirit' is). They could give us their insights and point out some directions we

---

*The Code of Canon Law has since been rewritten. The categories of religious and lay communities have been greatly if not finally clarified. Madonna House is now a Public Association of the Faithful, of diocesan rank.

might take with regard to them; but they themselves cannot directly affect us.

It is we who must first absorb what they offer, reflect on it maturely, ask the guidance of the Holy Spirit, and then decide what changes (if any) need to be effected. The whole process has to be done from *within*. And that requires a receptive heart! It is only those members of the Apostolate who are really dedicated that can effect these changes, not those who accept the Apostolate only as far as they like it and subconsciously reject whatever changes they wouldn't like to see happen. (I don't know if this makes sense to you; it is hard for me to put it in words.)

There's another point that I notice about the process of Renewal in the Church. The thinking today among religious groups seems to be moving more and more toward 'unity' ... in the ecumenical attitude of concentrating on "those things that unite rather than divide." This has led to questioning whether religious and lay groups should continue as they are, multiplying and duplicating themselves, not always to good ends. People want to eliminate the many diverse communities that exist, as well as the spirit of competitiveness which has unfortunately developed among them. They feel that the vocation to love (which we all have in common) could then be brought out more fully. *This,* do they know it or not, *can only* be expressed by a terrible amount of hard work, and a zeal to 'cry the Gospel' uncompromisingly. They also are focusing on Formation of Members (and such like), how to avoid the multiplication of houses of study and the consequent duplication of training (which is often poor because of a lack of good equipment and personnel). I agree with many of these insights, and applaud their efforts.

But I feel that there is a subtle danger in their thinking. Perhaps I am a bit conservative on this subject, but I fear decisions about religious communities which may go to the opposite extreme. It is one thing to de-emphasize whatever differences between groups have been overly stressed in the past. It is another thing to eliminate them altogether, and not allow for legitimate *movements of the Spirit of God* in the various communities. I think that there are many good and wholesome differences within groups. These special accents should remain, and be honored by the other communities as unique qualities. These would be valuable contributions to the 'whole' of religious life; and it would be a loss to the Church to have those gifts destroyed by a bland 'general unification' unthinkingly done.

Do you know what I mean? In other words, I can see a swing to 'unity' 90 percent of the way. But not 100 percent! I think there is still room for 'diversity in unity' as St. Paul says. What do you think?

Yes, there is much in what this person says. There is much in what I remember. So on this note I leave you, dearly beloved.

With much love, and even more patience and joy,

CORRECTION – AN ACT OF LOVE

July 19, 1965

Dearly Beloved,

Once again I come to visit you in spirit. Imagine that we are all sitting together, I and each group of you in whatever mission you may be. We are talking matters over, peacefully, as members of a community of love should.

In a sense, the Lord has given me the gift of 'bilocation' because I feel that I am with you wherever you are. I walk and talk and suffer and rejoice with each of you individually – especially when I am at the Love-Feast of Christ (the Mass) and we have become one in Communion. At night, too, I feel myself one with you. Perhaps that is why I need less and less sleep; for my love for you wells up in my heart. Yes, "I am with you always" ... for Love does such things.

Today I want to talk about, once again, the topic of *correction*. I say 'once again' because I do not know how many times we have already discussed this most beautiful subject. But as we grow together in wisdom and grace and love, we are able to look at 'correction' with a greater understanding –more sanely; more scientifically, even – and plumb the depths of its spirituality.

The dictionary defines the word *correctness* as "being in accordance with facts" (the practical aspect) or "being in accordance with a standard" (the ideal aspect). It refers to having "true, accurate, balanced, appropriate" thoughts, feelings, actions, behavior patterns, habits, manners, and dress. The word *correction* is defined as "admitting the possibility of error; being able to substitute the right version for the wrong version." (This suggests that both 'insight' and 'flexibility' on our part are required here.) The dictionary goes on to define the word *correction* as 'being a servant' ... one who serves ... meaning that correction *serves* "to reform, to reshape, to make straight, to make whole, to put into accord with."

I think these definitions are sufficient for our purposes, but I would like to make some illustrations of my own. Because I am a nurse, my mind goes to images of health. When a doctor looks at a medical deformity of any kind, or when a dentist looks at any deformation of teeth, they both use the word 'correction' when they speak to the parents or relatives of the patient, meaning that either this thing can be 'put to rights' or it can't.

Do you object to hearing word 'correction' when it is used by professional people in relation to deformity or illness? I doubt it. In fact, you are probably very happy to hear that your little brother or sister can get their teeth straightened, even if they have to wear braces for a while. You are quite willing to wear an uncomfortable back brace, if it's going to alleviate your pain and correct your spinal condition.

Take physiotherapy, which is used in many medical cases. A person's leg has to be 'made straight' – by massage, by exercise, by walking a certain way, by wearing special equipment – in a word, 'corrected.' Having worked with many patients, I can tell you that they are very glad to suffer the pain in order to have a limb that is straight and strong so they can walk without difficulty. I myself have been challenged to do this. As I've told you many times, my knee was exceedingly painful when I went walking. Yet the doctor told me, after my operation, that I had to walk first one block, then two, and to keep on increasing the distance. I did not rebel against his orders. Neither would you if you wanted to walk again. I just bore the temporary pain and did the exercises and walked, and kept on walking – no matter how painful it was.

I can use examples such as this endlessly. Many women 'correct' their figure. We all know how many people diet for this reason; they practically starve themselves to be slender, to stop the inroads of fat. In diets and therapies (often for beauty's sake alone) tremendous money is paid to professional experts who can help 'correct' wrong postures, pimples, fatness or thinness, deformation of any kind. And no one complains.

When a local director, a department head, a spiritual director, or I myself 'correct' you, however, it seems that you are unable to accept it in the same way. You become angry. You get antagonistic, hostile, and withdrawn. You have endless 'tizzies.' Why is this? You would probably be among the first to pay out lots of money to get your physical defects corrected. Why not accept *free corrections* in which there is no financial payment involved; on the contrary, it is love that is involved.

Think how much love must go into correcting another person. It's not an easy job to point out defects! Speaking just for myself and the local directors, I can say that some of you have been corrected by us for years, but you have not easily accepted it or gladly cooperated with it (inwardly anyhow, and some not even outwardly). This seems to be because of some emotional reason or other that you haven't yet put your 'insights' on. You have a tendency to revert momentarily to an infantile, childish, or adolescent response whenever it happens, to a pattern of thought that has no place in this beautiful exchange of love.

Why is it that some people can't face correction squarely? Why is it that, instead of immediately bursting into a flood of justifications, the person does not simply say, "Thank you; teach me how to do better." One common reaction I often encounter is this: When you are faced with some error on your part (which incidentally you acknowledge most of the time, because it's obvious that you are guilty of it), you often start 'putting the blame on others' for things that are connected (or utterly unconnected) with the point at hand. I have experienced this so many times with almost all of you; and now the local directors are experiencing these reactions. Why does this happen? You wouldn't object to great physical pain inflicted on you by doctors, nurses, beauticians, or dentists; or at least you would try to hold your response in check. Yet you object to the gentle and patient corrections of your superiors in Madonna House.

Why not read the dictionary definition over a few times? It objectively states what *correction* is, and approaches it with a mature, adult point of view (not to mention a spiritual one). Among other definitions I haven't mentioned is the one from the pocket edition of the Oxford Dictionary: "Admonish for a fault; counteract and eliminate or neutralize a harmful tendency."

Now a person who is trying to do this to you should be a well-beloved sight. You should have 'at hand' a desire for complete cooperation and openness. If you realize that you are being helped and your harmful habits are being neutralized, you should be 'in seventh heaven' that so much patience and love has gone into work of correction. It requires that the person-in-charge 'be present' to you and not neglectful of you, to engage in constant repetitious acts for your well-being – even as a brace has to stay several years to straighten out one's teeth, and as massage treatments often have to continue for months. The people who straighten out your teeth and give you a massage are paid for it; and you are grateful to them, notwithstanding. You realize that they have invested a lot of their knowledge into that skill and you benefit by their expertise.

Here's another puzzling situation. It is interesting to note that – no matter how much hostility and animosity and spine-stiffening, tear-jerking, tizzy-filled attitudes have been exhibited by a person (across the board, in every situation) (whether in a fieldhouse or at the training center) toward loving and patient correction – that very same person seems to respond quite differently when he or she put in charge of others. (Some of you on the staff will know what I mean.) Many persons who are made responsible for things, even temporarily, begin to – if you will pardon me (smile), I say this with great gentleness and understanding – *yell bloody murder* when all this barrage of emotional immaturity and this adolescent 'reaction to authority' gets directed at *them!*

How can I help both sides – the 'corrector' and the 'correctee' – from feeling hurt by this 'straightening out' process? I think that Father Briere's letter, written back in April or May 1961, can give you a fresh insight on this. I would very much appreciate if you would read it. I think it will bring new peace to all of you. And we need that sort of refresher periodically.

Remember that corrections (according to St. Thomas of Aquinas and the Old Testament) are acts of fraternal love and charity. Why don't you absorb that idea more deeply, my beloved, so that we can continue to grow as a community of love?

Love,

142

THE THEOLOGY OF 'CORRECTIONS'

Spring 1961

Dear Family,

Catherine has asked me to write down for you some
theological principles underlying the whole painful matter
of correction. I say 'painful' for such it is; not only for the
one who receives correction but *especially* for those who
have the grave responsibility of continuing the training of
our staff members, and are therefore required to give
correction.

Psychologically, it is painful to be corrected by others
because we too often consider it a 'total condemnation' of
ourselves. And it is painful to correct others because we
run the risk of losing their 'approval' (and perhaps gaining
their active enmity). If we are required to correct a whole
group of people over a long period of time, there are
moments when we may feel isolated, unsupported,
misunderstood, perhaps even unwanted. If we know the
psychological principles involved in these matters, we can
learn to lessen these irrational fears of ours and make them
manageable. Our knowledgeable intellect can take charge
of this.

There is, however, another area of knowledge which
needs to be considered. We have a tendency to ignore (or
forget) our *theology* on this matter. So let us establish some
points of doctrine here. Perhaps they will enable us not
only to 'accept' correction but to do even more – to 'desire'
it with all our hearts.

Point 1. When we embraced the three Evangelical
Counsels (namely: chastity, poverty, and obedience) we
were answering the call of Christ: "If you would be perfect,
sell all that you possess. And come! Follow me!" Because
we *wanted* to be perfect, we freely and joyfully made these
promises to the Madonna House family. We made a sincere
commitment to observe them in a particular manner; to do

so daily, to the best of our ability, for the rest of our lives.

Point 2. In doing this, we promised that we would *seek* after perfection right up to (and including) the moment of our death. The moment of death constitutes the high point of our dedication. Our whole life is really an exercise – a series of exercises, one could say – to prepare us for full immolation at the hour of our death. This means that, daily, we are duty-bound "to seek after perfection." (This particular phrase is a classical one found in all the spiritual books; but it is not one that I like.) I prefer the expression "to seek to love better and better." So then, we have promised that we would sincerely try to love, and to *improve* (with God's grace and the help of others) the quality, the intensity, the unselfishness of our love.

Point 3. The three Evangelical Counsels have one key purpose: to remove the obstacles in us that keep us from controlling and gradually conquering, gradually eliminating our main selfish tendencies. Now, selfishness uses three principal means to satisfy itself. These three passionate urges inside us produce many tentacles, reaching out and trying to grasp whatever is available. They are called, in traditional language:

A. The Concupiscence (or desire) of the Flesh, whereby we seek pleasurable sensual experiences. Its tentacles reach out for whatever stimulates our human body – food, drink, sex, drugs, comfort, ease, any feelings associated with the senses (sounds, colors, tastes, smells, touches). When this desire gets out of control, it is labeled as gluttony, lust, sentimentality, sloth, etc. By our promise of Chastity, we have seriously determined to control such desires and keep them in balance.

B. The Concupiscence (or desire) of the Eyes, whereby we seek to possess 'things.' The tentacles reach out for whatever 'good' our eye sees outside the body – such as: money, books, clothing, houses, cars, property, anything that we can collect and save, anything over which we can exercise 'ownership.' When this desire gets out of control, it is labeled as avarice, covetousness, greed, meanness, stinginess, etc. By our promise of Poverty, we have seriously determined to control these tendencies.

C. The Pride of Life, whereby we prefer 'ourselves' to other people (and sometimes even to God). Our ideas, our wants, our very 'existence' takes precedence over other people. The tentacles of this desire will reach out to gain *control* over others (in the form of power and authority) or to gain *approval* from others (in the form of dignities and honors) or to gain *independence* from others (in the form of false liberty and freedom).

When this Pride of Life gets out of control, it engenders a great mixture of passions. The label for each one will vary, according to the source from which it springs, the person against whom it is directed, and the action it precipitates. Jealousy, envy, greed, pride, vanity, etc., are focused on whatever 'things' we value and wish to have for ourselves. Anger, impatience, hatred, rancor, contempt, etc., are directed against those people who interfere with our possession of those 'things.' Killing, fighting, stealing, criticizing, snubbing, etc., are specific actions we may take to repel or punish those who interfere with our desires.

By our promise of Obedience we of Madonna House have seriously determined to keep this 'preference for self' under control. In a general way, we do this whenever we carefully listen to the 'voices' which come from outside us − from people, events, circumstances − and try to ascertain from them the Will of God for us. In a more direct way, we do this by 'subjecting' ourselves to those whom God has appointed to lead us, desiring always to fulfill their requests and desires with a heart that is 'cheerful, prompt, and willing.'

Point 4. Our selfishness is *always* with us, in one way or another, right up till death. We have to realize this important truth, because the great illusion of 'good' people is to think – after a few years of training, of spiritual struggle, of diligent practice – that they have pretty well conquered their selfishness. This is an extremely dangerous state of mind! It makes progress impossible; and *not* to progress in the spiritual life is to go backwards. Gradually, such a person will fall into a *worse* state than he was before coming to Madonna House.

Point 5. As we grow in the spiritual life, that many-tentacled threefold evil will manifest itself in *different* ways. At first, we will learn to overcome (or at least to control) the grosser manifestations. For instance, gluttony in regards to food and drink may long have ceased to be a problem. But 'holy' persons may become gluttonous in their desire for spiritual consolations. They go to God, not to honor him but to get a satisfying feeling in their own soul. Such persons may not be avaricious in regard to money, but they may become avaricious in collecting holy pictures or medals or rosaries or relics.

Point 6. Since we have promised that we would continually seek *to grow in love,* our directors have the very heavy responsibility of indicating to us the areas where our love is deficient, where we seem to be making little or no progress. They have to correct us when we are not 'doing little things well' out of a deep and abiding love. They have to correct us when our appearance is sloppy; when our moods are harming 'the common good;' when we are abrupt with one another, with visitors, with those whom we have dedicated ourselves to serve. Our directors have the right – indeed, the painful *duty* – to correct us in any and every area of our lives. We should pray for them that they may lead us ever more quickly to the God whom we love.

To Summarize: We can state the whole matter in a few words.

• Because we realize that God is 'the best' that is;

• Because we realize that God has in his great love called us unto himself, to a deep and intimate union with the Trinity;

- Because we realize that all the obstacles to that Great Union can be summarized in a single word: self-will;

- Therefore, we have chosen 'The Way of Obedience' as the best method to overcome this self-will, as the greatest protection against self-will.

- In consequence, we have *freely,* and *with great dignity,* placed ourselves in the hands of those who can best make known to us the Will of God for each moment of our day.

- And because we want God so terribly much, we are not only 'open' to correction but we are immensely grateful to those who take the trouble to correct us.

How fortunate we are, really! Let us thank God and our directors for the great privilege of being corrected whenever the need arises.

Best Blessings in Our Lady of Combermere,

Father Brière

GOD'S GRACE AND PROMISE TIME

July 30, 1965

Dearly Beloved,

The day of Promises is approaching. Over a period of years, I have noticed that the majority of you undergo, not only spiritual trials, but deep emotional ones as well.

To do so is perfectly normal, both naturally and

supernaturally speaking. Somewhere along the line, however, you get confused; this is not to be wondered at either, because this is also the hour of Satan. This is the time when he either walks about like a roaring lion seeking to devour you or, since he loves playing many roles, comes to you as a philosopher or a 'friend' with gentle manners and clever arguments.

He sets about proving to you, rationally and logically, all the reasons why you shouldn't make these Promises, or he confuses you with suggestions that you are making these Promises out of human respect. Perhaps he makes you think: "What will my parents say if I don't make them? ... What will the members of the Madonna House family say if I don't? ... What will my friends, who admire me so much for being here, say if I don't?" On and on go the clever suggestions of the former Angel of Light. This, added to the normal emotional strain and to a good and holy examination of your conscience and yourself, naturally causes a time of tension and questioning.

Part of this is as it should be. You are giving yourself to God for a year, or for two years, or for a lifetime; and it must be a *free, willing, joyful* gift. At no time and under no circumstances can your marriage with God be a 'shotgun wedding'! 'Shotgun' can refer to many intangibles. There is human respect, which I have mentioned already. There is a fear of failure, or of appearing to be a failure. There could be a desire for the love and security of a family like Madonna House. Thousands are the 'guns' that might seem to influence the freewill offering of yourself to God, for a time or forever.

Throw all of these 'guns' away. Grow in faith and trust of both God and those superiors to whom God has given the heavy, awesome responsibility of deciding whether or not you have this vocation. Dearly beloved, how can I find words that will pierce the emotional darkness surrounding you at this time? God knows that I implore him, not only for light, but for words to relieve the *unnecessary confusion,* the evil fears, the inability to think straight, the lack of faith, confidence, and trust that some of you suffer during these pre-Promise days!

Of course, a certain amount of wholesome fear has to

be there because fear is 'the beginning of wisdom' (Psalm 111:10). There is no bride-to-be or groom-to-be who isn't afraid of committing himself or herself to the other for a lifetime in the vocation of marriage. There isn't a religious or a priest who doesn't tremble with that holy fear, that wholesome fear, before ordination or the taking of temporary or perpetual vows. Whenever a person makes a solemn commitment to a task, a cause, a vocation, either for a long period or forever, this fear is present. Let that insight sink deeply into you. God uses this fear (which, I repeat, is 'the beginning of wisdom') to spur on your intellect, to clarify it, to help you make sure of what you are doing. The devil, however, tries to make this fear an emotional 'binge,' a means of escaping from life and from responsibility, especially from facing that great reality which confronts each human soul: *God's call to us.*

Surely those of you who are about to take Final Promises have been given every opportunity to examine this vocation. Surely the tremendous amount of spiritual and secular knowledge that has been given to you must have clarified your vocation for you. The world you live in and the spiritual knowledge revealed to you must have given you an understanding of God's great love for you, and the reasons for you to love him back. What of daily Mass, of retreats, of poustinias? What of the help and love you have given to each other that sustains you through many a dark day? What of the graces poured into your souls so constantly, so tenderly, so lovingly, from the hands of God through the hands of Mary? What of all of this?

Why, then, do you allow yourself to be possessed by fear and dark doubts, to be filled with mistrust of self, of God, or of your superiors? Why the emotional confusion? I beg you to stop. I beg you to pray as you have never prayed before. I beg you to sit down in a chapel or church and to write out all that you have received from God. Each gift is a proof of his special love that shouts (or should) to your soul that he wants you in this vocation. If you come to him with deep faith, with deep trust and confidence, he will walk on the sea of your emotions and quiet them. He will bid Satan depart. He will take you in his arms and allow you to listen to his heartbeats, and they should make it clear to you why you are making these Promises.

Remember also that the frail, sinful, weak human beings who are your superiors undergo similar trials about your vocation too. They have the awesome responsibility of signing their names to the petition that you so naturally (perhaps even casually) send them, thinking it is just a canonical procedure to be gone through. Before I sign my name to that little letter that sounds so official, I pray and I suffer. I have to 'make sure' to the best of my poor human ability – and in prayer that must be deep, sincere, simple, trustful, and full of faith – that God will give me the grace to put my name down on that letter of acceptance.

I beg of you the alms of your trust, confidence, and faith ... in me, and in all the superiors who will come after me. If I were to accept you for any other reason than my belief that you have been called to this vocation, I must face the fact that I will go to hell! Think of that, will you? Maybe it will help you understand the protection and tenderness with which God surrounds you, even unto the agony of your superiors and their love for you.

Because I believe in frankness and truth (which makes people free, for truth is God) I will mention a thought that may come to your mind as you read this letter: "How come – if our superiors have the grace of state – so many of the staff, even after Final Promises, have left Madonna House?" The answer doesn't lie in the fact that we have necessarily made a mistake in their vocation. The answer is threefold:

(1) They had free will. Some of them misused it. They shouldn't have left, but they did; and no one could stop them. It doesn't mean that they didn't have the vocation. Let us always remember that every person has the awesome gift of free will and can choose to accept a vocation or to reject it.

(2) We did not necessarily make a mistake about their vocation. We made a mistake about the depth of the emotional problems of a given person. God probably permitted it for the good of the Apostolate and for that person. In some cases, the question of vocation is still pending; a 'final choice' has not yet resolved the

situation. In all such matters, we must follow the primary diagnosis and explanation of competent medical authorities.

(3) Sometimes God will make it very clear that one vocation is a 'stepping stone' to another one, as he did with Father Cal and our other priests; they entered the priesthood first, and years later were called to our family as a secondary vocation. There is the case of a one of our lay members who went on to become a diocesan priest elsewhere; he probably would have been a priest of Madonna House had 'the timetables of God' been different. So a person may be called to be with us 'for a time' and then continue living the spirit of Madonna House in quite different circumstances. At no time can we say that such departures indicate 'a lack of vocation' to our family.

A vocation is a sacred thing. It is between God and a soul, and the soul must be free to make this decision. The directors are there to see that a person is free from any outside pressures. As for the inside pressures – doubts, fears, emotions, rationalizations, escapes, human respect, or what-have-you – well, all I can add is the sentence that Christ himself said to St. Paul when this mighty apostle, buffeted as you are, was crying out for help against such a temptation. Christ said, *My grace is enough.*

All I can do is to lead you to Christ so that you might hear that same answer in the depths of your souls.

Love,

Catherine

FREEDOM OF CONSCIENCE

August 19, 1965

Dearly Beloved,

Every time we clarify some point or other during our spiritual reading, someone suggests that I write a letter on that subject for you all to read. Thus it happened that, yesterday after the noon meal, we hit upon the question of flexibility, or malleability, or (to put it in plain Americanese) an ability to 'roll with the punches'!

We were reading something by Hans Kung, pertaining to 'the freedom of conscience' now being widely talked about in the North American Church. In our discussion we focused primarily on Madonna House, for we always move from the general principle to the particular one of "how to incarnate it in our daily life" here and now.

I made the statement that, as far as we are concerned, the aggiornamento, the Vatican Council, and all of the controversies we read about in the Catholic Press should not affect us unduly. Much of what the aggiornamento calls for, we have always been doing. I went on to report that we *already* have liberty of conscience at Madonna House. Here I paused for a second; then I pointed out that liberty of conscience demands men and women who are emotionally, spiritually, and intellectually *mature*.

In the context of the Catholic faith, the Christian faith, it demands 'mature Christians.' What do I mean by that? I mean that, when confronted with an issue that involves liberty of conscience, one must *act upon it*. But one must also give much thought, meditation, prayer – and, if necessary, fasting and time in the poustinia – in order to make very sure that: (a) it is truly a matter of liberty of conscience; and (b) one is mature enough to take the consequences of acting according to that liberty of conscience.

To illustrate: Some years ago when I was in Harlem, I

knew a convert, a black woman. She was a wonderful person, and very zealous about making other converts among her black friends. In the process of introducing the Catholic Faith to one of her lady friends, she brought her to a beautiful Catholic church in the Bronx, New York. It had a nice piece of ground and a garden in which some previous pastor had built lovely outdoor Stations of the Cross. While my friend was explaining these to her friend, the pastor came out of the church and walked through the garden toward them. In a very angry voice he ordered them off the premises, saying that black people were not allowed or wanted in the church or in the garden!

The two women arrived at Friendship House tremendously excited; my convert friend was exceedingly upset, and somewhat angry and desolate. I must admit that I was angry too, and with a 'just anger'! I picked up the phone and called Cardinal Spellman's secretary. (The cardinal was a good friend of ours.) I got an immediate appointment to see the cardinal.

I spent the money to take a taxi there with the two ladies, presented them to Cardinal Spellman, and let them explain the situation. The cardinal acted promptly. He took up the phone, told the pastor to come immediately to his residence, and had the secretary serve us tea while we waited. When the pastor arrived, the cardinal spoke to him privately. Then we were called into the room, and the pastor apologized to the two women very humbly and profusely. The incident was closed. The ladies were free to go to that church, as were all other blacks.

Now, suppose the cardinal had refused to act in this matter ... or worse, had upheld the pastor's decision! Now you are truly faced with a question of 'liberty of conscience.' Could you continue to work in his diocese, to have a Friendship House there, or be part of a such a setup in any way? If you had been confronted with that situation, would you have been prepared to close Friendship House and to face all that it would entail? Do you see what I mean? To exercise liberty of conscience, you must be both *courageous* (full of fortitude and faith) and *ready to lay down your very life* (the existence of your group) as a consequence of exercising this liberty of conscience.

So, having produced this example yesterday at spiritual reading, I went on to explain that closing the house is what I certainly would have done myself. I expect any of the staff of Madonna House to do that, if confronted with a similar situation; and I hope that all the coming generations of Madonna House members would do the same. We must be ready to 'lay down our lives' for the immovable, unchangeable mandate of God which has been given to us, which is the spirit of Madonna House that you know so well, and which includes in itself a true liberty of conscience. For the spirit of Madonna House is this:

- To live the Gospel 'with your life' ... personally, individually.

- To form a community of love, a family of Madonna House.

- To bring this love to individuals, *one by one,* never en masse.

- To take strength and example from Bethlehem, Nazareth, and Golgotha; applying them to oneself ... personally, individually.

- To silently preach the Gospel to the world.

- To do so through the childlikeness of Bethlehem; through the hidden life of Nazareth in 'small things done well' for God; and through the kenosis of Golgotha – in a total 'emptying' of self.

- To do all this so that *Christ may live in you.*

This spirit of Madonna House includes – more than that, embraces! – liberty of conscience. The spirit of Madonna House, by its very essence, tries to incarnate 'a true freedom' within each individual of our family.

Although the essence of this spirit can never be tampered with, the techniques of its application, the ways it can be presented to the world, must be intensely flexible. Our techniques must be malleable like wax that is slightly heated; or like good soft clay out of which so much can be done, if it is of the right consistency. Suppose I went back to Harlem today with the techniques of the 1930s. What a fool I would be! I would be disregarding almost thirty years

154

of growth and change that I see around me – in history, in technology, in mind, in spirit, in ways of living.

If we live the spirit of Madonna House in the proper way, then 'freedom of conscience' and all that follows after it will be ours as a consequence. Controversies about 'authority' and 'obedience' and all the rest of the new vocabulary will be wasted upon us. If we preach the Gospel with our lives, it means that *we believe in it,* since we live it! And that applies also to 'authority' because the Gospel shouts that authority exists to serve, or in other words 'to govern is to love.' It also shouts that 'to obey is to love' and that obedience among us – Gospel fashion – can only be based on love, a love that is freely given. There is no other way.

Lovingly yours in Mary,

A PRODUCTION MENTALITY

August 20, 1965

Dearly Beloved,

We continued to read "Freedom in the Church" by Hans Kung. Our attempts to clarify and sanctify its 'troublesome' points led to some very pertinent insights. It was as though the breath of an angel had 'troubled' its stagnant waters and made them come alive.

Somehow we got onto the topic of what it is that 'fetters' our sense of freedom, what 'imprisons' our liberty and keeps us from assuming our full responsibility as mature Christians. Yesterday we hit upon the word *production*. It developed into a key word, a shaft of light in an unexplored darkness. It turned out to be an 'open window' for us, like the aggiornamento of Pope John XXIII was for the Church. We discovered – vividly and perhaps suddenly – that production is *the great heresy* of the North American continent, of its culture and its spirituality.

Let us define what is meant by 'production.' In this case, we mean that we value ourselves *exclusively* by the tangible goods that we can produce for society. We discovered that we tend to estimate our 'self-worth' by the amount of these 'good works' that we can achieve. Truly, this is a poor way to evaluate a living human being who is created in the image and likeness of God.

One person gave us a most pertinent example. She was confused by our discussion, she said, and listed all the pressures that made us pick berries in the summer, under the lash of nature's cycle. She said that the Apostolate needed the berries to feed itself, to sell in the Gift Shop, and to provide for all the guests coming to the next Summer School of 1966. What was wrong, then, in estimating one's value by the amount that one could pick in a given time. Surely it was a valid measure of one's worth, at least in this type of work.

This was a good example of 'production mentality' and it was not to be denied an answer. My reply, as usual, dealt with the intangibles of the spirit. To respond to the needs of society (of a community, apostolate, nation or neighborhood) by 'producing something' is a holy and reasonable act. But such a production must be spearheaded by, or in answer to, *genuine* needs. In this case, the need was for berries, but it could have been vegetables or other foodstuffs for the Apostolate. This is a genuine need, for the family of Madonna House must eat.

The key word, however, is not 'production' but 'charity.' Charity and reason dictate that we gather the food which God has given us to gather, either on the farm or in the bush, wherever it is to be found. And if the nature of the fruit or vegetable is such that it demands immediate processing, then sometimes we may have to work 'round the clock' to do the harvesting, blanching, cooking, canning, or freezing. But we must not measure ourselves against the number of bushels or pounds of 'produce' we have gathered (except as a measure of our need, not of our worth). We should measure ourselves against the *love with which we have done this work*. This gathering and this processing is to feed our brothers and sisters and ourselves in the Apostolate, *in order to serve* God and our neighbor better; for food is necessary to human life.

Any form of 'loving service' will have an aura of peace and joy about it. But this heresy, the obscene heresy of measuring human worth against the amount that it can produce, can only create in people the joy of hell. Many saints were often utterly 'nonproductive' members of the Mystical Body of Christ. There was Gemma Galgani, a twentieth-century saint, who died at the young age of 25. She spent much of her life confined to bed, suffering for the Church and the people of God. That was her joy; that was her 'loving service.'

Take the ultimate human poverty of insane or psychotic persons; the blind, the lame, and the halt; the retarded and the Mongoloid; the useless ones; the despised ones. According to the measuring scale of 'good works' these people are not only unproductive, they are considered a 'burden' on the productive ones. Such thoughts are but a further extension of this heresy of production.

Yes, that is the way the world in general would view these people. But in the economy of Christianity, in the reality of God's love for human beings, these afflicted ones have become victim-souls on our behalf. Far from being parasites, they are the beloved ones of God and holocausts of love for us. If we had an ounce of sense within us, we would 'hold onto the hem of their garments' in order to be carried by them into heaven!

But the whole matter is deeper still. These intellectual attitudes engender in us the emotional disease of 'productionitis.'* First, let me share with you a letter I received from one of our members. She writes about her attitude toward production:

*The compulsion that `I must produce... I must produce... I must produce.' In later decades, it would be called the `workaholic' syndrome.

> I could never define what a 'person' is. If all your life you felt that you never 'existed' or even knew what it meant to *be* a person, and if you thought very poorly of yourself because society always measured you by production; if you had to suffer odious comments from others along with this low opinion of yourself, you have a double 'hell' to break loose from.
>
> At Madonna House, I learned of the dignity of manual labor. But it became another hell to plow through. Once I had become aware of this dignity, then guilt feelings began to enter in and I felt as if I had to *atone for everything*. I knew I wouldn't be able to stand on my feet all day long; and a worry about 'production' crept in, even though I knew that people wouldn't think less of me if I couldn't do a lot. Even now, I still have some of that attitude in me.

I could give no better example of 'productionitis' than this beautiful, sorrowful letter of a young American shows. What a tragic sentence: "My attitude on production is first of all that *I could never define what a person is*. If all of your life you have never felt that you existed, or knew what it meant to be one, when society has always measured you by production and you had to suffer this along with a low opinion of yourself."

Here, human dignity is destroyed within the mind of a person. Whenever people are measured only by production, they do develop a low opinion of themselves. And not only are they measured by the amount of work they have accomplished, oftentimes they are evaluated by the specific type of work being done. Along with a 'production mentality' there comes this idea of 'status' and the chains of misery grow heavier. The feeling of imprisonment grows deeper and the sufferer becomes more helpless.

By the very essence of the spirit of Madonna House, the essence of the Gospels that we try to preach with our lives, we spiritually and intellectually reject this 'production mentality' as a terrible heresy. But do we always implement that rejection? I will give you a factual example:

One summer all the members of our Yukon house

arrived in Combermere. That was very unusual. Long planning had gone into this trip. It was not easy to close a mission house for two weeks and drive 8000 miles, round-trip; but they did it. They arrived at a very tense, almost chaotic time. The house was filled with summer volunteers, unexpected guests, and a great variety of priests. We were preparing, with joy and great excitement, for retreats before Promises. It was also berry-picking time!

Everything demanded, screamed, pressurized us of Madonna House into that production mentality. There were so many people to deal with, and so many chores to do. Each department was virtually jumping with its own activities and responsibilities. As a result, the Yukonites, though welcomed warmly and lovingly, kind of got 'lost in the shuffle' for a while, until we sat down and discussed this tendency of *putting things (and the production of things) before people.*

This is just one example of what can happen, even in a house of God that most assuredly is dedicated to incarnating hospitality to all strangers, but might have taken 'its own' for granted when they should have come first. To know when to work hard, to know when to stop working at a moment's notice, to know how to accept peacefully the frustration of a hundred unfinished jobs because people (and situations connected with people) arrive unexpectedly – that takes wisdom and charity. And, I think, sanctity.

Yes, the pressures of work can push us into a production mentality. Unfortunately, into this picture comes another element – the emotional one which I call productionitis. So many of us find 'escape' in work and in production, escape from our own tensions and our own emotions. So many of us still have a very low opinion of ourselves. So many of us still measure ourselves by the amount we produce for the Apostolate. So many of us rationalize that these things are 'needed' for the common good (and so they are). We tell ourselves that we must fulfill our obligation to 'the spirit of Madonna House' by being useful. While we're being 'useful' we are also trying to be charitable and loving, of course; but the major accent of our work is still on its usefulness.

Sister Mary Andrew gave us an axiom of psychology. She said that, from childhood on, we measure our self-worth by the reflection of that worth in the eyes of those who matter, meaning that we value ourselves the way that we are valued by others. If our sense of self-esteem is very poor, if 'those who matter' did not give us our true value, our true dignity as children of God, then – since we cannot live and face our 'valuelessness' – we have to *prove to ourselves* and to the world that we have some use, some value, some shred of dignity. We seek to prove it (first of all to ourselves, and then to others) by our production. This is the disease of productionitis.

Do you see what I'm getting at, dearly beloved? The combination of our own psychological fragility and the psychic wounds inflicted on us by this civilization of ours can really create a situation almost beyond bearing. I have tried to combat it for years. The *poustinia* was one of my ways of alleviating the situation. I had hoped (and my hopes were somewhat realized) that these days of silence, mortification, solitude, and prayer would help us see our true value in the eyes of God.

But this is not enough, evidently. So we have to make a continual search of our minds, hearts, and souls. We have to use all of our insights and really start an *all-out war* against that 'production mentality' so inbred in us by the culture of this North American continent, and by the resulting psychological traumas.

Here are the areas that need to be attacked, some 'battle stations' in that 'war':

- Face yourself honestly; see yourself through the eyes of God, your loving Father. In the light of what you know about scripture, liturgy, theology, salvation history, re-evaluate your dignity and self-worth.

- Look at the world around you; see how and where its 'production mentality' has invaded your intellectual attitudes. Arrive at a basic truth: that your own 'personhood' and the people around you are more important than 'things' and 'actions.'

- Keep a watch over your heart; continually clarify the intentions you find within it. See clearly when your production is motivated by the need of charity, and when it isn't.

- Learn to accept the normal frustration of putting *people before things.* In our Apostolate, that means you will be quite a few unfinished or half-finished jobs 'left hanging.' Develop the ability to peacefully bear with this situation.

- At the same time, study carefully your work methods, looking for any slackness or inefficiency. Constantly review your routines and techniques for 'getting things done' each day. *The use of time* is God's greatest gift to each of us, and it must not be wasted.

I hope that I will hear from all of you, and that you will discuss this lengthy Staff Letter in depth.

Lovingly yours in Mary,

Catherine

REAL FRIENDSHIP

August 28, 1965

Dearly Beloved,

As usual, I begin with a definition as found in a dictionary. In this case, I chose to look up the word *friend.* This is what the Oxford Dictionary says about it: "One joined to another in intimacy and mutual benevolence apart from sexual or family love; a person with whom it is good to be; with whom I can be myself in a situation where mutually we are concerned for one another and truthful with one another; not trying to put our best foot forward, but being our real self." Such then is the approximate definition of a 'friend' by the cold semantic Oxford Dictionary.

Let us analyze the definition a little bit. The first thing that strikes us on reading it is that a friend is a person from whom we do not hide our weaknesses; before whom we can strip off all our masks; before whom we present ourselves as we truly are, expecting and (usually if it is a true friend) getting the same treatment from him or her.

Members of a family can be friends of one another, as can a husband and wife; but with the latter, sexual love prevails. The dictionary defines friendship as being between people who were formerly strangers, lacking any family ties. A friend is also a person who shares our interests. One can say that friendships are often based on mutual interests, causes, goals, or work.

Now let us look at friendships a bit more deeply. From conversations that I have had with members of Madonna House, it appears that each of you yearns to have a friend. Sister Mary Andrew says that this is normal, that besides family ties and love and marital relationships each person should have at least one friend – a good and true one. So the need (which each one of us in Madonna House feels!) to have a friendship with one person on some deep level is, on the whole, a normal state of affairs for all human beings.

I have listened *viva voce* and via mail to many of you who were desperately hungry for friendship, and I ask myself the question, "Do you understand the word *friendship* any better than you understand the word *love?*" And I didn't come up with a direct answer.

Let me take you back to a story that most of you may have already heard. At one time, I made a tour across the United States and Canada lecturing at Catholic colleges. After the lecture in each place, I would ask the same question, "What do you think is your vocation?" The majority of those present (numbering anywhere from 250 to 500 students) said, "Marriage." I asked the next question, "Why do you want to get married?" Inevitably, the answer was: *"To be loved."*

By the end of my lecture tour, I had a very clear picture of the tragic situation among modern youth. Each male and female of marriageable age wanted to *be* loved!

May I ask you, then, if that be the case, *who is going to do the loving?* Since each said that he or she wanted to be loved, and none answered, *"To love,"* I repeat, who is going to do the loving?

Now, the same question applies to friendship, which is just another form of love. From all of the conversations and letters from the members of Madonna House, I gathered the impression that they have a terrible need for a friend who will love them, listen to them, help them, spend their time with them, and share their interests. As yet, however, I have not found among the members of Madonna House an attitude of seeking good, holy, mutual friendships that is based on *loving.* For friendship, like love, begins in the heart of one person toward another. Friendship expresses itself, first and foremost, in *a concern for the other,* in a desire to be *of service* to the other; not in a desire to have a listening ear, a consoler, for oneself. No, a desire to *fill the needs of the other.*

The words of St. Francis apply to friendship: "Not to be understood, but to understand; not to be loved, but to love; not to be consoled, but to console." The paradox of this affair is that if one does those things – loves, consoles, understands – one will receive love, consolation, and understanding in return. But it will not be immediately.

Another area of confusion lies in the very word *friendship* – its heights and depths. Sister Mary Andrew told us that to bring up children who are emotionally healthy, parents must love them. Not with a permissive or possessive love, however. They must love them with a love that is firm and strong, yet tender and gentle at the same time – a love that always sees *in truth* (which means in God) the ultimate good end of itself. Thus, parents who truly love their children will lead them to God, their ultimate end. They will teach their children obedience, discipline, and truthfulness. Teachings such as these are like a scalpel in the hands of parents. They root out any cancerous growths which could blight the emotional, intellectual, and spiritual life of their children.

Such firmness and discipline with a child, at a certain

age, may appear as horrible. At first, the emotions will show themselves in tantrums, etc. But if the parents persevere, the child will grow in the tremendous security of that firm and strong love and will become the mature individual that he or she is supposed to be: a God-centered, love-centered person. In a word, a *whole* man or woman.

Now when the members of Madonna House speak of friendship, do they understand what true, strong, firm, gentle, tender, truthful, disciplined friendship means? The yardstick of any friendship among Madonna House members is a very simple one: Does it lead both persons to God faster? Or does it lead them toward one another with the dizzying speed of an astronaut in flight, or even away from God?

To put it another way: Do I seek out 'friendships' to satisfy my emotions or my soul? Is my friend an ear into which I verbalize my emotional miseries, my hostilities? Or is he or she a person to whom I open my heart in order that – through fraternal correction, through love and insight – this friend might cut out the little cancers that fill my soul? Do I stand ready to perform this service for the other and to let the other perform for me this act of friendship, of love, of service?

Until those questions are answered truthfully within our own hearts, we should examine ourselves very thoroughly and define well what we mean when we say that we want 'friendships' in the Apostolate.

Another aspect of true friendship is the painful fact that we will have to tear off the masks we wear (even in Madonna House) and reveal the total poverty within ourselves as well as the glory of God that is in us. We will reveal those to our friends, and they will do likewise. Are we ready for this kind of friendship? We of a thousand masks? We who are afraid to look at ourselves because of Jansenism, Puritanism, and a thousand other wounds which have been inflicted upon us ... including the measuring of ourselves by the yardstick of production? Do we dare, we who have such a poor opinion of ourselves, to tear away the masks which protect our inner selves, in order to have a real friendship? For only a maskless friendship is a true friendship.

In Madonna House, we are not afraid (as monks and nuns used to be) of what is called 'particular friendships.' People of former times, superiors especially, were probably afraid of homosexuality, if they knew what it was. But we are not, because the grace of God has been with us in these matters of chastity, and our approach is one of trust and love. No, we aren't afraid of 'particular friendships' in the old sense of the word.

Personally I pray for and longingly desire that friendships 'across the board' flourish and develop in this humble but lovely corner of God's vineyard called Madonna House. But to be brutally truthful, I don't want, for your sakes, adolescent friendships. These friendships 'peter out' as soon as both parties have verbalized, griped, or beefed about their hostilities toward authority, or toward some other member, or toward some ideas or situations within Madonna House. That is not true friendship.

No! I wouldn't want to see adolescent friendships, ones founded solely on immature self-centered needs. I would like to see friendships founded on concern for 'the other' ... for the other person's needs. Then it would be true friendship, one that seeks no other reward for itself than the 'well-being' of the friend. The family well-being, the spiritual well-being, and all the rest of the well-beings (emotional, intellectual or whatever) that belong to the human heart.

Lovingly yours in Mary,

CHASTE, CELIBATE LOVE

September 28, 1965

Dearly Beloved,

Right now I have an interesting letter here before me. It is from one of our members who went to a meeting where a celebrated nun talked about the 'reformation' of her order. This nun was saying that she is very broad-minded about the changes, the opening up, the reexamination of all the facets of aggiornamento which apply to nuns. She went on to advocate "deep love relationships between men and women who are celibates as a way to wholeness and holiness."

This Madonna House member, smartly and intelligently, states in her letter: "I can't blame people who are teaching these ideas. Maybe I'm not understanding them correctly. Maybe it's my own fault for not questioning what a promise of chastity really means."

That is a good comment and a good letter and I answered it. I thought perhaps I would share it with you.

You ask a very intelligent question which is very important to all of us here at Madonna House, especially in these times of aggiornamento: the question of celibacy and chastity, of love in the broad sense of the word *caritas,* and how this applies to interpersonal relations of people under vows.

First and foremost, you missed the obvious: namely, that you belong to a group called Madonna House; a place where a good and wholesome relationship already exists between 'celibates under vows'; a place where the priests, the other men, and the women all love each other deeply; a place in which this love of ours leads to wholeness and wholesomeness, as well as to holiness. We are known as being 'a community of love' – a place to which hundreds of priests, nuns, and lay people come each year, from all over

North America, mostly to see and touch what your lecturer-nun is talking about. Madonna House is unique in this respect, and the bishop himself said that we are a 'laboratory' for the whole Catholic Church in America. You heard him say that, but perhaps you didn't catch the celibacy aspect of it.

What is happening in the Church nowadays is very simple, my child; being a convert, though, you might not appreciate it. Catholics of the North American continent were influenced not only by Jansenism but also by some Protestant thinking, especially Puritanism. Some of this took deep root in the souls of many Christians, both Protestant and Catholic. These ideas were: sex is dirty; the woman is Eve tempting man with the apple of her sex appeal; the only way to remain pure and sinless, especially for people under vows, is to build thick convent walls to separate the men from the women; and never allow the twain to meet, except under supervised and controlled circumstances. It is almost a tired old joke that the sins highly emphasized in the Catholic Church were those against the 6th and 9th Commandments (adulterous acts and lustful thoughts) while *charity* – whose other name is love, and who is God – was very much neglected.

Well, the aggiornamento came. Now all of the nuns and priests are discovering true Christianity, in which friendships of a chaste and holy nature can and should exist between people of the opposite sex. There is much *discussion* about this, but it is often done by people who lack sufficient *knowledge*. When people learn a little more about psychology, anatomy, and sexual instincts, they will begin to understand how to control their passions. There is no denying that the sexual attraction between women and men is extremely strong and that, generally speaking, people who talk about 'deep love relationships between celibates' are treading on dangerous ground.

What all those good nuns and priests must also talk about – before they implement this lovely and natural Christian way of loving – is *Christian maturity*. Now how does that sound? Very simply, it works like this: first and foremost, they need to reflect thoughtfully on that fact that it is *God* who calls people to a life of celibacy. It is definitely a vocation; it is so stated in the Gospel. Christ himself was chaste, but was not opposed to marriage or to friendship.

What is amazing (this is an aside) is that virginity – total consecration to an ideal or to a cause – is both known and respected by pagans. From the earliest recording of human history, practically all religions knew of and practiced virginity or celibacy, and some form of dedication under vows. In classical times, Rome and Greece had their vestal virgins dedicated to the service of the temple; and this was true throughout pagan history. Today various pagan religions have men and women who choose to be celibates or virgins, or to remain widows and widowers, and to dedicate their continency to their god or gods. Some people in the Old Testament had this calling; and it seems to be an inborn trait of the human race because it has been a continuing thing.

I have to smile at some of the Catholic magazines and their discussions of married clergy. There is nothing in the Gospel against married clergy. Celibacy for priests has been a law of the Church for quite a number of centuries; but it could certainly be abolished, should the Church ever decide to do so. St. Peter was married, as we know; and likely the other apostles, with the exception of St. John, were also.

In all Eastern Churches, before a young man reaches his deaconate, he is asked if he wants to remain a celibate or to get married. If he chooses the latter, he is allowed to leave the seminary and seek a wife. It's interesting to note that, in Russia and Greece, *over sixty percent* choose to be celibates because of the deep calling they feel to follow Christ in his celibacy. So it will be to the end of the ages because God gives that call to men and women, and hence gives the graces to answer it.

But the artificial, unwholesome, psychologically unhealthy fear of sex, and the separation of the sexes that existed in the Catholic Church from medieval times on, is not good. Why do you think so many priests visit us? Because they find a family atmosphere and a spirit of love; because they find 'a community of love' ... and they need it, as you and I need it.

As you know so well from my letters, our changing

times need *both psychological and Christian maturity.* Yes, a great deal of maturity is needed because in North America sex has been suppressed for so long; and now it surrounds us through television, secularism, and materialism to a tragic degree. It has become such a novelty to people that they have developed 'sex on the brain'; they simply do not know how to handle themselves. So one has to be careful to understand what Christian maturity and emotional maturity are, and how the two complement each other.

Chastity is a tremendous flame. It not only lights people's way but warms their hearts. It is like a foretaste of heaven where the saints love one another as Christians should begin to love one another on earth. Today chastity is ridiculed, and there is a lot of criticism about total dedication, vows, and what-have-you. All that is just 'whistling in the dark' because humanity continues to respect those who embrace this state of loving so tremendously. People look at our young members and they marvel. Almost in spite of themselves they are filled with admiration and respect. If you only knew how many souls have been saved from themselves by this 'foolish spectacle' (foolish to the world, that is) of good-looking young men and women (and even my celibacy with Eddie) living a chaste life, you would be surprised.

Like the strange glowing light that caused the Magi to follow it to Bethlehem, so on the horizon of the North American continent is the (comparatively) small Apostolate of Madonna House, shining like a star. As one priest told me rather poetically: "Because there is such a wholesome and holy love between men and women here, hope is born anew in many hearts, both Christian and non-Christian. Your greatest work, Catherine, is not in what you do but that you have been able, by the grace of God and the help of Our Lady, to form that true 'community of love' between men and women which should exist between all Christians. You are a living example of what can be."

Lovingly yours in Mary,

Catherine

I GIVE YOU THE WORD

December 11, 1965

Dearly Beloved,

Once again the incredible, wonderful season of Christmas approaches. Once again I turn to the Christ Child for words to express my love to you. And once again, in his silent, tender, merciful, compassionate way, he seems to give me *himself,* for he is The Word!

Now I hold him, for he makes himself small enough to nestle in my arms. Once again, haltingly, shyly, humanly, I try to pass on to you himself – The Word. I try to do this through my poor human words. I hope you will be able to read between the lines since through these words, poor as they are, I desire passionately to give you Christ!

I have been thinking about Advent: What is it? What does it stand for? And it came to me that Advent is the fulfillment of the promise of Yahweh, for his pardon is our peace and our redemption. The sign was a woman – a woman who had to say *Fiat,* for she had to be with child. And the Child was the Son of God, the longed for Messiah whom the Jews awaited with such expectation. We, the people of the covenant, possess that sign now. Our Advent has come, showing us that that other Advent will lead us to the new Jerusalem, the Parousia, our joy and our glory.

We are the baptized ones; and baptism and Christmas merge scripturally, for *Christ has come.* He lived on this earth as a youth, a man, a teacher, and he was baptized; having been baptized, he went through his passion and resurrection. We also are baptized in water and in faith, in his death and in his resurrection. Advent and Christmas, therefore, are a sign to us of the pilgrim, the servant, the suffering Church going into the Parousia, our heavenly home.

We have another sign; on Good Friday, we have the Cross. But to every believing Christian, the Cross has a backdrop, the tremendous light of the resurrection. The third sign is Easter, the feast of the Resurrection, on which the shadow of the Cross falls again for us. For remember, I repeat, that even after his resurrection, and because of it, because of his birth, his life, his death and resurrection we live in a constant Advent toward the Parousia.

What does this mean? What should it mean to us of Madonna House, dearly beloved in Christ? It should mean that we are children of joy, for there is no such thing as a joyless saint; but our joy is cradled in the poverty of Bethlehem, the poverty of creatures. We must accept this, as we must accept and integrate the passion and death of Our Lord in the daily pains, conflicts, and struggles of our lives. I must remind you once more that we are beggars; we are the poor man of whom the Scriptures speak. But our poverty should be our joy, and our conflicts should be our joy because they are all rooted in his love and his plan for us, in his death for us.

How rich we are! How much can we give our neighbor, we who are fed with the Bread and Body of the Child who is born unto us this day; of the Man who, in a passion of love, died naked for us on the Cross! We can give him to others, if only we die joyously to ourselves, to our little ideas, our little conflicts, our little difficulties. Then we can offer him to all those we meet as a ripe fruit from the tree of life. For in offering him, we shall possess him more than ever. These are the words that come to me on the eve of Christmas, 1965. This is the meditation that I want to share with you.

What can I bring to you as a gift through the Christ Child? What do my poor empty hands hold that I can give you through him and his Blessed Mother? I can give you nothing, children of my love, except a poor human heart filled with love for you, a heart that offers itself with a simple humble 'fiat' to God, for him to do with as he wishes, so that all of you and I myself might become truly a community of love.

So take my heart, my weary pain-filled joy-filled heart, as the only gift left to me to give you this Christmas of 1965.

Lovingly yours,

DEATH – A BEAUTIFUL MOMENT BETWEEN LIVES

February 25, 1966

Dearly Beloved,

Recently, one thing has struck me rather forcibly; namely, the death of so many relatives of our staff. All of this has brought vividly before me the thought of my own death, because I myself am not getting any younger. That is not really important, however, for we all walk in the shadow of death. Sometimes a youth meets death face to face before old age does.

As I meditate on death, it seems to me that we of the Apostolate do not talk or think enough about this topic. We should, you know, because death is one of the most beautiful moments *between lives!* God has been so good to us all in the Apostolate. The deaths of Cathy and Mary Ann were his vivid, glorious, tender lessons to us as to what death is really like for a Christian.*

Since man divorced God – say, for the last four

*In June 1964, Cathy Maynard died a slow death from cancer at 37 years old. In April 1964, Mary Ann Gilmore was killed instantly in an auto accident at 32 years old. Both were members of Madonna House.

hundred years or so, especially in the Western world – and since the pre-Vatican II Church surrounded death with a sort of grimness, with Requiem Masses all in Latin so that nobody understood their beauty, Catholics became rather fearful about death, just as pagans were and still are. Some of the attitudes and customs that are definitely un-Christian are still with us.

Let's face a few truths about the Scriptures. Death is awesome; there is no denying that. It is the cessation of 'being' as we know it in our experience. And behind it, of course, is the idea of the 'just punishment' that God meted out to Adam for his original sin. We have remembered all that; but we have failed to remember that *Christ has conquered death* and that, from the moment of his resurrection, death has lost its sting.

We should keep in mind that we are about to enter into 'the fullness of life' – a life of pure love, a life of intimate union with God, of overwhelming happiness and joy. When we realize that we are awaiting the Parousia – where there will be perfect happiness because the universe (this earth and everything in it) will be restored to a new life – then we will understand the value of death.

The early Christians may not have read Teilhard de Chardin* (smile) but they knew about the Parousia better than he did. And in the Eastern Churches, the fact that "God is in the cosmos and all the cosmos (all of it!) is in God" is known even to the illiterate. Because of this, Christians have always considered the day that people died as their 'birth' date. That's why, throughout the liturgical cycle, you read about the martyrs not on the day of their earthly birthday but on the day of their death, which is their birthday into heaven.

To die in the state of grace means to go to heaven. We're not interested here in purgatory because it is, at worst, a stopgap on the way to heaven. So let's talk about heaven, which is not a 'place' but is a state of union with God. It is a state of such joy and happiness that St. Paul says that "ear has not heard, eye has not seen what God has reserved for those who love him."

---

*A Jesuit priest who was a theologian, poet, and paleontologist. His writings were very popular during the 1960s.

In faith, then, why are we so afraid of death, except for psychological and human reasons? If we believe ... and we do profess to believe, since we call ourselves Christians! ... if we believe that Christ came to redeem us so as to bring us to his Father, so as to give us this life of union with him; if we believe that all of our earthly pilgrimage (not only of us personally but of the whole Church) is directed *toward that one goal* of union with God, why are we so reluctant to accept this fact, this joyous and beautiful fact of faith? The central point of our belief is that *since we, too, die with Christ, we shall resurrect with him!*

Because our faith in this central tenet is so weak, we push the thought of death away from ourselves instead of preparing for it. And we do that, not only with regard to our own death personally, but with the deaths of our mothers, fathers, brothers, sisters, relatives, and friends. If we believed as Christians should in the resurrection of Christ, and in our own resurrection, we would be dancing. We would be wearing white garments of joy. We would have music and wine. Hosannas and Alleluias would resound in our hearts and in our homes when someone goes to God.

Why should we begrudge all these wonderful people (to whom we belong and who belong to us) the tremendous happiness and immense joy of union with God? Why mourn for them? It is understandable if we mourn for ourselves, of course. In the natural order, we will be bereft of their earthly companionship, of the knowledge that they are on this planet. We will no longer be with them, in the sense of living in the same place.

This sorrow is part of the natural progression of life; after all, children leave their parents' home to work, to get married, to form new families. Whenever we are bereft of someone's immediate presence, especially in the case of those with whom we have close family ties, it is natural for us to mourn. That is understandable. *That is being human.* Remember, though, that we are mourning for ourselves. To mourn for those who have made their final leave-taking and have gone to God is strange for a Christian, to say the least. If we stopped to think it all out in the light of the Gospels, we would understand better how to accept the loss of a loved one.

174

Yes, we have this contradiction within us between our beliefs and our practice (or non-practice) of those beliefs when someone close to us has passed away. But we also have strange attitudes to death as such. These probably are inherited from the superstitions of our ancestors to whom death was a great mystery, as even birth was. In this case, I am speaking of primordial man and his early descendents. Let us call it our anthropological and pagan inheritance. In more modern centuries, however, we Catholics have become so very much divorced from the sources of our Christian religion (and practically from God himself) that we not only fear the reality of death, but we fear the thought of it. Read Evelyn Waugh's *The Loved One,* and you'll see what I mean. Certain men, such as funeral directors and morticians, capitalize on all of these fears. They traffic in death, or rather, in our non-Christian attitude toward death. This trafficking flourishes all around us.

We fear pain also. True, there is a type of pain that is almost unendurable, but oftentimes we want to immediately abolish every little hurt that comes our way, all the little stings and discomforts that barely pass for pain. We want to do this regardless of the source of it, so we reach out for a tranquilizer, an Aspirin, some morphine or its derivatives. Whenever we have a psychologically painful mood, we want a mood lifter! Where is our faith? We have been redeemed *through pain;* are we not willing to face some of it ourselves? Do we need always to be assuaging it, instead of bearing it? But I am really writing about death, not pain, so I better stick to the subject.

Frankly, this is what I most wanted to say: Let us turn to God and ask him – who has already taken the sting out of death, who has conquered it – to help us to see the face of his love. Let us beg him to increase our faith so that we would desire to be with him, even if we must die to do so. We should echo the words of Teresa of Avila: "I die because I do not die."* She was so in love with God that

*In one of his poems, St. John of the Cross (a compatriot of St. Teresa of Avila) repeated this sentence nine or ten times, placing the phrase at the end of each stanza.

she really wanted to die to be with him, but she was so in love with people that she was also willing to live forever if it be his holy will. That is the proper attitude to death, my dearly beloved.

And now some practical matters about death in our Apostolate. There seems to be a confusion among us regarding this. I have been asked again and again what is the spirit of Madonna House as to letting members of the Apostolate go home when there is a death of parents, brothers, sisters, and close relatives or friends. So here is my answer: We must turn our face to the Gospel to find the spirit of Madonna House regarding death. How did Christ reply to the young man whom he asked to follow him when the man said, "Lord, give me leave to bury my father"? Christ said: "Let the dead bury their dead. You come and follow me." What does that sentence really mean? Was Our Lord harsh, unloving, demanding? What does Jesus mean here? For Christ never contradicts himself; and since he said that every iota of the Old Law has to be observed (and the Old Testament already considers burying the dead as a work of mercy) why did he utter that sentence? He was not referring to the literal act of digging a grave and putting a body into it; or having a wake, weeping over the body of the beloved person; or doing all the things that pertain to mourning over oneself at having lost a beloved one.

No, he meant that, since he is the resurrection and the life, the man in question should detach himself *inwardly* from the physical burying of the dead, because his dead were not really dead. Christ would resurrect them if the man believed enough to 'let go' of all things and follow Christ. He proved that statement of his by allowing Lazarus to be buried and in the tomb three days (which in the hot climate of Israel was really a hell) and then he raised him forth from the dead.

Nor is he opposed to our mourning over ourselves, that is to say, exhibiting tears and all other signs of human sorrow. In his humanity, he himself wept over Lazarus. No. One has to understand that passage in deep faith, and so do we at Madonna House.

How does that add up? Very simply. If you are

stationed at a distant mission, and simple financial considerations or complex travel arrangements prevent you from being a mourner when you should be, you remain where you are. You let the dead be buried by others. You follow Christ, inwardly and completely, and your dead will profit from that act of detachment in a thousand ways unknown to you. So will all humanity because you will have brought forth in your life the truth of Christ. At that moment the Apostolate, for you, is Christ. In faith, you have followed him, just as the man who did not go to bury his father.

When my mother was dying in Belgium, my brother telegraphed me that, if I wanted to see her, I should fly to Brussels. The Doherty family in Chicago offered me money to do so, but my spiritual director said that I couldn't go. I had to choose Christ, meaning the Apostolate, because future members of the Apostolate would not have any Dohertys behind them to 'shell out' the money.

When I arrived in Edmonton and found that Eddie was going to be operated on for his kidneys – a dangerous operation for a man of his age and heart condition – my first instinct was to turn back and be at his side, but Father Cal sent me on to the Yukon to finish my visitation. Again it had to be the common good over the personal good of Eddie and myself. That is what Christ meant when he said what he did to the young man who wanted to bury his father. That is what we apply in Madonna House in the circumstances mentioned above.

Whenever the opportunities are such that the common good does not demand priority, however, then we follow the corporal work of mercy, and our personal inclinations, and the culture of the country we are in (in this case, United States and Canada). We go to the bedside of the dying and to the burial of our parents, brothers, and sisters. All things must be considered. I simply say that, whenever a death occurs, these things must be measured against the common good of the Apostolate in charity, in justice, and in common sense.

I repeat, let us act with common sense and with love for the brethren, but let us have a joyous faith at all times. We shall all continue to pray for our deceased families. Let us rejoice with them and for them.

Lovingly yours in Mary,

ENTERING THE RESURRECTION

April 1, 1966

Dearly Beloved,

The immense and beautiful mystery of Christ's resurrection is upon us! Alleluia! Alleluia!

I write this on the Friday preceding Palm Sunday, but already the light of the resurrection shines blindingly on the coming week, the darkness of which we know is temporary. The darkness exists in time and history, and in our lives, only to show us the face of Love who died and resurrected himself so that we, too, may enter into that resurrection. Such is the truth of our faith. Applied to the everyday life of our Apostolate, it is so clear and joyous that my whole heart sings and sings a hymn of gratitude to God the Father.

Think, dearly beloved, just think for a moment how wondrous and how beautiful it is to be a Christian, to live in faith, to know in that faith – with a knowledge that transcends all intellectual knowledge – that we are now, today, living in the resurrected Christ and going rapidly into the heart of the Trinity in a union of love, joy, and happiness that "ear has not heard and eye has not seen, and mind cannot understand."

All of this simply adds up to one little word: *Love!* We must love ... love with our burden of emotions, of miseries and doubts and confusions and temptations, because those emotions are the door through which we are going into the Parousia. That door is cruciform, true; but the cross is bearable if we have the faith that is necessary to accept it and 'live it out' this very moment, this very day, in the resurrected Christ. He is with us at our typewriters, our laundry tubs, our meal times, in our darknesses and lights, in our little hurts and our big days. For it is "with him, in him, and through him" that we are going to know that elusive happiness which escapes all those who do not believe in him.

This happiness is not illusory; it is real. Go into yourself and ask yourself, "What do I see?" And the answer will inevitably be *happiness*. Happiness is with you, happiness is in you; happiness and love beyond understanding, yet real and touchable. It feeds you daily on itself, for the Lord is with us. Alleluia! Alleluia! Perhaps my heart is too full to explain the joy, the longing, that fills it. I hope that your hearts are also filled with that joy and that longing, even though you may live in the midst of trials and temptations.

This year all that I have to say to you, outside of wishing you a glorious Easter, is this. Let us pray to the Father: "Abba, give us the gift of ever growing in faith in you, your Son, and the Holy Spirit. Abba, Father, take us in your arms now and hold us tightly. Let us know your Son daily better and love him more, for in knowing him we shall know you – you who are our beginning and our end, you whom to be with is Parousia. Yes, Abba, give us faith and the gift of prayer."

Dearly beloved, it is all very well to study psychology, to learn many secular subjects, to be an expert in the aggiornamento. This is all necessary; but it should come only after we have understood that we are truly the poor of Yahweh, the poor of the Beatitudes, and that without Christ we can do nothing. Our Apostolate will begin when we cease to measure and weigh ourselves by human production or natural worth, and begin in faith and in love to recognize our poverty, which is so gloriously filled with God. Let us begin to lean on God *constantly,* as the just men of the Old Testament did, and as the poor ones of the Beatitudes and the New Testament should do.

So I pray that on the great Feast of Easter we will all understand our poverty and rely only on God. Then, we will be rich indeed, and we will restore the world to him.

Lovingly yours in the
resurrected Christ,

THE HEART OF THE APOSTOLATE

May 16, 1966

Dearly Beloved,

At the request of some of the priests, I have decided to write a Staff Letter so that each of you can have a copy of God's Mandate to me. You may find it a good source of meditation, and it will be on record in these letters. Factually, it was what made me leave all things and go to live in the slums of Portland Street in Toronto, in the 1930s. So here is the Mandate as I perceived it:

> *Arise – go. Sell all you possess ... give it directly, personally, to the poor – being poor – being one with them, one with Me.*

This is the original message which pursued me

through several years. *Pursued* is the word. It would not leave me alone!

Accompanying it was a deep, inner, unshakable conviction that this arising, this going, this traveling, was a journey 'to Bethlehem' ... and yet that my life would be spent 'in Nazareth.' There was no inkling of what the future would bring; no foreshadowing, no presage, no movement of my soul or in my soul. I simply went forth! And when the will of God seemed to lead me from the obscurity of Nazareth into the hustle and bustle of the marketplace, I did not 'understand' ... I just went.

Then came additional 'words of God' that my soul heard through the following years. When I say *heard,* I don't mean that I had any visions or heard voices. I simply mean that, somehow, in some manner that I can't explain, I 'just knew' that this was so.

Little – be always little ... simple – poor – childlike.

Preach the Gospel WITH YOUR LIFE – WITHOUT COMPROMISE – listen to the Spirit – He will lead you.

Do little things exceedingly well for love of Me.

Love – love – love, never counting the cost.

Go into the marketplace and stay with Me ... pray ... fast ... pray always ... fast.

Be hidden – be a light to your neighbor's feet. Go without fear into men's hearts ... I shall be with you.

Pray always. I WILL BE YOUR REST.

These 'words of God' don't occupy much space on a piece of paper, but that's all that I have to give you; that's all that God gave me personally, and that is what I have lived for. That is to me all that matters, for it is to me the soul, the heart, of the Apostolate.

Lovingly yours in Mary,

Catherine

ON BEING RECALLED TO COMBERMERE

June 18, 1966

Dearly Beloved,

It has been a long time since I have written a letter to you. Since I am getting back to normal these days,* I have been tackling my overdue correspondence with the staff and everyone else. Now that I am catching up, I have a moment to share with you the results of my observations, meditations, and prayers.

One thing struck me very powerfully and, if I may say so, it has made me a little sad. It is the attitude of our members – senior, intermediate, or junior; but especially seniors – when they are transferred from a fieldhouse back to our training center in Combermere. It seems that, to most of them, such a recall is akin to some sort of punishment.

Why should that be? Are we or are we not a community of love? At least, are we or are we not *trying* to be a community of love? If that be so – and this is the only thing that really matters in the Apostolate! – then why this fear, this shame, this sense of failure, of punishment, and of guilt? Frankly, I find it hard to understand. As you know, I often talk of 'openness' and I feel more strongly, as time goes by, that we have to share both our joys and sorrows, both our failures and successes – in fact, our humanity, our lives – with one another. Otherwise, it is a mockery when we say that we are trying to be a 'community of love' ... in a sense, it would be blasphemy!

So let us face a few simple facts relating to a primary truth: *We are anawim,* i.e., the 'little ones' of God. We are the poor of Yahweh and of the Beatitudes of Christ. Let us face the fact that we are sinners, creatures who are totally

*In February, a medical checkup indicated that Catherine was overworked and under great tension. The doctors ordered her to stay in bed most of the day and 'rest' for a few months.

dependent upon him. He knows quite well all our pains, our sins, our weaknesses as well as our strengths. He loves us not because *we* are good, but because *he* is good. *When we acknowledge all of this, he deals with us tenderly and lovingly.*

Let us face a few more facts: Being what we are, it is quite possible for some of us to take a little longer than others in getting over our emotional difficulties. It may come to pass that these emotional difficulties may create a burden in a small fieldhouse. As a result, you may be recalled to our training center here in Combermere.

Why be ashamed of that? Why feel guilty? Why feel a failure? Love is calling you back to help with whatever problems you may have. In Combermere there are priests who know you well and who can help you over this 'hump' of emotional difficulties. From Combermere you can have access to psychiatrists, if there be a need to do so. Why be ashamed of that? It is love again, acting to help you. Lastly, there is myself. I love you with a great love and stand ready to help you and to be of service in any way possible.

So it seems to me that – if you are out in the field and have an emotional problem that needs 'straightening out' and are called back to the training center so that we can help you – you would have a sense of joy at all this assistance now being given to you. You would share this joy with your brothers and sisters in your fieldhouse, and throughout the Apostolate. Instead, you all too often feel depressed, afraid, guilty, ashamed, or what-have-you.

You may be recalled here for quite a number of reasons. One is to further your training, for our training is never finished and 'the vision of the whole' must always be expanded. Remember that any fieldhouse assignment is temporary ... unless you have proven to be unusually valuable in your particular house and should remain there for an extended time. Another reason is that you are considered as good 'material' for training others, and so you are brought back to Combermere as a mentor for initiating young people into our life.

Another reason for a recall may be to give you further academic training. As you work in the field and the picture of your talents becomes clearer, the directorate must consider how to foster those talents and use them where they will do the most good for the whole of the Apostolate. Or you might be recalled for a 're-evaluation' because we notice that in one fieldhouse you are not as happy as you might be in another which has more scope for your talents. Never forget that you are continually growing and maturing; so greater fields will await you.

Yes, there are thousands of reasons why you may be recalled. Even if the reasons are your weaknesses or some of your other problems, there is nothing to be ashamed of or to feel guilty about. Remember that we are a community of love, and that this recall is done with deep tenderness and love. It is done to help you overcome your difficulties. Who of us is without them? So be at peace. Do not have a childish or worldly attitude to this simple act of love which comes from the depths of the hearts of those whom God has chosen to take care of you ... you as a *total you:* the physical, spiritual, and emotional you.

So be at peace. Come back to Combermere joyfully, whatever the reason for your recall. For you come to a place where hearts, arms, and souls are wide open to welcome you (no matter what!) with understanding, tenderness, and gladness, and above all, with love.

Lovingly yours in Mary,

A COMMUNITY OF LOVE

October 5, 1966

Dearly Beloved,

Once again with deep love and tenderness I come to talk to you, my spiritual children, about the essentials of our Apostolate. Perhaps I should call this letter *A Report on our Directors' Meetings*. But it is so much more, because it doesn't deal with particular resolutions or decisions so much as with 'the essentials.'

From the very first day there was a wonderful unity among us, and I think I can truthfully say that we felt the presence of the Holy Spirit in a very special way. From the first day on, we examined the whole Apostolate and each of its missions from one point of view only. Or perhaps I should say that we concentrated on 'the essence' ... and the essence is very clear: *Madonna House exists to become a Community of Love.*

A community of love will produce 'islands of peace' wherever its missions are established in this stormy, war-torn world of ours. Madonna House and its missions are meant to be *a sign of the Lord to his world.* Each of us has been chosen to 'show forth' that sign of which we are the bearers. What are we a sign of? First of all, *himself!* We are to show his face to the world. And the only way that we can do that is, first and foremost, *by showing it to each other.* We show it by forming a community of love in which we see his face clearly, and then we turn around and show it to the world.

At these directors' meetings, we discussed the fact that we are likewise *a sign of his existence.* A great theologian said recently: "Today it is impossible to prove the existence of God by reason and intellect alone. Today, one must live the Gospel without compromise. Then, and only then, will men know that God is not dead but very much alive."

As each director made a report on the past year's

apostolate in his or her fieldhouse, those 'essentials' were the main considerations by which they (the reporting ones) and we (the listening ones) evaluated each house. It was truly a beautiful, positive, encouraging, joyful way of doing it. Gone were the difficulties that used to 'bug' the local directors and the directorate. Each brought to the meetings a newer and deeper vision of a growing spirit among us – a spirit that prays, strains, hungers for 'the essentials.'

It became evident that the message which everyone will have to bring back to the fieldhouses will be that message of 'the essentials.' In a sense, it amounted to several Gospel passages:

- *Total reliance upon God.* "Without Me you can do nothing."

- *A sense of priorities.* "Seek ye first, the kingdom of God and the rest will be added unto you."

- *The primacy of love.* St. Paul's hymn on charity says: "If I speak in the tongues of men and of angels, but have not love, I am a noisy gong or a clanging cymbal. And if I have prophetic powers, and understand all mysteries and all knowledge, and if I have all faith so as to remove mountains, but have not love, I am nothing. If I give away all I have, and if I deliver my body to be burned, but have not love, I gain nothing."

- *Long-term commitment.* That same hymn also said: "Love is patient and kind ... Love bears all things ... endures all things."

Each local director, and we at the training center, realized that 'the essential' thing for us to do is to become this 'community of love.' But it also means that each individual fieldhouse, each department and subdepartment of Madonna House – in fact, any group (however small!) that is involved in any part of the Apostolate – has but one main task: to achieve among its members, by God's grace, a 'community of love.'

For instance, I reported that I had taken over running of the Gift Shop. Busy as that department happened to be, what with the preparation of a 'pioneer house and museum' for next year's Canadian Centennial and the great influx of tourists during this year, the most important job I have had (as head of that department) has been to create a 'powerhouse of love' among those members who work in the Gift Shop. Everything else has been subservient to this.

I need not tell you, my dearly beloved, that in order to form a community of love, each of us must undergo a *kenosis,* the 'emptying of self' that we talk about so much but often do not implement in our daily lives. The local directors, of course, realize that they themselves have to implement it first. It was beautiful to the point of pain to see their openness and their desire and their hunger, no matter what the cost, to really take hold of this joyous yet crucifying task. They realized it was no easy task to take group of human beings, with all of their foibles and emotions and problems, and make that group (as well as themselves) into a powerhouse of love.

That is why it became so clear to all of us that none of us can do it alone! That is why the words of Christ finally began to speak deeply in our souls. For we knew with a new knowledge that, both naturally and supernaturally, *without him we can do nothing.*

At the end, we discovered that unless we are totally and completely surrendered to God, we cannot really be 'united' with him. Only in proportion to that surrender of ours to his most holy will, and to the particular God-given vocation we have received, would we become useful instruments for his love. *For we cannot give to the world what we don't possess ourselves!* Unless we love each other the way he wants us to love, we cannot show His Face of Love to the world around us. Unless we have peace, which is the fruit of that love among ourselves, we cannot give His Peace to anyone else.

Yes, the essentials became very clear to us during these meetings. We understood, in a deeper and move vivid sense, our own human weakness ... and God's mercy, tenderness, and compassion. We understood that *every moment is the moment of beginning again.*

Yes, the Holy Spirit was definitely with us during these meetings. He was guiding this beautiful, open, humble gathering of directors and department heads, who exist to serve God and you. Pray that each one of us (and that means all of you, collectively and individually) begin to see more and more and to 'live out' more and more the love that alone can form a community of love. Let us do this, first, with each other; and then let it spill out lavishly over the rest of the world with whom we are in contact.

Lovingly yours in Mary,

A VISION IN THE NIGHT

December 9, 1966

Dearly Beloved

This year I tried to write my usual Christmas letter to you; but somehow words did not come easily. I prayed to the Lord and it dawned on me that perhaps, in my utter poverty, I could only offer you my agony.

Agony is not a very good gift to offer on Christmas, so I should add to it a particle of joy. For when one is in agony for the Church (not simply the Catholic Christian part of it, but all human beings for which Christ died), there comes a point when a strange 'joy' begins to bind up the wounds which agony has made. It is a beautiful and serene joy.

This gift to you is one more step of the enlargement, the growth, of 'the vision of the whole' of the Madonna House Apostolate. This is all that I have to give you. Accept it with my deepest love – the depths of which so many of you do not suspect, but which stays with you and follows you and understands you, no matter what your own understanding of it may be. So, with deep love for you, I send you my Christmas gift ... a letter that I wrote to myself on November 16, 1966.

In The Dark Valley

The night of November 14-15 has been a very strange one for me indeed, for I spent many hours between sleeping and waking, with long periods of being fully awake. Yet, awake or asleep, I was taken up into what I must call a 'deep vision' or an intellectual insight that gripped me during that time and without any surcease. There is no beating about the bush that I was in the throes of a sadness beyond description, a fear beyond the telling of it, a numbness and yet a clarity of mind that strangely blended all together.

It came to me that *the Catholic Church is in grave danger!* We Christians are like a snowball that is rolling down an immense mountain and, in the process, becoming a juggernaut. And all of this is falling on the Church and, in some manner, crushing it. The Church lies in ruins underneath the cold snow, which symbolizes so many cold hearts of so-called Christians.

The conviction grew upon me that *the Church is at the crossroads.* And by 'Church' I mean all of us. Yet it is more than just all of us, the 'People of God'* (bishops, priests, and lay people) – it is also God! For the Church is the mystery of the Bride of Christ, and he is its Head. It seemed to me that the People of God have forgotten this aspect of Church. We have set aside the fact that the Church is the Bride of Christ. We have not taken into consideration the tremendous *mysterium* of Christ's Headship.

We are beginning to treat the Church as if it were only human. It seemed to me that so many of us are tearing that humanness apart, cutting the Church down to our own level, treating it as if it were just another institution – an *organization!* – and forgetting the awesome fact that it is also and predominantly an *organism,* a Living Body, the Head of which is Christ.

*A key phrase in *Lumen Gentium,* the Vatican II document on the Church, promulgated in November 1964.

I realized, in some inexplicable way, that if one tears the Body apart, then the Head must die. So it came to me that Christians are crucifying Christ again, in ourselves! How this could be I don't know, but it was very clear and vivid to me; and it was exceedingly fearful. Fear shook me like a fever. Suddenly it came to me that God the Father was intensely angry at this recrucifixion of his Son, at mankind's total forgetfulness of the Church, which is his Son's Body; and that his Son is, at the same time, the Head of it and its Bridegroom.

Our faith teaches us that our God is a 'jealous' God. The word *jealous* is not to be understood in a purely human way. It is to be understood as *a passionate concern* about our ultimate happiness as well as our present tranquility and peace; for God loves us simply because God is good. It came to me, therefore, that God's anger was a 'just' anger, because we ourselves were tearing apart all that makes for our peace. His justice has given birth to an anger over our blind, absurd, willful, hostile, stupid ways of treating the immense graces he had sent us through the Holy Spirit, through Vatican II.*

It came to me that God was continually giving his signs to us, writing on seen and unseen walls many awesome words of warning – calamities such as disease, floods, hunger. These natural disasters we try to explain away scientifically; but we have had wars, and I don't mean only the Vietnam War.† I mean the terrible, unholy wars in which human beings rage, one against the other, *in their souls*. The fragmentation and division of the People of God, their hostilities and hatreds toward one another, their rejection of the Gospel in a most obvious way – all of this was before me with a startling, fearsome clarity.

---

*The sessions of this ecumenical council, attended by over 2000 bishops, took place between October 11, 1962 and December 8, 1965.

†*During 1965 and 1966:* A series of tornados devastates the central portion of the USA, killing 300 people, injuring 4000, and causing billions of dollars in damage. In Turkey, an earthquake kills 3000 and leaves 100,000 homeless. In East Pakistan (where Madonna House has a team), cyclones cause 38,000 deaths and leave 7,000,000 homeless. In Nigeria, the beginnings of the Biafran War; 30,000 Ibo tribesmen are massacred and 1,000,000 people become refugees. The USA begins sending its first ground combat teams into Vietnam. (Over 8,000,000 US troops will see action there; in the next ten years 58,000 of them die, 364,000 are wounded.)

Everybody was becoming a reformer! But each person was a reformer, not according to the Spirit of the Lord but according to his or her own spirit, which was often impregnated with the spirit of evil. I saw the Church crumble, its Body torn to pieces, its Head crucified, not as Christ was crucified as a whole man, but with little bits and pieces of him (namely, ourselves) nailed to some immense grotesque cross.

It is said that we are a prophetic people. I fully understand that this does not mean we prophesy the future. But it appeared to me that the future is, or could be, exceedingly dark, depending on how many 'just men' God could find among us. By 'just' I mean, in this case, 'loving' men. Men who love their enemies. Men who love each other according to God's order, and therefore love God.

I'm not ashamed to say that I trembled before this sight. It came to me vividly that we of Madonna House must truly increase in love, must hasten to make that community of love which my heart urges me to talk about so constantly, so violently, so passionately.

I fully understood the words of God that the Church will continue to exist and that all hell will not prevail against it. But it also seemed to me that Catholics especially, through the communications media and all the intellectual turmoil that now exists, are slowly but surely driving the Church, which is already in the diaspora, into the catacombs. I shuddered, almost wept, at our responsibility for those who are tearing the Church apart. These people are our elite; they are endowed by God with many graces of intelligence, with talents beyond the average. I trembled at their misuse of these gifts, at their shirking of the true responsibility these talents give them. The words of the Gospel that came to me last night were: *Woe to those who scandalize the little ones of Christ!*

A Vision on the Mountain

I saw the immense changes that were coming; again, fear overcame me and a sadness beyond words. Instead of leading men toward God, instead of making it easy for people to find him, these changes were leading them *away* from him.

When I had reached what appeared to me the point of no return, when I wanted to run away from it all and hide someplace (knowing there is no place to hide from God), I seemed to see with a sort of blinding clarity what the role of Madonna House must become, in the face of what appeared to be the future ruin of the Church.

It seemed that God has placed us on a mountain top the better to see the whole perspective of this battle between men and God, between good and evil. Down below, there in the valley, men were building another Tower of Babel. Here on the mountain top, we of Madonna House were being called to build a community of love.

Because this community was a community of human beings, it seemed to me that it was composed of the things that human beings primarily need – shelters, buildings, etc. Yet each dwelling, each house, also had a *symbolic* meaning. Each was a parable, representing an instrument of God to repair, restore, heal, call, help those men in the valley who were creating a Tower of Babel, who were fragmenting the Church, who were crucifying each fragmented piece of the Body of Christ on the grotesque cross and thereby again crucifying its Head. But it also seemed to me that these buildings, as well as the community of love which they sheltered on that mountain, were placed there by God to console, heal, and in some way *die for the little ones of Christ* who were being scandalized by others.

So, there was a mountain. And on that mountain were dwellings, real dwellings, which to me signified the fruits of this community of love that Madonna House must become – or perish!

In one building were gathered experts (both priests and lay persons), very special people chosen by God. Like others who will come in the future, they were endowed with the God-given talent of intelligence. They were very proficient in their fields of canon law, scripture, theology, etc. Some scientists, interested in integrating the Gospel with their particular intellectual disciplines, were there also.

These priests and lay people were all busy in their fields and, because of their extreme competency as well as their love for God and desire to serve him, they were drawing up from the valley their colleagues. These latter were slowly beginning to climb the mountain because they could not participate, or were tired of participating, in the fragmentation of the Church and its crucifixion.

In a second building, I saw writers, painters, artisans, people interested in all forms of art (including handicrafts and the dramatic arts). They too were filled with a great love for God and a deep knowledge of their arts and crafts. They also were drawing up from the valley their colleagues who, like the scientists, could not continue to fragment and crucify the members of Christ's Body.

In a third building, I saw priests burning with the love of God and man, making ready to serve both – either by returning to the valley, or by going to other valleys throughout the world – to witness to Christ by 'being' and by loving, and then by 'doing.' They were leading our lay apostles into places where God was either not known or had already been rejected.

I saw smaller dwellings scattered around those three big buildings. They were 'mothers' to future poustinias all across the world – ashrams in India and prayer huts in Africa. In them, living alone, were priests, laymen, laywomen. They had embraced solitude, prayer, and penance in order to uphold others and to atone before God for the men in the valleys. These people had an open door. I saw the little ones from the valley come in great numbers to 'eat of the fruit' of their silence, contemplation, and penance.

I saw other buildings in which many people, both men and women, were living and working and being 'trained' (if that is the word) in the formation of a community of love – a community in which all the others I mentioned above could exist. I saw the whole of those buildings as one single candle, a little candle shining in that terrible darkness which is becoming darker every day. But even a little candle is a great light for those who dwell in Stygian blackness.

It seemed to me that *this was what God wanted* of Madonna House. We must become that little candle in the terrible darkness which is already here and which will intensify in years to come. It seemed to me that this was

God's loving answer to the chaos that man has created within himself; this was God's peaceful response to the hostilities, to the anger, to the unpeace, to the forgetfulness of the essentials of the Gospel, to the terrible cutting up of the Body of Christ, of the People of God, which increases in violence from day to day.

I understood that this community of love was placed on a mountain top so that the burning candle, even though little, could be seen from everywhere in the darkness below. I realized that the buildings were humble and poor, and very simple. And all who dwelt in them had to be equally as simple and little and childlike. For the 'Goliath' down in the valley can be killed only by a 'David' ... a young boy clad in simple shepherd's garments, who has a slingshot of love and the little stones of simplicity, humility, and childlikeness.

And so it was. The community of love that dwelt on the mountain top were all clad in the garments of service (which are the priestly robes of the Good Shepherd) and were using their talents only as tools of service. Besides their 'weapons' of love and humility and simplicity, they each held a towel, a pitcher of water, and a basin ... so that they could wash the feet of all those who came to them.

Those who went down into all the valleys of the world carried nothing but a slingshot of charity and in their pockets the pebbles of childlikeness and humility. They were girded with the towel of service, but they possessed neither pitcher nor basin ... knowing they would find 'in the marketplace' a vessel to capture the clear waters of love flowing from their hearts, wherever they went to witness to Christ.

Such was the vision I saw in the strange night of November 14-15.

Lovingly yours in Mary,

THE GIFT OF MY LOVE

March 15, 1967

Dearly Beloved,

You have been with me through all of Lent. When I say that you have been with me, I mean it almost literally. Each one of you walked with me and talked with me, and I with you. Somehow, we were all together in a strange, deep, mysterious, and incredible unity. It was, therefore, a beautiful Lent for me.

There was pain in this unity and pain in this love. Yet somehow (don't ask me how), there was tremendous joy in all of it, including the pain. I understood the words of the Gospel as I have never understood them before. Indeed, *his yoke is easy and his burden is light,* because he-who-is-Love makes it so.

We walk in the resurrected Christ! We live in the resurrected Christ! We have our being in the resurrected Christ! We are the children of love and light, alleluia! I give you joy, the joy of the resurrected Lord. I give you love. I give you Christ, for he is risen. Verily he is risen. Alleluia!

Throughout this Lent, I yearned with a tremendous yearning to tell each one of you how deeply, totally, and completely I love you. I love each one of you separately, individually, uniquely, for each one of you is unique. I long to tell you that I love you *as you are,* accept you *as you are;* that I trust you completely, for trust is the unmistakable fruit of love. I want to tell you that every day I pray for you and lift you up to the Lord so that he may take you from me into his strong Divine Arms.

My heart wants to explain to you that my love sees deeply into you because the Lord leads me to do so. He bids me by his Mandate to "go into the hearts of men without fear; I will lead you there." I realize that you cannot always understand the ways of my love, because it is the love of a *surgeon* who cuts to heal, to cure, and to make well. It is the love of a *teacher* who, knowing your potential, endeavors to bring it forth by always asking more of you than you think you can give. I know what you have to give, and I love you enough to call it forth.

I also love you as a *pilgrim* does – the pilgrim who leads the pilgrimage – for in my country there is always such a leader. The leader is chosen by the pilgrims themselves or by someone in authority; in my case, I think it is God who puts me there. He wants me to be a crutch for the tired, a counselor to the upset, a carrier of the sick, and to keep the pilgrimage on the move. A surgeon, a teacher, a leader of a pilgrimage – it seems that I try to be all of these things; but above all, dearly beloved, I wish to be your servant.

I have learned two things well (even though I am weak and simple): (1) That to govern – which means to serve – is to love; and (2) That if one can suffer and continue to love, then one can do almost everything, even things which seem impossible.

As I write all of this, I want you to understand very clearly that I can do none of these things by myself alone. In truth (I write deeply from my heart), I am the poorest of you all, and so I have to lean on God much harder than any of you do. So, with the joy of the Lord and the love of the Lord, I give you my poverty and my weakness; for I know well that it is his strength that I am giving you then. It is only "in him and with him and through him" that I can love you as I try to do.

I know this is a strange letter for me to write; and many of you, perhaps, will not even know why I write it. I speak a different language from the one that you are accustomed to; but, some day, you too will speak that way to others, and then you will understand. For some reason, which I cannot explain, I have had to write this letter. This Lent I went into the depths of myself and found these things I write about; and I had to express them, whether or not they are understood.

Yes, they had to be expressed as my humble gift to you for this Easter of 1967. This letter is addressed to each and every one of you; for what gift can any of us give the other, except *the gift of love?* It is a gift which is expressed simply, in a childlike way, by one heart that holds another in love. My heart holds each one of you in a love that surpasses understanding and explanation.

Of such love is unity truly built, and a community of love formed. A community of love is so needed in these days of darkness, hate, and war. My heart is wide open to you, dearly beloved, and I pray the Lord that our hearts be open to one another, so that we might love him ever more – first, in himself; secondly, in all of humanity; thirdly, in created things in which he has his being.

The Lord has truly risen, alleluia! Verily he has risen, alleluia! Love walks among us. Where love is, God is; and Love is God. Let us bring God to one another and to the world. Alleluia!

Lovingly in Mary,

LOVE IS A HOLOCAUST

March 20, 1967

Dearly Beloved,

It is only today, after I wrote my 'love letter' to you as my humble Easter gift, that I come to visit you. I want to talk to each of you about a few things that I have kept in my heart for a long time – things that I have shown only to the Lord but which now I can share with you.

They concern what I call the 'formation' of a community of love. Again and again you have heard me talk about it. I know that, with the grace and help of God, you are all working at it. But we have not yet talked enough about 'the little things' as well as the big ones which go into the formation of that community.

Let us look at ourselves together, and let us do it in the name of the Lord, trying to see what it is that holds us back from implementing the desire of God's heart for us; for it is he who called us to form that community.

One of the greatest obstacles, of course, is our humanity – our humanity wounded by original sin. We have to recognize this. But among us the expression of our wounded humanity takes various forms which could, if we were really open with one another, disappear as quickly as fog disappears before the sun.

It is a question of personalities. No one person is like the other; we are all unique. Yet God created each one of us to make up a beautiful mosaic, a picture puzzle in which the very uniqueness, the very differences, become the key to fitting the pieces together. He has blended each one of us so that we can become firmly wedded to the other in that beautiful design of his divine life which we call love.

Are you a young local director, afraid to be rejected by your staff, who may be older in seniority, education, experience, and knowledge? What have you got to fear, once you understand that *you* do not direct your fieldhouse? Christ does the directing! So be open with your staff and simply say to them: "I'm young and inexperienced; correct me if it is needed. But, at the same time, obey me; because you're not obeying me, you're obeying Christ."

Are you a new director, overwhelmed by the responsibilities of creating a community of love within your house, while attending to a thousand needs that clamor at the doorstep of your mind, heart, and soul? Be not fearful or depressed. Pray and fast. Acknowledge your newness, your weakness, and draw out the more experienced people in your house. Never be afraid to 'lose face' as the world calls it, for each one of us in Madonna House is of good will and desires to grow in wisdom and grace.

Are you a member who has problems with your director, or with the other staff? Do you consider yourself unappreciated, misunderstood, or evaluated only by your performance? Stop it! Stop it right now, dearly beloved, because in very few places of the world will you ever be loved as you are in Madonna House. And if you are misunderstood and seemingly rejected because your brother or sister has an emotional problem, that is one of *their* travails; so go out to them in your love. Be open with them. Do not withdraw from the group, for a withdrawal wounds the common good.

Do not make comparisons; they are odious. It truly doesn't matter that someone has a Ph.D. and someone else has barely finished grade school or high school. These are all worldly yardsticks which are not important. So when we greatly desire to establish a community of love among ourselves, let us take it for granted that we are all 'neurotics' together, in the informal sense of the word.* We are people who live in a century of atom bombs, of vast technological changes, of great renewal in the Church – all of which has shaken the foundations of many of our securities, both cultural and spiritual. Let us realize that, with this background, we will have many stresses and strains, and that these tensions will affect our emotions. Let us rejoice at this realization, for *our weakness is God's strength.* It is he who has selected us and brought us to Madonna House. He has done this so that we may learn to love him and each other and, by doing so, bring that love to a world which hungers so deeply for it.

Let us not be dependent upon any one person, but dependent on God alone. At the same time, let leaders 'lead' and the strong ones 'lay their strength at the feet of others' to be a lamp to those feet, leading them to God, not to themselves. Let no one 'feed' his needs on another, but let everyone allow himself to be 'eaten up' by the other. Every morning we eat God, and so must be eaten up ourselves. That means we must give ourselves without reservation to everyone who needs us at the moment, especially to our own brothers and sisters.

In peace, in love, and in trust toward one another, we can solve all things; for when one can suffer and also love, then one can do almost anything – even things which, in

*"Mild mental confusion characterized by anxiety, unrealistic ideas, and sometimes erratic behavior; it is caused by a sensitivity to one's surroundings rather than by a specific neurological disorder."

this world, seem impossible. All of this means that we finally understand the 'price' that a community of love entails. It starts whenever an individual human being turns his or her face toward God (for the Trinity is the original community of love). We must first form that 'community of love' within ourselves because, unless we are one with the Trinity, we will not be able to be in true relationship with one another.

There lies the secret of a community of love – oneness with the Trinity first – a oneness that will give us the strength to 'pay the same price' as the Second Person of the Trinity paid for ransoming you and me. For it is he who is going to love in us when we have finally surrendered to the fact that love is a holocaust. In it, the *I* in us is totally burned out and we no longer use that pronoun selfishly or self-centeredly. Then, our community of love will begin to have its being and we will appear as a clear flame for all to see, and men will come to touch our wounds. That will be the greatest pain, but it will also give us a *joy* beyond all understanding. Yes, these are the little things (but they are really so immense), that go into the making of a community of love.

If you want to find out the progress of your little family in the missions, it is very simple: just observe how much joy is in your house, because joy is the yardstick of a community of love. Perhaps it is foolish of me to give you the well-known prayer of St. Francis in this letter, but here it is:

Lord, make me an instrument of peace!
Where there is hatred, let me sow love.
Where there is injury, pardon.
Where there is doubt, faith.
Where there is despair, hope.
Where there is darkness, light.
Where there is sadness, joy.

This is the first part of the prayer, which lists the fruits of the second part. Unless we have accepted the second part, we shall not produce the first. The second part is:

O Divine Master, grant that I may not so much seek
To be consoled, as to console.
To be understood, as to understand.
To be loved, as to love.

These three requests of St. Francis to God sum up the ways of making a community of love. Once they are understood, and implemented or 'fleshed out' in our lives, then comes the immense reward that God promised us in his Beatitudes:

For it is in giving that we receive.
It is in pardoning that we are pardoned.
It is in dying that we are born to eternal life.

You know this prayer of St. Francis, but I implore you to meditate upon it during this glorious season of Eastertide. It holds all that God wants to say to you, and it holds all that I want to say to you. I know that, in your heart, there will be an echo, "Yes, yes, this is the way, Lord. Help me to start on it."

Lovingly yours in Mary,

A MEDITATION ON POVERTY

March 22, 1967

Dearly Beloved,

I enclose herewith a meditation of mine which was published in the Spring 1967 edition of *Spiritual Life,* a Carmelite magazine. I thought that it would make a good Staff Letter and clarify a little further for all of us what true poverty is really like:

Poverty is the *Sword* of the Spirit with which it slays the 'flesh' that wars against God – the 'flesh' of Self that nurses at the breast of pride, vainglory, and vanity.

Poverty is the *Fire* of the Holy Spirit that burns down the thousand mansions which Self has built in the caverns and deep places of the soul – wondrously appointed mansions of vanity, greed, and avarice.

Poverty is the *Light* of the Holy Spirit that disperses the night, which hides so well these mansions built in the soul of man by Self; and the lust, gluttony, and sloth that have come to dwell in these mansions under the soft cover of this dark night.

Poverty is the *Pruning Knife* of obedience that is held by the husbandman, God the Father. He comes as a mighty power to cut deeply, to trim and strip the bark from the tree of the soul, until it stands white and stripped of Self before his face. Then, with the gentleness of a Father, he grafts it onto a mighty tree – his Only-begotten Son. Trembling and bleeding, the slender tree of the soul is annihilated. It beholds its utter stripping, unworthiness, nothingness, and is lost to all understanding and comprehension. It knows only that it has become, in a manner inexplicable, part of an Immensity and Infinity that it knew not existed. Now, in truth, poverty has done its work, and all the soul can do is to 'stand still' in the darkness of a new night of obedience and to 'be a holocaust' to love.

Poverty is the *Treasure* of the Most Holy Trinity – a treasure reserved for the soul of one who, in the dark night, grows into a mighty branch of the Tree-who-is-Son. Bedecked with all the richness that poverty and obedience possess, the branch becomes the bride of Christ and in a sense 'enters into his kingdom' while yet on earth!

Lovingly yours in Mary,

WHO AND WHAT IS A SPIRITUAL DIRECTOR

September 16, 1967

Dearly Beloved,

There seems to be some kind of confusion arising in the minds of several of our family as to what and who a spiritual director is. I will answer that as briefly as I can:

- A spiritual director is a man who is also a priest.
- A spiritual director is a priest who, with the grace of his priesthood, has also received the grace of guiding souls to the Father, through Jesus Christ, our Brother.
- A spiritual director does this guiding through the Holy Spirit.
- A spiritual director is not a psychiatrist.
- A spiritual director is not a doctor.
- A spiritual director, humanly speaking, might not guide anybody anywhere.
- A spiritual director is a man, a priest, who must be utterly open to the work of the Holy Spirit in the person whom he has accepted for direction.
- A spiritual director must literally efface himself, so as to allow the Holy Spirit to guide him to see the works of that same Holy Spirit in his directees.
- A spiritual director is a priest who has only one aim in view: namely, to obey the promptings of the Holy Spirit in himself with grave humility, and to pass those promptings of the Holy Spirit on to his directees, no matter what the cost is for them both.

Having tried to express briefly what a spiritual director is, I'm going to try, just as briefly, to express what a spiritual 'directee' should be. There are three key points:

Point 1. When you seek spiritual direction, you must pray much to God and ask him to direct your choice of a spiritual director. Sometimes this most important part of obtaining a director is omitted. This is tragic, for you must not choose a spiritual director because he has an attractive personality, because he seems to have a similar view of life as you do, or for any of those superficial reasons. You should pray to God to get a priest who will lead you to God firmly and constantly.

Point 2. When you find, after prayer, the priest that God wants you to have – God seldom (to my mind, never!) refuses that prayer – you must put yourself totally into the hands of this priest and give him your love, trust, and obedience. Once this spiritual director has accepted you as a directee, you should never question his actions with regard to you. Every action of this priest is presumed to be for the good of your soul; here is where the aspect of 'trust' must come in.

Point 3. When you receive spiritual direction from the priest, do not expect 'understanding' from him as well (in the natural sense of the word). He understands you much better than you may suspect; but, illuminated by the Holy Spirit, he may not act toward you as you may wish that he would do. Let him work with you according to the lights of the Holy Spirit.

Love, trust, and obedience – these are the three keys to fruitful spiritual direction. Because people under spiritual direction are dealing with a mystery that is exceedingly profound, it demands complete faith, complete trust, complete obedience – not to the man but to the priest who, *because of his priesthood,* is illuminated from Above.

Therefore, you must leave yourself completely in the hands of your spiritual director. If he answers your letters, fine; if he doesn't, fine. He must have a reason. You continue to love, trust, and obey. He is not there as a psychiatrist or as a doctor of any kind. He is there, watching the work of the Holy Spirit in you and opening himself to that Work of the Spirit within you. Unless you understand this, and cooperate with it, it might be better not to have a spiritual director.

Lovingly yours in Mary,

THE ALPHA AND THE OMEGA

November 21, 1967

Dearly Beloved,

It has become quite evident that Madonna House has reached another level of grace. To put it another way, our hearts have heard the call of God, "Friend, go higher."

The meeting of the local directors here was full of grace, as you know by now, and it vividly brought forward that now our primary work is to form a community of love among ourselves. Everything else that we decided at this meeting was secondary. For the more we love one another, the better we will serve. Our work will be more orderly, more efficient, more loving, in depth. The more that we achieve this community of love, the more widely these works will spread into the secular world, into politics and economics, into the renewal of communities and cooperatives, into the corporal and spiritual works of mercy.

I have been praying almost constantly since my return from the Third World Congress of the Lay Apostolate, because one part of it struck me, almost as St. Paul was struck when he fell from his horse on the road to Damascus.

For a while, perhaps, I was as St. Paul: deaf, dumb, and blind. What hit me so much was the fact that what we at Madonna House call our 'techniques' (if that is the right word) were constantly discussed, approved, acclaimed at the Congress, especially by the poorer nations. There wasn't a single workshop (and there were many of them) in which they did not beseech, implore, demand that the rich nations remember that all activity – political, social, economic, pastoral, etc., (the Congress embraced the gamut of the world's problems, within the Church and outside of it!) – must be done with the help of *prayer*. Mass must come first; periods of silence, solitude, meditation, and contemplation must be second. It became apparent to the white races, the rich nations, that the words of Christ once more were taking flesh before their eyes, "I thank you, Father, that you have revealed this to the little ones of this world and not to the wise."

Workshops on the Missions – represented by India, Ceylon, Africa, Latin America, Polynesia, the Philippines, Hong Kong, Formosa, Vietnam, and Sweden – loudly and clearly outlined *the way of the missionary.* Representatives from third-world countries said: "Come and live with us for several years. Become our friends. Identify yourself with us as much and as far as your culture, bodies, and minds can. Then pray to identify yourself more – perhaps even dying among us in that adjustment to our ways. Do nothing for several years until we learn to trust you; your western ways impinge upon us continually, and oftentimes we have been 'sold down the river' by you.

"We need your help. We want you to heal us and to help us learn a thousand things. You can be nurses, teachers, social workers, etc.; but we, the Catholics of these countries, want you to bring us Christ *first,* and to do so through person-to-person contact and through identification with our life. Give us *yourself* first, and then all your programs of help afterwards. Then everyone will know our God better because you will be 'living the Gospel with your life'... and that is the loudest preaching."

That's when I was struck! That's when I felt deaf, dumb, and blind for a while. I must admit that, in a sense, I was terrified and awed. I felt as if I were the prophet before the burning bush in the desert – the prophet to whom a voice said: "Take off your shoes, for this place is holy." It isn't given to everyone to have such a confirmation of what appears to be crazy ideas. In a manner of speaking, I have 'laid down my life' for these ideas, and I still try to do so. I confess that I began to shiver as though I had a fever or a chill. This was the very thing I had been praying for almost constantly, hoping continually to be able to convey what it is that we must implore God to help us to understand. Who can define what a community of love is? Yes, who? Unless one steeps oneself in the Gospel and lives it.

Haltingly, and with humility, I must attempt to express

what is in my heart. (Though I might be steeped in the Gospels and have to try to live them, I feel unworthy to do so.) When I got up to speak at one of those workshops, I mentioned our idea of what a 'community of love' is, and tried to describe it briefly and succinctly, a woman with a beautiful face (she was from Calcutta) got up and exclaimed: "That's it! What we need today is the sort of apostolate this lady speaks about. It will be like seeds blown by the Holy Spirit across the world; and wherever they fall, they shall draw all things unto themselves, because they won't be doing it, Christ will do it through them."

After a while, she came and said (and again I quote this in humility, for humility is truth): "Of all here present from the West, you are the only one who spoke to my Hindu-Catholic heart. I work with the Bishop of Calcutta. Would you come there?" I answered, "By the grace of God, we may."

I share with you only my own vision. Let it fall like a seed into your heart and grow there as the Holy Spirit may teach you, if my vision be from him. As I see it, in order to form a community of love, we must first form a community of love with the Trinity. In each of our missions, in each of our departments, in the heart of each member, we must be a community of love with the Holy Trinity first. As we approach the fire of that love that the Trinity is, we must allow that fire to burn out the dross that is in our own hearts.

We must follow in the footsteps of our Brother, Jesus Christ. We must lean on him, as anawim should, when 'the going gets rough.' He will take us to the Father's Heart. We know that the Father, through the Son, has sent us the Holy Spirit who will guide us in 'crying the Gospel with our lives,' for that's what it means to walk in the footsteps of Christ. We know that the Holy Spirit will teach us and reveal to us, step by step, what we might not know or might not have understood. This is the beginning of our grace-filled understanding of where our place – that unique place of each one of us – should be in forming the community of love that Madonna House must become ... or perish!

As we follow and hold onto our Brother Jesus, we

must pray, beg, and implore him that we may follow him into the totality of this kenosis – the 'emptying' of himself – which began at his birth when he took our flesh; the kenosis of his whole lifetime in Nazareth; the kenosis of his preaching and training a band of followers; the kenosis he completed on the Cross as he died for love of us. We must undertake the 'journey inward,' knowing it will be painful, yet believing that it will become joyful, for God is joy. So is love! Both lead to utter freedom.

We must guard against one of the more subtle wiles of Satan: that of *escaping into a false or inappropriate 'good.'* If the devil cannot tempt us with evil, he will tempt us with 'good.' It is so much easier to get involved in the hippies, in the underprivileged, in world poverty, in anything and everything except this kenosis, except this following of our Brother Jesus to the Father, into that fire that burns out all that isn't of God in us. But if we fall into the above temptation, our work will be as nothing.

But if we are leaning on, holding onto, following Jesus Christ to the Father, we will empty ourselves totally and be filled with the Holy Spirit. And then we will fall in love with God, with the Most Holy Trinity; and we will become part of Them, part of the eternal, primary Community of Love.

Then we can walk into the secular world, clad in charity, truth, humility; and we will renew it. Then we can enter into politics, economics, any facet of the world-at-large that needs restoration – even the far-distant universe. Interplanetary life will be easy for us, as will the latest technology; for love can penetrate all of these, as it can penetrate all creation.

Let us, therefore, begin at the beginning, with the Alpha and Omega, with our Brother Jesus Christ who will lead us to the Father and who gives us the Holy Spirit: and all of the rest will be added to us. Amen. Alleluia!

Lovingly yours in Mary,

ON INTERPERSONAL RELATIONSHIPS

November 22, 1967

Dearly Beloved,

Is this letter just a follow-up on my previous letter about forming a community of love? Or is it a letter that springs from my heart because these days I seem to be constantly praying for all of you, and for the Church especially? The Church is so deeply wounded that I feel compelled to share with you much that cries out to be shared.

Time after time I ask myself how I can help you to incarnate our Little Mandate more profoundly. Sometimes it seems to me that I am constantly looking at various facets of some strange, diamond-like situation. If only we could consider together how to 'reshape' this strange diamond, how to make each facet hold its own beauty and yet contribute to the beauty of the whole, then we could advance (or perhaps the word is understand) a little better how to deepen this community of love.

One of the facets that need replaning, reshaping, and repolishing is the interpersonal relationships in our midst. I know I walk on difficult and dangerous ground here. I do not want to bring in the old psychological and so-called scientific facts of maturity, of desire for approval, of competition, of withdrawal and what-have-you. I feel strongly that the staff of Madonna House are familiar with all of these.

I want to talk about this question of interpersonal relationships on a *spiritual* basis. We all desire to escape from facing ourselves spiritually, or should I say from facing God in depth. And where do we escape? Naturally, into our work. There we meet people and things that demand our attention. But though we might be meeting them daily, we do not have to live with them as we have to live with ourselves or with close family members.

We can feel deeply about all the tremendous needs of this tragic world of ours, and the poor we serve, and the social conditions in which so many injustices are still prevalent, nationally and internationally. All of this is beautiful and it should be so, provided that we have honestly and in the depths of our hearts examined the relationships we have with one another in the Apostolate!

I find, for example, that local directors feel threatened by their staff. I discard the emotional reasons for this because I am sure they can deal with that if they really wish to do so. But when I pray, I try to consider why any director should feel threatened by the staff when we are already a community of love, and must work only at deepening this oneness, this unity that is the fruit of love. I search for the reason and continually turn to God for the answer.

Conversely, when members feel threatened by the local directors or by me, I again to turn to God because something is just completely incomprehensible in this situation. Each director has been a staff worker, has 'started from scratch' like everyone else, has needed comfort and support while growing more deeply in the Madonna House spirit. A director, therefore, realizes what other members must be going through, and can offer them love, understanding, and support.

There cannot be a division of loyalty in Madonna House, because where there is love, there should be a single unifying loyalty. Just recently a situation arose in one of the houses in which the staff there became very hostile. It seemed to them that I was attacking their beloved local director in some way or another. But how was that possible? The local director is one of my spiritual children, someone whom I love tremendously and have carefully trained, and for whom (without exaggeration) I would lay down my life. So how can such a strange idea enter into the minds of those members of Madonna House? I wouldn't know, but it does; and it leads to a misguided sense of loyalty. This proves that, in the depths of our souls, we must work on our community of love.

As I said, other members don't seem to be able to understand their local directors and, consequently, they feel threatened by them in some way. There are thousands of intangible situations which arise between the staff and local directors, between heads of departments and their trainees, assistants, or whatever you wish to call them. Why should that be in a community of love? Surely they should know that the director loves them and wouldn't harm them, and that the director counts on their continued support, love, and prayer. Interpersonal relationships between staff show such a gamut of problems that it would take a book to enumerate them. Why is this? Fundamentally, we all love one another deeply. If any of us goes away on a vacation or a trip, we feel very deeply the absence of those who have gone. Then why those tensions between members when they are present to one another?

It all comes down to this: we do not understand grasp what is meant by 'openness' of heart. We haven't quite understood that we are all involved in *one* Apostolate. We seem unable to be objective about any criticism (or what appears to us as criticism) of a fieldhouse or of a member of Madonna House. To many of us, correction still means *rejection*. It is sad to see that we still work on so natural a plane. We do not use the tools that psychology has given us to eliminate, or work upon, our little psychological problems. If we did, we would then be free to face our shortcomings and those of others with an 'open' heart. While lovingly accepting ourselves and others, we could help one another to overcome these difficulties.

I really don't have the answer, except to say that it lies in the growth of the community of love; but that growth has to be taken seriously. It would be a great joy to me if we could be openhearted to one another, and if we really concentrated on the things that are so vitally important throughout the whole Apostolate. It is fantastic how difficult a challenge this seems to be. We are a family. We are a community of love. All I pray is that we grow in the family spirit and in this love. Please. Help me to help others in the family.

I am enclosing a poem that I wrote for one of our members. It tries to show that it is all very well to take the whole world into one's heart, but that the most important thing is to take the person next to you into your heart. In this poem, I am the local director, the member of Madonna

House, the head of a department or a director general – take your choice! I am a member of our Madonna House family who is sitting next to you. That's what the poem means; and unless you understand and love me, all the rest will not be quite in truth, no matter how marvelous your works (or mine) may be.

I don't remember if I were white or black or red.
I had forgotten, too, where I came from ...
Was it from Poland? Or Timbuktu?
From the jungles of Vietnam? Or China?
The memory of all was lost somewhere back there!
All I knew – I was a woman or a man
Created in the image of my God,
In search of love.

As I walked the noisy city streets
And lonely roads of forest and of field,
I met a thousand people.
They spoke to me in many tongues.
They probed.
They asked where I came from and who I was.
They wrote thousands of thick books about me,
And slender poems.
But they never knew me
Because, you see, they didn't love me as I was.

They marched for me.
They wept for me.
They shed their blood for me.
But, still, they didn't love me.
They were so busy finding out who I was
And who they were.
So busy helping in thousands of ways
But one –
They did not meet me as I was and as I am
Because, you see, they didn't love me
With the heart of Him Who told them to.
It was difficult ... too difficult.
It would break them up.
They didn't understand that love was the beginning
And the end.

All the rest could only come from it –
Acceptable to me.
All they did was bitter, unimportant without it.
As I exist, I pray to Him
Whose image I am ... that they see Him in me.
Then we shall meet in Him.
Then, and only then, we shall begin to speak.

Lovingly yours in Mary,

Catherine

LOVING SURRENDER

December 9, 1967

Dearly Beloved,

Before I begin this next letter, I want to ask you to pray for Alma Beauchamp. We don't yet know the final diagnosis, but she just had a lung Xray, and it showed spots. With her history of cancer, I must admit that we are worried. So please pray.

Her spirit is tremendous. Upon returning from the doctor, she told us that in her there was great joy. She said she placed herself, and whatever diagnosis might be forthcoming, into God's hands. She offered herself for one intention only: that Madonna House and each one of its missions, especially the one of which she is a part, may truly become a community of love.

Greater love has no man than to lay down his life for others. This is what Alma has done for all of us. Whatever the diagnosis may be, this total surrender for others, this laying one's life down for us, is a fact. Meditate on that. Meditate deeply; for it follows, strangely enough, upon my last letter about being a community of love in Madonna House.

This kind of witnessing by one of our members is an awesome confirmation of God's will. For he alone can give a person the grace to make this total offering of oneself. We are before a sign of God that we cannot disregard. It brings me back to the forming among us of this community of love which haunts me night and day with a strange, relentless urgency.

Many thoughts come to me. Some come as a result of your letters; some, I think, as a result of my constant prayers. These days I spend at least an hour a day in my poustinia; sometimes more. I am like a leaf tossed in the storm of the Holy Spirit. I repeat, there is a strange urgency in me, and I keep thinking of one of my favorite Scriptural sentences: *The charity of Christ urges me on!*

Once again I want to speak of the community of love in Madonna House. Sometimes it appears as if the staff depend a little too much on the local directors and even on the directorate. I sense that over-dependence. True, those in authority should always be trying to pass on the spirit. I especially should; by example, mostly, but by words too, since I can't be with you all everywhere.

Nevertheless, a community of love depends, primarily and constantly, *on God himself.* All of you know the spirit of Madonna House. If you have forgotten some of it, there is the Little Mandate to remind you of it. You can read the Staff Letters and, above all, *the Gospels.* So you must realize that you do not always have to turn to the director general or the local director to ask how the spirit is to be applied to this or that situation. If each one of us has the spirit, there will never be a 'breakdown' in the team spirit, which is but another way of saying the spirit of the community of love.

Even though you understand the special graces that the directors general and the local directors are given to carry the responsibility of integrating that Madonna House spirit, I hope you realize that it is also the responsibility of *every* member of the community to do this as well. There should be no separateness or distinction in this matter between the staff and the local director. In fact, the staff must remember that they are many, and the local directors or directors general are few, and everyone has to work together to carry a house and all of its responsibilities.

The community members must support those in charge of a house with their love and understanding. At the same time, I hope to God that no one thinks of the local director or the director general as 'the brass' or 'the boss.' Such an attitude would be unthinkable in a community of love, for one does not think of God in these terms. The Trinity is God who is our Father; the Son, Jesus Christ, who is our Brother; and the Holy Spirit who is our Friend, the Friend of the Poor, and our Advocate. Their authority is the authority of a love that serves. Christ died for us; what greater service could he have rendered to mankind?

So let us not slip into a 'boss-helper' relationship. Let there be a community. If you want, the local directors and directors general could be looked upon as the 'suffering servant' of others, but never as a boss. They should never be talked about in conversation among the staff as *he, she, they*. In a community of love, there is no anonymity or estrangement. We are *we*.

I need the feedback of your reactions, your reflections (be they positive or negative); and I am sure that the local directors do too. That will help to form a dynamic, realistic team. There is a need to relate to one another and to communicate constantly, no matter how great the risk involved in this approach. Be not afraid of risks. In the spiritual life they abound, especially risks to our emotions. But as St. John of the Cross says, "I jumped into the abyss and caught my prey." It is from one of his poems; he is talking about God, and refers here to the abyss of faith.

I know that a community of love is not achieved in a day; it is the work of a lifetime. But let us seriously begin it now, for who knows how much time each one of us has. Also, because it is evident even in our youngest members, who knows what effects our loving each other will have on those who come in search of answers to their confusions and bewilderment. You realize, of course, that none of us really give them answers from the intellect, that is to say, from discussions, clarifications, dialogues, encounters, and what-have-you. Our answers are *rooted in our lives,* the lives of us all, local directors, directors general, and all our members. We have a priest visiting us at present. He spends his day at the farm. He needed many answers; but no one with whom he talked seemed able to give them to him. After he started working at the farm, however, he came to me and said: "I got my answers in watching those people at the farm, seeing how they live and pray and work together, and love each other. It came to me without words."

That is what I mean.

Lovingly yours in Christ,

HIS INCARNATION IS THE ESSENCE

Christmas 1967

Dearly Beloved,

What can I say on this Birthday of the Child? What can I say that has not already been said a million times better?

Perhaps I can share a few thoughts with you for that is all, in my intense poverty, I still possess – a few thoughts and an immense love for you. But I have already given you my love; it is yours to have and to hold until you die, until I meet you in the Heart of Love. But here are a few thoughts I wish to share:

Christ desires to be born in the manger of our hearts. Are the doors of those hearts of ours wide open to receive the shepherds, the Magi, the stray visitors ... in a word, humanity? Are they open to receive one another in the Apostolate as Christ would receive each one of us? Are they open to receive those around us whom we have come to serve everywhere in our Apostolate? Or do we think it enough to make a manger of our hearts so that we might hold Christ unto ourselves exclusively? If so, that was not what he was born for, and he might bypass the manger of our hearts.

Christ told us that unless we *become like a child* we would not enter into the kingdom of heaven. We tend to associate children and Christmas in a very sentimental fashion; we do so almost against our will. A newborn baby is 'cute'; children are 'lovable' creatures. So they are, but that is not what Christ meant. At least, I don't think that he did. He wanted us to have the *heart* of a child.

What does it mean to have the heart of a child? A child is utterly trusting. He will put his hand into the hand of a stranger and follow him, maybe even to his own death. A child is totally open, uninhibited, simple, direct, and, unless given fear by his elders, unafraid. A child believes without reservation.

Every morning, after Communion, I go to pray to the Infant of Prague. I say but two sentences: "Give me the heart of a child. Give me the awesome courage to live what it demands." That's what Christmas means to me, too.

We split hairs these days. We are busy about unessentials. We ask: "Should we have Mass with guitars? ... Should they be electrical? ... Should we adapt Eastern music for our liturgy, or use the African melodies of the Missa Luba? ... Should we receive Communion under two Species? ... Should we hold the bread in our hands, as well as the chalice? ... Should it be the left hand or the right hand?"

We ask: "What of the virginity of Our Blessed Lady? ... What about the role of the priest? ... What about birth control? ... Abortion? ... Religious Orders? ... Religious habits versus secular dress?" All of these and a thousand other questions occupy our minds and feed our endless discussions.

God has become Man. What does this mean? What does it mean in my daily, ordinary life? How does it apply to monotonous routines? What change does it demand of me? How must I witness to this great event of God's becoming Man? *These* are the questions to ask!

God spoke while he walked the earth. What, in essence, did he say? Do I accept it, or do I rationalize it away? What does his resurrection mean to me in the Apostolate? To any Christian, anywhere? As I start on my pilgrimage toward his crib, I find myself weeping (spiritually at least) that everyone everywhere constantly skirts *the essence* contained in all these questions that I pose.

What does it matter about guitars, etc.? What does anything matter, except that God became Man; that he gave us a commandment to love him and one another; that he died that we may live that commandment and be one with him; and that his resurrection is our hope. His incarnation is the essence, for it leads to his resurrection, in which we live. That places a burden on each one of us, the sweet burden of living out his incarnation, his commandment. To me, Christmas is my sharing in the witness of this Glad News, by proclaiming it with my life, by shedding all the unessentials and living in the very essence of the Child, the Man, and the God.

This is a strange letter for me to write, but these are the only thoughts that come to me. All my recent travels to London, Rome, Brussels, etc., as well as the quiet of Combermere and the solitude of my poustinia cannot erase from my mind and my heart the sight of poverty; the knowledge that men kill one another all over the world; that violence and hatred are rampant in the hearts of men.

No, nothing can erase this knowledge, these sights. Yet I know that he has come, that in a very few days we are going to celebrate his coming, and that unless we live the essence of his incarnation and resurrection, we shall not bring his peace and his love to the world as we should.

So, as of this Christmas, let us be done with unessentials. With Christ, *every moment is the moment of*

218

beginning again! Let us go together to kneel at the crib of a Child, to receive the heart of a child, and to live accordingly.

Yes, these few little thoughts are all that I have to give you. They are wrapped in my constant love in the Christ Child.

Lovingly yours,

AUTHORITY FIGURES AND EMOTIONAL REACTIONS

December 14, 1967

Dearly Beloved,

Ever since I came back from Rome, my heart has been filled with many thoughts and ideas. I have been praying about them, and it seems to me that this is the right time to share them with you. I know the season of Advent is a busy one for all of you, but these thoughts seem to clamor for release. As I see it, I have to throw them out like seeds to the four winds of the Holy Spirit. I have to allow him to sow them wherever he wills. I leave the reception of them to you, hoping that sometime, someday, you will have time to read these thoughts and to apply them, if they be worth applying.

Lately, as you know, I have been talking about the community of love. Europe hit me very hard; Rome especially. It hit me through my senses; it penetrated my mind and filled my soul with the unshakable conviction that we must truly remember that – first, foremost, and last – the world needs communities of love. It needs them to be like the early Christian communities, places that people can come to, to be healed of their emotional anxieties and to have their shaken faith renewed. The world needs a loving community in which to rest, and to find understanding. Today I want to talk on that subject.

As I have already suggested in a previous letter, what bothers me is the relationship which exists in our Apostolate between what might be termed authority (or the 'authority figure') and the other members of Madonna House. It begins early. When young people come to Madonna House, they seem to stand in awe and admiration when they encounter their first authority figure. This is usually the head of the department where they are assigned to work. It is here that whatever relationships they might have had with previous authority (such as fathers, mothers, teachers, or employers) begin slowly to be revealed by association. Emotional reactions occur for various reasons; there is the desire for approval, the fear of the unknown, even shame at not knowing some skills. Sometimes there is a heavy pressure created in those undergoing their formative years at Madonna House, an inner tension caused by the fact that the Gospel is being constantly applied to daily living. When that happens, it seems that God's smiling face gets distorted by their misplaced emotional reactions.

Then comes their relationship with me or whoever is the supreme authority, even though he or she is elected by the members themselves. This person also gets a share of emotional and spiritual reactions, as do spiritual directors. All of this is understandable ... up to a point! But after several years in Madonna House, after several years in a field house, people should begin to realize that they have been *called* by God to this Madonna House life, which is fundamentally a novitiate of the Lord. They have to assess (as we have had to do) the positive sides of our Apostolate and this vocation. I am not going to enumerate them because you know them. The graces of God and of Our Lady of Combermere, the tender care you receive in your weaknesses, the development of your personality, the spiritual care that you can receive here from our priests – all this provides you with insight and knowledge.

Father Cal wrote you that there comes a time when, with the knowledge acquired in psychology and your personal growth in spiritual life, you must begin to understand (with the help of prayer and the grace of God) that whoever is a figure of authority is indeed the servant of the others, and a suffering servant at that. You must include the heads of departments, the local directors, the directors general in your community of love. This situation might not apply to every house and every person; but, on the whole, it does, unfortunately. That is why I write about it, pray about it, and implore the Lord for gentle, tender, loving, and healing words to share with you what is in my heart.

This Christmas, why not meditate on the role of a director? Do you ever stop to think of the burden that this person has? On his or her shoulders lies the responsibility of a given house. On the shoulders of the directors general lies the responsibility of the whole Apostolate. But a house or an apostolate is not a 'business.' Each person in a given apostolate must be of special concern to the local director. Each must be treated differently, and truly everybody in that position strives to be aware of this and practice it.

The same people are responsible for the financial running of the house. They are responsible for its physical, mental, and spiritual order. They are responsible for clogged drains, broken dishwashers, leaking walls, and leaky roofs. They are responsible for the daily programs which I prefer to call the 'service' of the house, which are directed toward those whom we have come to serve – our neighbor. Above all, on their weak all-too-human shoulders rests the responsibility of leading and forming (or helping to form) this community of love that we are talking about.

Who are those people? They are men and women, some young, some in their middle age; they are ordinary human beings, lonely with their own needs, which few notice. They are people who must always be aware of other people's needs and forget their own human needs; they are the ones who have to carry the brunt of any tragedy, misery, or difficulties that arise in any house. Theirs is the terrible responsibility of decision making on the spot, and all of the time, first one, then another, shows them signs of hostility, or noncooperation. It may not be true of your house when you read this, but tomorrow it might be.

I remember a young girl in training to whom I casually remarked that I was tired. She looked at me with her big eyes as if stunned, and said: "You, Catherine, tired? I thought you were never tired!" She knows better now ... but how do you think I felt? It falls on the shoulders of those who are directors to carry their own weight, plus the weight of the Apostolate, plus the weight of every person in their house. For this they have grace; but remember that they are human. So look at them as human beings.

Again I find myself bereft of words, for I speak of such intangibles. Most of you have passed through the hands of the director of the kitchen, but few of you have seen her in the dorm, when she lies on her bed sobbing and exhausted by the barrage of hostilities and difficulties that the young ones had brought to her. It is not because they were evil; they even loved her. No, it isn't that. It is a strange sort of thoughtlessness which presumes that the person in charge is a superhuman being, a superman or a superwoman without needs.

I guess this letter doesn't make much sense, unless your heart is attuned to what I am saying. And I hope it is, because my heart understands both sides. Yet unless the staff really take the head of the department, the local director, or director general into their hearts and love them, our community of love is not going to grow. And grow it must, or we shall perish!

As I finish this letter, one final thought comes to me: Can you project yourself into being a local director tomorrow? Because that may happen.

Lovingly yours in Mary,

Catherine

ON EMPTYING ONESELF

January 4, 1968

Dearly Beloved,

As time goes by, I want more and more to share with you some of my experiences. Perhaps I should call them 'spiritual' ... but then what is a spiritual experience? One does not really divide the spirit from the flesh; at least I don't. Let's say that I really just want to share myself with you.

You know that my trip to Rome has shaken me up in more ways than I can express. It has set me to thinking about many things. Among them, as I have said, is the need for communities of love; or perhaps I should say *a* community of love, specifically ours of Madonna House.

I told you how, after I had listened to the so-called underdeveloped countries and observed the developed ones trying to reply to them, I realized that there is only one thing the world needs today; it needs people who 'live the Gospel.' A community of love is a group of people living the Gospel of love; living it *for all the world to see.* That is what the world is crying for − to be able, like St. Thomas, to 'see and touch' the wounds of Christ. For where there is love, there are wounds. You cannot separate love and pain.

As Advent approached, and then during it as well, my thoughts, meditations, contemplation, prayers − call them what you will − kept going more and more deeply into this idea of a community of love and how to reach it. I had already realized that, in order to form a community of love with another human being, I first had to become part of the primary Community of Love, the Trinity. I already wrote this to you. I just want to repeat it, because it was a starting point of my meditation.

Throughout Advent, slowly and painfully I began to

understand in a deeper fashion that the price of this formation of a community of love, person-to-person and throughout the whole community, was kenosis. (I need not remind you that the word kenosis means 'emptying' oneself.) We know from St. Paul's words that Christ emptied himself to take on the slavery of our humanity. All that I kept centering upon was that he *did* empty himself for love of me, that he *did* become Man. He, the incomprehensible, the inexpressible, the unencompassable, entered the womb of a woman, was born, lived, preached, and died. And then he rose again.

As I advanced more and more deeply, my thoughts centered on one word or two. If I spoke English, I said: "I am emptying myself." If I used the Greek word, I said "Kenosis." What did this word mean to me? Why was it in my heart like the Jesus Prayer, a refrain to every act, an echo to every movement ... and even in my dreams?

As Christmas approached, I began to get an inner understanding of what God was asking of me. I could put it another way: What was one of the prices – perhaps the greatest – that had to be paid for forming a community of love with another, or with the others? I saw myself as a channel, the bed of a river, a chalice, a cup, a vessel, which had to be cleansed from all the things that were not of God. I imagine that these things differ in each person. I knew slowly, by the grace of God, what things I had to get rid of so that he could go through me without impediment. I understood that no one forms a community of love without Jesus Christ, our Brother and God. He said, "Without Me you can do nothing." You know that he is the bond of love that wants to bind us together; but he does not force us, he leaves us free to open ourselves wide to him and hence to our neighbor, to the other. This is especially true in Madonna House. So what I had to do was to cleanse this 'vessel' that I am, so that Christ would find no obstacles in passing from me to you who read this letter!

Yes, that's what was meant by kenosis, by emptying oneself. St. John the Baptist put it another way. He said he came to make straight the paths of the Lord. This too is meant symbolically; he had to make them straight in the hearts of men, but first and foremost he had to do so in his own heart.

I thought and thought about how I could express to you this feeling, this searching, this profound grace, namely: that I must continue to empty myself for the sake of the Madonna House community of love of which I am a part. Two days before Christmas I had the answer.

Most of you in the field remember my Christmas decorations. I always had the same ones: a small creche on the top of the filing cabinets, with little animal figurines around it, and Christmas cards hanging on the walls. It was beautiful, lovely, and proper; but not for this year.

This year the opposite is true. There are practically no decorations. I took off the walls almost everything that was on them, with few exceptions. I made a manger out of my fireplace, put straw in it, and made an infant in swaddling clothes. Two barn lanterns now hang from the shelf of the fireplace. Four special vigil lights, larger ones, are burning before it. My filing cabinets were covered with a brown cloth on which there stands the Bible, and a red candle. On the table is a gift of love from the kitchen – a Russian Church made of gingerbread, some fruit, and a candle inscribed with a Slavonic cross.

Those who come to see me find the room exceedingly peaceful and restful. It is so simple and so poor, yet so full of kenosis that I learn from it every day more about this 'emptying of oneself' that I have gone through, and which I hope to pass on to you.

I ask your prayers, however, because even at this late date it is not easy to empty oneself. The struggle goes on within me and the eternal *I* raises its ugly head. So pray for me that I will truly find my *only* happiness in being empty, so that some day I might understand better and, before I die, dare to whisper: "I live not, Christ lives in me."

I don't know whether or not this makes a real letter. To me it is just a sharing with you of an experience that I had during Advent. Perhaps it will help some of you. If so, I shall thank God for it because graces are never given by God for oneself; they are always to be shared.

> Lovingly yours in him who emptied himself for the love of others,

(signature)

TIME BELONGS TO GOD

January 12, 1968

Dearly Beloved,

There is one problem or question (call it what you will) that seems to keep recurring in the house correspondence, newsletters, and in personal diaries. I would like you to think and pray about it. We will definitely have to discuss it because it arises too often, and it troubles my soul too deeply for it to be treated lightly. Allow me to put it this way: Constantly I am faced with the fact that you still divide the 24-hour day into work time and free time, into time for the Apostolate and 'my time.' This appears to me passably strange, and I speak now as a Christian, not only as a foundress of an Apostolate and the teacher of its spirit.

Do we have any time that belongs to us? Let us take Alma, for I have some sad news to impart to you. The tests finally showed that she has cancer of the lungs. Now Alma knows that time does not belong to her. *Time belongs to God and is part of eternity.* None of us knows how much time, or how little, we each have on this earth.

A Christian is a lover. A Christian is one who says: "My brother is my life." (You like that quotation yourself; it is so very modern!) And your brother is Christ, who gave us the commandment of loving one another as he loved us. If this be so, then I must give myself totally to my brother as a Christian, wherever I am, whatever I do; and that includes time.

The Young Christian Workers have always focused their discussion on the Gospels, in their basic approach to the apostolate of *observe, judge, and act*. New YCW members found almost immediately that they had lost all their manipulation or disposal of what was known to them as 'my free time.' They very soon discovered that all their time belonged to the apostolate; or to put it your way, to the brother who was their life. They found out that they had to spend a lot of time listening to youth. They had to sacrifice recreation often. They had to give up their 'free time' lavishly.

Alcoholic Anonymous groups, who do not exactly speak of Christianity, but of believing in a *power* greater than themselves, also have no jurisdiction over their own time. Married men and married women leave their families to go to the aid of a new recruit, or of the old AA member who once again has 'fallen off the wagon.'

In a family, a mother doesn't have free time that she can call her own. It belongs to her husband, to her family, to her children. True, when all is well she can arrange some free time for herself. But if you have ever dealt with families, or remember your own, you know that a mother's free time always depends upon the needs of her family. She relinquishes it without a moment's hesitation. A mother who nurses a sick child doesn't do it as a hired nurse might, on an eight-hour basis. She is like the good shepherd that the Gospel speaks about – the one who never abandons his sheep, because he is not a hireling.

When I was a waitress, a laundress, a salesclerk, I understood (by the grace of God) what it meant to be a committed Christian. I wasn't in any apostolate at that time, but was just trying to 'keep body and soul together' – for myself, my sick husband, and my little son. Nevertheless, I knew intuitively that if my fellow waitress was in misery, I had to help her, even though I was as physically tired as she was. Perhaps it meant going into another restaurant and buying a cup of coffee and listening to the tales of her misery until eleven o'clock at night. Perhaps it meant spending the lunch hour that I had intended to use to buy something, or to just take a walk. Instead, I would sit in a stuffy cafeteria and just listen. Love compelled me to do so. A loving, mature, adult Christianity compels millions of Christians today to do likewise, even though they are not dedicated to any particular apostolate.

We at Madonna House speak of ourselves as being 'totally consecrated to God.' I think that most of us understand that means our time is also consecrated to God, and we can never count on 'my' time or 'free' time as being sacrosanct "to me, and God help anyone who interferes with it!" If we do this, we are not totally dedicated, totally surrendered, totally involved in that brother or sister who is supposed to be our life!

The Communists know this aspect of life very well. They are organizers and deeply trained for any eventuality. People who live out their daily life for love's sake, or the sake of humanity, or the sake of a cause (like the Communists) know this for sure. Why then is there so much discussion among us about this free time? I truly begin to wonder.

Now let me make it very clear that I am not denying that the local directors, the directors general, the heads of departments, and the community in general must realize that – when possible – a change of pace and some free time must be given, just for the mental and physical health of the members of the community. That is not the point of the discussion in this letter. What I want to bring out is quite different. What I want you to pray and think about is having a state of mind and soul – this is a spiritual affair! – in which we all are ready to surrender our so-called 'free time' at the drop of a hat; we must not consider 'time off' as our due, or something to cling to as an inalienable right. Rights and love are somewhat unrelated terms. He who loves surrenders all rights within himself and thanks God for any free time, any privacy that God may vouchsafe him, especially when he is in the Apostolate.

I repeat: I want each one of you to pray and think about this very important question of Time, not so much your actual use of it as your inner attitude toward it. Let us discuss it thoroughly so that there will be no misunderstanding there.

Lovingly yours in Mary,

Catherine

OUR CRUCIAL PROBLEM

February 12, 1968

Dearly Beloved,

I am writing this to you as I travel from island to island in the West Indies. For once I begin my letter with several quotations from the Scriptures, because I am a little tired (and I think that the Lord is too) by the flow of words and the noise that those words are making everywhere these days.

Some of the words are holy words that we should be uttering on our knees, for as Scripture says, "take off your shoes because the place is holy." Words like 'community' (to take one example) can be twisted by the devil into a thousand beautiful shapes until we Christians forget that community is *communion* and that we cannot establish a community without first communicating with Christ. In this case, I do not mean semantically communicating, but *becoming one with Christ* through eating his Flesh and drinking his Blood.

One of the most obscene uses of this word *community*

and its derivatives is the word *communism,* which Satan has twisted beyond recognition. For while the communists profess love for humanity, and do have (as far as can be seen in the natural order) a desire for people to possess an equal share of the earth's goods, their bond is not of God. Their bond is not his Flesh and Blood. Their bond is not Love, the Second Person of the Most Holy Trinity, who is a Person above all emotions or humanitarian concepts.

I have been writing about a 'community of love' quite often since I returned from Rome. But, as I make my visitation to the fieldhouses, I see that even my humble interpretation of that 'community' is being twisted to serve people's personal needs. That sort of twisting and turning of my interpretation – let alone that of Christ in the Gospel – is what is playing havoc with the people who do it. This can happen in any of our houses where people indulge in this, even on a very small scale.

Before quoting the Scriptures to you, I would remind you of a legend (some of you already know it): In hell, there is a richly-set table, but everybody is given a spoon with such a long handle that they cannot feed themselves with it. And so they sit starving at that rich table. In heaven, the same rich table is set. The same long-handled spoons are handed out, but each person *feeds the other.* The moral is that, in heaven, no one fills his own need; all feed the hunger of others. And now for the Scriptures:

> You are God's chosen race his saints; he loves you, and you should be clothed in sincere compassion, in kindness and humility, gentleness, and patience. Bear with one another, forgive each other, as soon as a quarrel begins. The Lord has forgiven you; now you must do the same, Over all of these clothes, to keep them together and complete them, put on love. And may the peace of Christ reign in your hearts because it is for this that you were called together as parts of one body. Always be thankful.

> Let the message of Christ, in all its richness, find a home with you. Teach each other and advise each other in all wisdom. With gratitude in your hearts sing psalms and hymns and inspired songs to God; and

230

never do or say anything except in the name of the Lord Jesus, giving thanks to God the Father through him. (Col. 3:12-17)

So then, we are definitely God's most holy and well-beloved chosen ones, or none of us would have been called into his service of love. None of us would be his special 'little flock' to whom he said, "Fear not."

An Archipelago of Loneliness

This letter of St. Paul to the Colossians then goes on to outline clearly what a true community of love should be. What are the signs of this community of love, of his chosen people, of his well-beloved, as shown by people today? They are to be filled with compassion, kindness, humility, meekness, and patience. *Are we?* If, for instance, one of you feels that the others around you are 'islands,' you might suffer because your needs are not being fulfilled. A deeper reason for your anguish may be because God has given you a special grace to suffer with him in this house of ours, where the community of love is slow to form because of our sinfulness. What then is your reaction if this be the case with anyone of you across the Apostolate? What is your response to this gift of pain?

Whatever it be, let us *not* refer to the situation as a problem in 'interpersonal relations.' That phrase is 'for the birds' as far as Scripture is concerned! Forgetting your own needs, you hold in mind that you are well-beloved person – someone chosen by God! – and you are clothed by him with compassion and kindness toward the other. You remember that you have been given the garment of humility, meekness, and patience; so you are not so much concerned (as St. Francis was not concerned) about *being loved,* but are focused totally on loving the other. You are not interested in *being understood* but in understanding the other. You are not interested in *being consoled* but in consoling the other!

How do you do that? The first step is forgiveness. "Bear with one another and forgive whatever cause of complaint you have against one another!" Then, and only then, can you speak the Lord's Prayer and ask forgiveness from God. Even *that* is not enough to form a true Christian community of love. I implore you to remember that I am not speaking about 'community' as used in the modern sense by some in the Church. I am speaking of a community of love *that is truly Christocentric.*

So even the above is not enough. As St. Paul says, "But above all, clothe yourself with love. It holds together and perfects all these things." Unless you have that kind of love, unless it is this love who is a Person, who is Christ, all of your conversations about community are a lot of hot air. Not only are they an unpleasant noise in the ear of God, but they are a delight to the devil.

If, perchance, God has given any one of you the immense grace of sensitivity (his sensitivity, that is) and his pain over the fact that in your house this community of love is slow in forming, then rejoice with a great joy and be glad. Go and dance before the Blessed Sacrament. Don't fall apart at the seams. You are being called to stand with Christ, humbly, meekly, and patiently before the heart of a human being or human beings.

Why is there so much talk about communities, but so little talk about love in its true sense as *God?* Even if we do add the word 'God' to our pitter-patter about forming Christian communities, we are in a sense liars, consciously or unconsciously; for we are not ready to bear with one another, to forgive, to be humble, to be patient, and to bear the pain of Christ, should he choose to give us that special grace.

The Eastern Fathers have this to say about God and love:

> God can do all things except constrain man to love him ... In the expectation of being loved, God renounces his powerfulness and assumes kenosis under the figure of the lamb who has been slain from the foundation of the world. His destiny among men depends upon the fiat of humanity.

So let us in Madonna House stop thinking about community, Christian or otherwise, until we have said our *fiat* to God's love. Let us get busy about clothing ourselves – for we are chosen people – with compassion, kindness, humility, meekness, and patience. Above all, let us clothe ourselves with the love that asks nothing of the other and gives everything to the other. While we are engaged in all this painful dying to self in order to live in the resurrected Christ, we must do as the letter to the Colossians says: "And in your heart let stand supreme the *peace* of Christ to which you are called as members of one body. And *be thankful.*"

Bridge of Understanding

So where does it bring us? It brings us to look into our hearts and clear them of all desires to fulfill our personal need for love, understanding, consolation, etc. What is our Apostolate all about? Well, we know that today, with even increased communications, people are more and more becoming 'islands.' Our Apostolate, therefore, following Christ and his apostles (and the Letter to the Colossians), is to be *a bridge between those islands.* But we will never be bridges to anybody outside of Madonna House unless we first become bridges to one another.

When we have begun to put our feet on that road – sincerely, honestly, with an open heart, and with our minds in our hearts and are not busy rationalizing ourselves away from Christ – then, and only then, can we lift our voices in this community of ours because our voices will be voices of love and not of selfishness. We will not be busy fulfilling our own needs and doing semantic juggling with the latest modern vocabulary (dialogue, encounter, etc.) to hide from ourselves the fact that we want a Christian community of love *without paying the price.*

Being an advocate of audiovisual education, I suggest that you try a little of it on yourselves. Let each one of you hold in your hands a crucifix. Look at it carefully; meditate on it; realize that, in order to be able to make a real contribution to the community of love, you must be crucified on the other side! With this picture in mind, you will soon realize that the 'dialogue' between crucified persons is short and to the point because their 'involvement' has already reached a great height. He who is crucified with Christ has involved himself with all humanity, because he is a servant, a friend who is there when needed, just as the Master wants him to be. It is obvious that crucified persons, 'encountering' each other, have such deep 'existential experiences' that their silence shouts to the world!

So let us be done with thinking that the formation of a community of Christian love in Madonna House means forming a nice little club where 'interpersonal relations' can take place on a pleasant but superficial level. That is what the devil wants us to do! Let us get down to hard brass tacks, with a crucifix in our hands. Let us stop moaning and groaning and wasting a lot of words about how much *we* suffer because other people are 'islands' here and there.

There is another letter of St. Paul's from I Corinthians 1:26-31. I would like to finish this letter with it:

> Take yourselves, for instance. At the time when you were called, how many of you were 'wise' in the ordinary sense of the word, how many were influential people, or came from noble families? No, it was to shame the 'wise' that God chose what is 'foolish' by human reckoning, and to shame what is 'strong' that he chose what is 'weak' by human reckoning. Those whom the world thinks common and contemptible are the ones that God has chosen – those who are nothing at all to show up those who are everything. The human race has nothing to boast about to God who has made you members of Christ Jesus. By God's doing, he has become our wisdom, and our virtue, and our holiness, and our freedom. As Scripture says, *if anyone wants to boast, let him boast about the Lord.*

In case you think, dearly beloved, that my Staff Letters come to me easily, I just want to point out to you that this one is torn out of my heart. I can truthfully say that it is written while I hang on the other side of the cross, or try to.

I will be seeing each of you, and I hope that you will have read this letter by the time that I get to the houses, because this is the crucial problem of our whole Apostolate. Unless we understand the essence of this, we shall perish. Therefore, discuss it and examine your consciences before

God. Let us go over it together when I see you. Above all, pray; and if you can, do some fasting about it. *For these things are learned mostly by prayer and fasting;* and the powers of darkness are also exorcised by prayer and fasting.

Love,

Catherine

THE GIFT OF JOY

April 9, 1968

Dearly Beloved,

Alleluia! Alleluia! Christ is risen! Truly he is risen! Let us rejoice in this incomprehensible, unfathomable reality! For it is in the resurrected Christ that we have our life.

While I was on vacation at St. Teresa of Avila's,* I came out with one word and that word was – *joy!* I didn't make a poustinia but relaxed and enjoyed myself in a perfectly human, simple way. Yet it was quite evident that God came to share my vacation with me and, lavish God that he is, at the end of it he gave me that word joy to have and to hold and to share.

At first glance, it seemed a strange word to get from God. For it was the week before Passion Week and it was Lent, when usually the human sufferings of Christ

*Not Catherine's usual cabin and workplace on her island, but a small house a few miles outside of Combermere.

overshadow us and make us sad and sorrowful. And, at that time, we realize our sinfulness and the weight that it put on the Man-God. We realize this better than at any other time of the year.

Yet, during my stay at St. Teresa's for a little vacation and rest, I suddenly realized that joy was born on the Cross because God, notwithstanding his incarnation, his humanity, his hidden and preaching life and his passion, was filled with immense joy *at all times* – the joy of doing his Father's will! This joy he gave to us on the Cross; this quiet joy that lies in his peace which no one, except ourselves, can take away from us. This joy that bursts forth in an unbearable light in his resurrection.

He gave us this joy so we might comprehend a little that the sufferings, tensions, difficulties, and problems which must perforce fill every life have a remedy – joy! His joy whispers to us, shouts to us, that life is worth living, even with all of its sufferings, even with all of its difficulties; that it all has a purpose and a reason; and that it leads to perfect happiness, if and when borne with him, through him, and for him. It leads to *union with him.* By this I mean not only the union with him we will have after death. If we accept his gift of peace and joy amid suffering and pain, we will be united with him *here and now.* And we will be like him if we follow in his footsteps. We will understand his joy in doing his Father's will, and we, too, will possess that joy.

I am bereft of words to describe this joy that now fills me. I see its million facets, for he has opened my eyes to them; and yours will be opened too if you turn to him and ask for this insight.

I think of the joy of having been with you during the visitation. I think of the joy of being back in Combermere, yet still united with you in a thousand ways. I think of the joy that every step we make can give us. I think of the joy of going to bed and relaxing, knowing that the day has been God's, no matter what happened. There were doubts; there was pain; there were upheavals inside and out, in me and in the Apostolate. But always, always, this quiet joy fills my heart, and I hope, it will fill yours. Because, you see, each one of you and all of us together are God's miracle – God's miracle of love for us. For we are here in his house still, doing 'little things' no matter what the cost. Doesn't your heart feel like singing an alleluia for the day that is past, and thus make ready for the day to come? That is *joy*. Ours is an adventure with God, with life, with people, with each other. If only for a second we stopped to look at our life through his eyes, we would know it full well.

But I think I'll give up; I cannot describe it. I can only share it a little, send you straws through that wind of the Holy Spirit which is always around us. Yes, that is all that I can do. As for the rest, you will have to read between the lines and meditate upon it. No wonder that Leon Bloy (or some other writer, whose name I seem to have forgotten) once said, "Saints are never sad." Of course! They can't be!! And St. Paul, in his Epistles calls us Christians *saints*. Now, how can one be sad when one is a Christian?

So for Easter, the Easter of 1968, I give you the word that he gave me on my vacation: *joy*. He is risen! Verily he is risen! And we live in the resurrected Christ!

Lovingly yours in Christ,

THE DEATH OF MARTIN LUTHER KING

April 17, 1968

Dearly Beloved,

There really are no words of mine that can do justice to Doctor Martin Luther King, Junior. When we heard of his death, we had a Mass for America and the Americans. Alas for the land that kills its prophets and its saints! The only answer that comes to me is that the blood of saints and martyrs is the seed of faith. Let us pray for America.

This is the time of prayer and atonement, for in a sense, we – the whole white race – held that gun. The hand that held the weapon of death is the hand of all those of us who have any prejudice of any kind against anyone. We are all guilty, and none of us can say, "It isn't I."

Here is the fruit of my meditations on the death of a great man.

America now has two martyrs: John F. Kennedy and Martin Luther King.* A white man and a black man. Their blood is now mingled with the earth of this beautiful land. What will the people of the United States do, as they behold their land watered with the blood of their martyrs – one white, one black?

The death of those two men has shaken the world. How can racial injustice, how can the tearing apart of the brotherhood of man continue among the American people when they look at these two tombs? One is buried with all the pageantry given to the president of a great nation; the other in a plain coffin, drawn by mules. But both are signs of God to a nation's conscience. On the answer of the people of America to the death of their martyrs depends, in a sense, the future of the world. Because the only way to wash their hands clean of the blood of martyrs is to

*President Kennedy was assassinated on November 22, 1963; Dr. King, on April 4, 1968 ... two weeks before Catherine dictated this Staff Letter.

implement what they died for. Both died, not only for God and for their country, but for all of humanity.

They both stood for truth. For peace. For love. For God. Their lives are proof that God exists. The speeches of Martin Luther King proclaimed the existence of God and showed the face of Christ to the whole world. Did the world listen? Did America listen? Did the world see that face of God in the beautiful black face of Doctor King and the handsome Irish face of President Kennedy? Did it? Or is it another nation that kills its saints and prophets and closes its heart, mind, and soul to their love and their charismatic gifts? Which is it? On the answer hangs history and the fate of nations as well as individuals.

Do prophets and saints have to die to 'shake us up'? If so, why? I did not know Dr. King personally. I had met Mr. Kennedy briefly in his youth. I have lived for ten years in Harlem, however, and my love for the Negro people transcends my ability to express it. In a small measure, I foresaw, way back in 1938, what now has come to pass. But I did not realize that the final answer had to come through death, through the death of two people who were (I do not hesitate to say) 'the hope of the world' along with Pope John XXIII.

To me personally, the death of Martin Luther King is the death of a man I would have followed to the end of the earth. Fearlessly, he preached the truth; unafraid, he implemented the Gospel of Jesus Christ in a world which thought that God was dead. As I watched his funeral on a TV screen, I was reaffirmed in my belief in the resurrected Christ. Dr. Martin Luther King is not dead; he lives in that resurrection. He speaks to us as Christ spoke; he speaks the very words of Christ. By his simple direct life, he refutes the whole theology, philosophy, or what-have-you which teaches that "God is dead." We hear this sort of talk presented to us by some of the intellectuals of our day.

Today I cry to God out of the very depths of my pain and the pain of millions like me who mourn Martin Luther King, while thanking God that he was in our midst. Yes, I cry to God for my beloved Negroes of America. For they are poised on a decision that is excruciating, as all mighty decisions are. They are poised in the center of two crossroads. Which will it be? Will they take vengeance into their hands and sack and burn and kill and maim the whites who have lynched them, stoned them, denied their rights, persecuted them, and taken their human dignity from them? Or will they forgive? Martin Luther King was a martyr, and without hesitation I add the word 'saint.' Will they follow in his immense footsteps and implement the hardest commandment of Christ, who lived so gloriously in Martin Luther King, that commandment which says, "Love your enemies." Will they accept the non-violence which Martin Luther King preached (and which Jesus preached before him) and conquer the whites with *love* instead of violence and civil war?

This is the moment of the Negro's greatness; it is the moment of his greatest choice. I pray for the Negro of America with my whole heart, my whole soul, and with all of me because I love the black race. I think the whole world is praying, too; at least those who still know how to pray.

I cannot write an obituary on Doctor Martin Luther King, Junior, because he continues to lives. He is alive; he speaks; his spirit is with us. All I can say is *alleluia!* He is not dead, because martyrs and saints do not die.

Two men were killed. One was white; one was black. They were both Americans. Their blood mingles in the soil of that beautiful country. Will its people, and the world at large, understand that never again can it deny the brotherhood of man under the Fatherhood of God?

Lovingly yours in the risen Lord,

LOVE ONE ANOTHER

May 21, 1968

Dearly Beloved,

I love you with a profound and deep love. But, strangely enough, God himself seems to prevent you from understanding its heights, depths, and widths. For sometimes even love can overwhelm a person, especially one to whom this small four-lettered word is not yet comprehensible, or about which one might have a variety of reactions as well as a variety of misunderstandings.

Be that as it may, I love you very much. Granted, it might appear a strange love to many of you. Especially, perhaps, because it is expressed in 'waiting before your hearts' day after day with a constant, silent prayer for you. A prayer that holds you in my heart and never lets you go. It is because of this that I am writing this letter.

Recently, God gave me the immense joy of being with you in each of the houses that I visited. I came after much prayer, and with deep humility. I came in utter simplicity, as open to the Holy Spirit as I possibly could be, and as open as my poor heart could be open.

When I was in your midst, I never felt that I was giving you much. Oh, the fruit of an apostolic experience of 38 years, the experience of life lived under somewhat extraordinary conditions. Yes, these practical things I could share with you. But, above all, I constantly prayed and hoped that I could free the channels of my mind, heart, and soul – in a word, my 'person' – in order to allow the Holy Spirit to pass through me without too much hindrance.

Some two months have passed since that journey took place. The main theme of my visitation, if you remember, was the deepening establishment of the community of love. In some houses, it is bearing wonderful fruits. I know that we are all human but it seems strange that, barely two months after the visitation, the essence of it in some houses seems already remote and, if not forgotten, at least not absorbed.

The most tragic thing that can happen to us is a break in the charity that binds us, the bond of which is Christ. Let us keep this charity constantly before our eyes and our hearts, and let us do nothing against it, at least willingly.

You might wonder why I am writing you almost symbolically (as the Scriptures say, 'in figures') for this letter may not make much sense to many. But I hope that it will make sense to a few and help them to hold onto the graces of the visitation, to enlarge their hearts, to get out of themselves, and to look with new eyes at the Apostolate, at this community of love that we are trying to form. It is the most important thing we can do in this world of hate, division, and of brother killing brother.

Let us forget the pronoun *I;* let us think all the time about the other, the other brother or sister. Let us, above all, pray that we may be able to share this love and peace to others.

A strange letter, is it not? And it is a very hard one to write. Because I love you so much, I want to bring you "spotless to the Lord" as St. Paul says. In the mystery of God's choice, you are entrusted into my sinful hands, at least for a little while yet. That is why I write this strange letter and finish it with the words of St. John when he visited Asia Minor: "Above all, little children, love ye one another!"

Lovingly in Mary,

242

OUR ATONEMENT – 'THE DUTY OF THE MOMENT'

June 7, 1968

Dearly Beloved,

Two members in one of our fieldhouses had a problem. I wrote a special letter for that house, trying to answer both of them. I thought my letter might help all of us, for it clarified my mind; and I always try to pass on clarifications to you. I am eager to answer any question that might help one person or a group, or the whole Apostolate. This particular response of mine should be of help in a normal and constantly recurring problem, namely: how are we to 'see more deeply' as we grow in wisdom, grace, and love of the Lord?

Satan tempts people by good when he cannot tempt them to evil, and here is the temptation which I try to answer in this letter:

———————————

I know, dear heart, how difficult it is for you to see right away what was 'wrong' in getting the other member of Madonna House interested in the problem of those women who come to the city and who need much care, and in taking her down to the bus station to see the influx of same. I think I should 'spell it out' for you. It is time that I spelled out a few things to my spiritual children, one by one and all together, whenever such a question arises.

First of all, realize that your companion is a very young member of Madonna House. As yet, as with all who are at this stage, she is a sensitive and very unsettled person – some of the seniors are too, (smile!) – but the young ones are especially so.

Secondly, remember how I try with my life and my words to preach one thing and to preach it loudly and clearly. I guess it hasn't been clear enough or loud enough, probably because of my sinfulness, weakness, or what-have-you. I will repeat it once more, however. Madonna House is the place of 'little things done well' for the love of God (reread the Little Mandate). In order to create the community of love, that Christian community we're aiming at, we must do the will of our Father *always* – as Christ did!

How do we know the will of our Father? *By the duty of the moment.* We must give our whole self to that, because when we do so we can be certain that we are living in the truth, and hence in love, and hence in Christ. Doing the duty of the moment means focusing our *whole* person – heart, soul, body, emotions, intellect, memory, imagination – on the job at hand!

Let me give you an example: When I heard about Bob Kennedy being shot, I experienced a tremendous shock as everyone else did.* But because of my personality 'makeup' and my background, this shock was tied up with a tremendously deep spiritual trauma. I love America, the United States, with a great love. I love the American people with a great love. And to think that this beautiful country, this beautiful nation, was killing its prophets and its saints! It came to me that America had become the fighting ground of Light and Darkness. It was as if Satan and God were locked in a fight, almost like Jacob with the Angel.

In a sense, God is 'powerless' because he has surrendered his power in order to make us *free*. He doesn't want to use his power to *force* us love him and to obey him. No, Christ allows himself to be crucified out of love for us; and in crucifying his flesh, he crucifies his 'power to make us love him.'

He wants the love of *free* people. He wants to give us true freedom, as children of the Father. He wants to give us the freedom of his brothers and sisters. So he sends many graces to the American people. Some of his graces are human beings: John Kennedy, Martin Luther King, Bob Kennedy; and others who have not been killed but who go to jail, such as the Berrigan brothers do.

On the other hand, there is Satan. He can incarnate

*Robert Kennedy, the younger brother of President John F. Kennedy, was assassinated on June 5, 1968 ... two days before Catherine dictated this Staff Letter.

himself only if people choose to allow him to be incarnated in themselves. He has no power of incarnating himself as God has done. Evidently there are many who want this Satanic incarnation, even though they don't believe in the devil's existence. Because of this, violence and death (not only of the great but of the small) have taken hold of America and its people, and a cancer has begun to grow in the soul of that nation. I cannot behold it without weeping.

So now we are praying at special Masses for the people of America. Yesterday we had a Holy Hour in atonement for the people of America. As Eugene McCarthy said on TV: "It wasn't only a foreigner who held that gun; it was every American."

After I heard of the news of this latest assassination, I was in a sort of shock – spiritual, mental, physical, and emotional – so deep that I could have asked permission to go to the dispensary and sleep it off. I could have taken a bunch of tranquilizers to try to forget for one or two days the horror of it all. But I didn't; it wasn't the will of my Father.

The will of my Father was that I *offer* the day, that horrible panic-stricken day, that terrible time of pain, of tears that wouldn't come, of a feeling of being in a strange hell of my own ... I had to 'offer it up' according to the Duty of the Moment. And the duty of that particular moment, on that particular day, was to begin sorting our Drama Room, something I hadn't done for seven or eight years, and which had become an unholy mess. So, taking myself by the scruff of the neck, I went to the Drama Room and started looking at the costumes, the props, the theatrical makeup, the swaths of material. I sorted it out, box by box, dress by dress, item by individual item, because this had to be done. Each movement of my body became an act of atonement for the world.

Now we are back to you and the other member. For her (and also for you) the Duty of the Moment is whatever has to be done in your fieldhouse; this is especially true for her, for she is new there. And the tasks set before her must be done with a *totally concentrated* mind, heart, soul, and body.

If she goes around the office (or whatever the duties of

the day are) thinking about the needs of the women that you spoke to her about; then she is *not* fulfilling her Duty of the Moment. Her body may be in the office, but her soul and mind are somewhere else. That is 'what was wrong' with this situation. She is *not* doing the will of the Father. She is fragmented. (I know, because I can read in her letters how distracted, how fragmented she is.) Don't you see that a senior member, above all, must know how to teach a younger one to be immersed totally in that Duty of the Moment where God has placed her; and, I repeat, *totally,* not partially, not fragmentedly.

There is no reason why you shouldn't have told her about those women. That would have been all right; but you should have added: "This is a wonderful work for someone else. We in Madonna House are dedicated to the works of our Apostolate and the mandate of this fieldhouse in particular. The way to assist these women is through *total concentration on the daily Duty of the Moment.* That is the will of the Father for us. To follow his desires puts us in truth, and therefore, in Christ. And that is how we can best help those women. *This is part of the mystery of love."*

Yesterday we gathered around the statue of Our Lady of Combermere. We recited the rosary, read from part of the Gospel, sang a few hymns, and prayed in silence. In the eyes of the world, our 'contribution,' our atonement, our expression of love for the American people didn't amount to much. But in the tremendous mystery of God, who can tell what he did with this little Holy Hour which a group of unimportant lay apostles made around a bronze representation of his Mother? It is of such things that I want you to think; and think deeply. *For each moment of our lives can be an act of Christlike atonement.*

When each of us in the Apostolate fully understands that the simple little things – the Duty of the Moment in a particular department or fieldhouse – is the royal road to that atonement; when we realize that there's no use in *getting emotionally involved* in people's lives by wanting to participate in some other apostolate than the one we are mandated to (or trying to combine the two apostolates, to the detriment of both), we shall truly begin to form a community of love.

In a sense, I am grateful for your mistake. It is the kind that Thomas the Apostle made when he didn't believe in Christ's resurrection. Felix culpa. (Oh happy fault!) It made me clarify a situation and give an answer that may help many others. So you see, much good has come out of this. Let us thank God.

Lovingly yours in Mary,

THE ROLE OF NUNS

July 25, 1968

Dearly Beloved,

This letter comes to you a little late. I should have written about my trip to the United States and my talks to various houses of religious women. Usually I am pretty prompt in recording my impressions of the places to which I have to go. However, this trip was a little like the one to the Third World Congress in Rome. It didn't hit me as deeply and as pervasively as Rome did, but I must admit that it took me time to recover from it and to sort out my impressions. I *think* that I 'blocked' about writing this letter.

I can just see many of you smiling because you probably do not think that I block out many things! I am human, however, and I understand your 'blocking' because I also block things out at times. Anyhow, I think I blocked it. Why did I do this? The nuns were most hospitable and open to my talks. Their questions were good. True, the physical workout was quite heavy as usual. There were conversations between lectures and an extra public lecture at night: but that was to be expected. It is always thus. So why did I block?

The answer is fairly simple. Again and again, I'm faced with people who have sort of lost their way in the maze of modern post-Vatican thinking, and probably don't understand their emotional reaction to the heady air from the 'open windows' of Pope John XXIII.

It was a little difficult to listen to nuns worrying about their 'role' in the Church and in the world. Yet compassion and tenderness flooded my heart as I listened to them speak. They were frightened about the future of religious orders, male and female, but especially the female ones. They weren't even sure that religious orders were necessary!

In the midst of these deep fears, they had begun looking for answers *outside of the Gospel* as it were. There was much talk about living in apartments, living in smaller groups, inserting themselves into the secular society, into the marketplace, and especially into all kinds of ghettos. There was much talk about habits and wearing apparel, about the need for Catholic schools, colleges, hospitals. They were a bewildered people in many ways, asking what their 'role' for tomorrow (or the day after) would be.

A deep sadness took hold of me before this virtual Niagara of questions and worries and what-have-you. The sadness was that no one asked the essential questions. Perhaps they hadn't yet talked of them, or hadn't even been exposed to them! Truly I do not know these *whys*. But my sadness grew.

So for three days, I gave a lecture three or four times a day to representatives from 36 religious organizations (mostly teaching and nursing orders). In between the lectures, for an hour or more, I answered questions from the floor ... plus the questions thrown at me during the coffee breaks and during the so-called rest period. They were heavy questions and were getting heavier all the time.

The Basis For All Our Works

Do I need to sum up the gist of my lectures? I talked about the Gospel, about the need for crying the Gospel with one's life, about the absolute necessity – the basis of all the works of a nun (and for that matter, any Christian) – of loving one another. This is true whether in the postulantship, in the novitiate, or in the convent when professed! I said to the nuns that, unless they build a community of love (which they were anyhow supposed to be from the very beginning of the institutions of religious orders in the Church) they would achieve nothing.

I quoted St. Paul, or rather, I paraphrased him by applying it to their situation: "If you live in apartments in the very heart of the ghettos, or in the secular society of the marketplace, and have no charity, you are like tinkling cymbals. If you give your life in these ghettos, at these apartments, and have no charity, you are like sounding brass. If you wear modern clothes, dressing as the poorest of the poor or as the richest of the rich, and have no charity, in the sight of the Lord you are as nothing!"

Well, after that lecture, into which I had put all of myself, I sure had a lot of questions in the next period. They were interesting questions and ran something like this: "How can we have this 'community' of love when we are physically separated ... with postulants in one place, novices in another place, and these two have no contacts with the professed nuns or with each other?" I tried to put myself in their place, to 'identify' myself with their problems, to listen to their needs. What they seemed to be saying was this:

True, during our postulancy and novitiate, we each learn to love those around us a little bit; but this is a sort of 'potluck' because we are very young and are emotionally high about entering religious life. Once we are professed, we may find ourselves spending most of our time in academic studies (if we belong to a teaching or nursing order), and we may come together only once or twice a day – in the recreation room for an hour or so, and in the chapel for Mass or other prayers. Teaching in the winter, learning in the summer, or just going to college year-round, we come back to our individual cells to correct papers or to study our textbooks.

How can we learn to love each other when we practically never *see* each other, when we are expected to 'do well' in our studies, when we have given most of our time to either learning or teaching or correcting papers; and then to nursing and studying some more (for we have to be competent). We often go from the B.A. or B.S. level up to Ph.D.; and by the time we have gotten there we are already middle-aged and have acquired the habit of living in our cells, apart from one another.

The Value of Dormitory Living

They had something there. The more so in that I must admit their cells were very comfortable (I was living in one, myself, during this week-long Renewal Program). Their apartments had become nice places to hide in, with all the comforts of suburbia, let's say that of a family with a two- or three-car garage 'status.' It reminded me of the Indian Hostel in the Yukon, which Madonna House ran for a while at the behest of the Canadian Government. The government had built separate rooms for the staff, and we found that this setup was devastating for the 'community life' which our staff were used to in Combermere and in the missions. Having a room of one's own seems to kill community spirit, to destroy the ability to really be open to God and to loving one's neighbor. (This is a good thing to remember for the future that we not *seek out* this type of privacy, because it seems to kill a lot of the spirit!)

When I suggested to the nuns that they have dormitories without partitions, there was a sort of dead silence. I felt that I was being dismissed inwardly by each nun as a damn fool. I was asking far too much. In another lecture, when the question of poverty came up, I brought this dorm business up again. I pointed out that they were talking a lot about the Negro being poor, talking a lot about the orders being rich and having big houses and establishments, without realizing that it was *their own desire* for private cells which made those houses so big (or bigger than they would have been if they were sleeping dormitory-style). Of course, some missions and some small religious convents do have such dormitories, usually with partitions. Nevertheless, the nuns seem to feel it very strongly ... that it is supposed to be very heroic.

This question, therefore, of opening oneself to another

in those convents is really difficult. They don't seem to have a chance to 'be with one another' in any real sense of the term. My impression was that *efficiency, production, status, and competency* had become their yardstick, both individually and collectively as a religious order. It was so evident that this almost broke my heart! I cannot as yet be very coherent about all of this, but I came back to Canada with the realization that we have to be extremely careful in Madonna House about 'poverty' in its literal and physical sense, i.e., in regard to not possessing our own premises.

Recently we refused to accept the property of one of our houses. We told the bishop that we decided to leave the property in his hands, and we will just live there and do our work. From now on, we intend to do that in our other missions whenever it is possible. There will be exceptions, of course, but the fewer exceptions the better. Let's think very seriously about one important point of poverty – the lack of privacy of the poor. I think the nuns are in this difficult situation because they sought, for some reason or other, the privacy of their cells.

A Question of Clothing

After the public lecture, we had a coffee break with the laity. One mother, who had a daughter in the convent and nine other children besides, casually asked a question that had not occurred to me. Her words suddenly, like a needle, passed through my heart. She said: "My daughter belongs to a very big religious order. When she was visiting me recently, she told me very excitedly that they now have six models of what they call 'new habits.' One resembles the old one but is more streamlined; another is a tailored suit with a blouse, and she went on to describe several others." Then the woman continued: "I've been wondering. What are all those newfangled ways in clothing going to do to the finances of a religious order? Our own family has great difficulties in making ends meet. It's not that easy to clothe our nine children, my husband, and myself. But these fanciful changes of the nuns are going to take thousands of dollars, especially in the big orders, and this money could be used for the poor. I don't even mention the cost for new underwear they will need, and the hosiery and new shoes! There is so much poverty in the United States and the world; so many people go half-naked in America. What do you think of it all?"

Frankly, I could barely answer her. I hadn't thought of it at all. But since then, I haven't ceased thinking about it. It is one more unessential point that can occupy so much of the nuns' time and discussions, and even generates hostility among them.

All the while – having listened and spoken, and spoken again – I found that no one began with the essentials: *love one another, and love yourself 'well' in the Lord!* Everyone seemed to eschew pain. Many wanted to do what they wanted to do; and what they wanted was not, perhaps, the best for their religious order or the Church. It kind of frightened me. Don't misunderstand me, though. There was much beauty and goodness there too. But this terrible confusion was so prevalent that I was shaken by it, for it seemed that the nuns had forgotten the words of the Gospel: "Seek ye first the Kingdom of Heaven, and all the rest shall be added unto you."

As you can see, this letter is not very coherent. I'm still, if not blocking, sad. Perhaps with the sadness of the Lord (a little sliver of it) as he looks at those good nuns who are so enchanted by the superficialities of the aggiornamento, so attracted to the new siren-like voices of post-Vatican II. They don't seem to hear the soft and gentle voice of God calling them to reality and to sanctity, and to their vocation to love. Perhaps that is why I cried on that podium.

One thing I know. There opened before me a great temptation in faith! Thanks be to God, with the help of my spiritual director, I have overcome it. For there were days and nights when it seemed to me that the same slowly-growing cancer could enter our Apostolate sometime in the future. If we were not watchful, the little mice of ease and comfort would gnaw away at our foundations. If we surrendered to the two desires of 'taking things for granted' and of wanting 'extra privacy' of the wrong kind (and all of this *could* happen to us), then where would we be?

Pray for the religious – both women and men. They are certainly at a crossroads, for they will have to learn to reform themselves from the inside out, and not from the outside in; or else they will become sick in their hearts and in their emotions. Let us pray for them. They will have to learn to love one another, or perish.

Love,

Catherine

DIFFICULTIES WITH AUTHORITY

August 24, 1968

Dearly Beloved,

For the last few days, in the quiet of the evenings, I have been able to pray a little more. As I prayed, one thought began to form in my mind, and I want to share it with you. It is that there are, among us, quite a few people who evidently have difficulties with authority. Perhaps 'hang-ups' with authority is another way of putting it.

It has been very difficult for me, even during these times of prayer, to understand this situation. If it were only the guests or the very young members of Madonna House, I would understand this; but, strange as this might be, these difficulties seem to linger on, mostly among senior members of Madonna House. Some of the very young ones, who spend their first year in a mission, may also have difficulties with authority. This is to be expected and will pass away very soon; but why should these problems linger on among the seniors?

You and your directors are all about the same age. You have all gone through Madonna House training together.

Many of you have been in other fieldhouses where the same problem has occurred. Why does it seem so difficult for you to exorcise this emotional problem that has no place among us? Why, for example, are you afraid of another person of your own age-group? What can he or she do to you? In what way can he or she hurt you? If you were a younger person, say of sixteen or seventeen, and your local director was thirty or over, I could understand it. But you are practically the same age, and you are living (or trying to live) in a community of love. Could it be that those of us who feel that way have neglected to really turn to the Lord and to the Holy Spirit and to his beloved spouse, Our Lady ... and to beseech them earnestly to exorcise this strange, infantile, useless, unrealistic fear?

Another point that comes to my mind, perhaps because I am more familiar with it, is this: Do you ever think that tomorrow you yourself might be a local director and some of your own classmates in the Apostolate, or even your seniors, will suddenly be filled with a fear of you? Those members who were your equals yesterday and shared with you their joys and sorrows, took walks with you, recreated with you, and worked with you, have disappeared. And now one or two, or a group of fearful people, are facing you as their new local director. Be honest with yourself, dearly beloved. How would you feel if, instead of friendship and loyalty and help, you were confronted with diffidence and fear? You would not feel very well! I am sure that you would not understand *why* this has happened to you. You would be bewildered, hurt, and lost.

I often write about local directors. As I get letters from members who have difficulties of this type after many years in the Apostolate, I feel sad, terribly sad, because love is somewhat stymied in those hearts by this fear that needn't be there at all.

Again my heart asks a question from all of you: "At what point in the Apostolate will we – all of us! – finally realize that, in these 'hang-ups' and fears and little emotional 'messes' that we seem unable to shed (some of us, that is), we stymie the work of the Lord? We do not see the whole picture of our humble, little Apostolate. Do we ever really think, first of the Apostolate, and secondly of ourselves?"

Sometimes in the evenings and nights, I cannot sleep. I see Christ under various guises, waiting for us in our various missions; waiting for us in so many guises, while we are occupied with ourselves. We spend time tearing off our little scabs to see if our emotional wounds are healed. We feel that we are not understood, not loved, not appreciated, etc., and we begin to *brood* about it. A voice comes to me across the centuries, a beautiful Italian voice that was speaking French, the voice of Saint Francis of Assisi. It sings that real joy is not in being understood or in being loved or in being consoled; *real joy* comes to us whenever we reach out to understand and love and console the other.

Please, dearly beloved, do not take this as any kind of criticism, or even correction. I am just sharing with you some of my bewilderment, my sadness, that 'the freedom of the children of God' has yet to come to some of you. I pray to Our Lady for you to be liberated from those cords that bind you and keep you from being free.

Truly, prayer changes things. Perhaps if you thought of Jesus Christ in your local director, you would 'look up and see no one but him' (Matthew 17:7-8) ... and then things would be easier for you and his laws of love would be incarnated in you. He said to love God above all things and always. This to me does not present any stumbling block. Yes, God is not visible to our eyes. He is intangible; and we can maintain that, perhaps as yet, we haven't come 'face to face' with him. But every day we see our neighbor, who is an icon of Jesus; even 'the least of them.'

Jesus said, "Love your neighbor as yourself." Could it be that we have difficulties with our neighbor because, as yet, *we do not love ourselves properly?* Do we transfer this non-acceptance of ourselves to others, including our local director? Jesus also said, "Love your enemy." Surely a local director cannot be an enemy in Madonna House. If you find that you have a difficulty in loving the local director as Christ wants you to, then turn to prayer; for prayer alone will make the change.

Jesus said, "By this men shall know that you are my

disciples: that you love one another as I have loved you." We must truly love our neighbor (and our local director also) with the heart of Jesus. We cannot do this unless we love ourselves in the right way. We cannot show our discipleship to Christ unless we love one another with his heart, which means that we must empty our hearts of that egotistical self that stands like a high wall between us and God. We must enter this kenosis as Christ emptied himself; prayer alone can give us the fortitude and courage to do that.

Jesus said, "Knock and it will be opened. ... Ask and it shall be given. ... Whatever you ask the Father in my name, you shall receive." Do we believe this? Could this whole question of fear, maladjustment, lack of love, this resistance to surrendering all to Christ and to the Holy Spirit ... could it be *a question of faith?* Do we really believe that the one who asks will receive? That to him who knocks it shall be opened? Perhaps, at this point, we should pray for an increase of the Gift of Faith, because that is where our difficulty may lie.

My heart is filled with many other thoughts on the subject, but they are not formulating themselves too well, and I will have to pray more before I write again (if God wants me to do so). In the meantime, rest assured that I shall pray for every one of you in whom that fear abides. And I beg you to begin to pray ceaselessly for the Gift of Faith – and for its fruits: love and hope – so that you may become free of fear and attain to perfect love.

Lovingly yours in Mary,

THE RICHNESS OF POVERTY

December 13, 1968

Dearly Beloved,

I often wonder if I put across to you what I mean by that simple greeting, *Dearly Beloved.* I wish that I had words that would tell you the width, the depth, the height of meaning those two words contain for me and how in truth you are deeply and dearly beloved by me!

But how can one communicate the word *love* by words? Sometimes it is possible, but at other times words seem to mock me, to shrivel up and suddenly just vanish. Though I often go in search of them, I cannot always find them. When that happens, I know that this is the doing of the Lord; that he wants me to love you in prayer and silence; and that it will be he himself who will then bring to you this strange communication in his own tender and mysterious way.

This is my Christmas and New Year's letter to you. At the threshold of the cave of Bethlehem, which is also for us the threshold of another year in the vineyards of the Lord, I stand in a sort of strange poverty before you! Never in all the years of my life in the Apostolate have I been so poor; not even during the Bolshevik Revolution when I was stripped of all the goods of this earth and became this tragic figure, a poor woman running for her life and hiding, running and hiding; not even when I landed on the shores of the New World, only to find there the abject poverty about which so much is being written now.

Today, having enough food, having wonderful shelter and a tremendous spiritual family, I find myself poor in a different way, while I am exceedingly rich in another way. I know that I am rich in poverty. It is my poverty that I want to give you this Christmas – all of it. What kind of poverty? It is not easy to explain. It could be called the poverty of *detachment,* but that is such a puny and unimportant word.

Perhaps I should say that I give you the poverty of 'a pilgrim in search of the Absolute.' Such a pilgrim carries nothing with him. Yes, I think that would be more nearly what I mean. Yes, that is the gift that I want to give you. But there is a strange and mysterious accent to my gift. The pilgrim of the Absolute has nothing of his own. The road is too steep, the mountain of the Lord that he has to reach is too high for him to be able to carry anything. And yet, strangely enough, this type of poverty can carry the whole world with it. I'm not sure that I carry the world, but one thing I know, with a certainty that no one can take away from me. It is that I carry each one of you in my heart. I know your name. Individually, uniquely, in the Biblical sense of the word, *I know your name* as God knows your name. For he told it to me when he brought you to Madonna House.

The poverty of the pilgrim of the Absolute is, therefore, immensely rich in love. Not because the pilgrim is good or holy or intelligent or in any way extraordinary, but because *anyone* who starts on such a pilgrimage to the Absolute already possesses the Absolute in a hidden and mysterious fashion. It is said that *he who desires God already possesses him.* It would be useless for me to hide from you that I not only desire God, but I am passionately in love with God, obsessed by God, hungry for God. And so, poor pilgrim of the Absolute that I am, I already possess him, at least in part (if one can ever 'partly possess' God).

But enough about me. I just wanted to share with you what is in my heart and be truly open with you, with that openness that we talk so much about but which often eludes so many of us. That type of openness can also be my gift to you, for it is part of that poverty that I speak of.

I beg you very humbly to look at the year of grace 1968 which is just reaching its end. Let us together thank God for its pains, its joys, its doubts, its temptations, its cold and its heat. It has been a year of miracles, one of which is that I am writing this letter and that you are reading it!

Let us be open and truthful about this: it is a daily miracle that each one of us is still in Madonna House. This miracle is a gift, a tender loving gift of our Lord and

Brother, Jesus Christ. It is the gift of perseverance for each day, each hour, each minute of our life in the Apostolate. I pray that when Sister Death* comes to take us by the hand and lead us to the Father, the Son, and the Holy Spirit, the fullness of that gift will be ours. I pray that we will not be somewhere else – where he does not want us to be but where *we* thought we should be.

Let us thank him for the thousands of graces he has given us. Grace is a shaft of light that comes to each of us from his loving hands, according to our needs. To some, it is like the brilliant light of Mount Tabor. To others, it is like a beautiful lamp to be put on the desk of one's mind, heart, and soul. To a third, it might be a candle, with its soft and gentle light. But each will receive, and has received, according to his needs. These lights are growth in love. Slowly, slowly, they merge together and help us to form that which he wants us to be: *a community of love.*

As the days run by, it becomes crystal clear that what the world needs is just what we are trying to achieve with his gifts of light: communities of love; communities of little people like us; ordinary 'grass-roots people' who know that all that they have, all that they are, come from him. And all these talents he has given them must flow like a thousand little brooks, like quiet streams or turbulent rivers, into one immense sea – the sea of love!

Men – besieged by a million robbers, wounded to the quick, lying all along the roads of the world, the hard pavements of our cities, the dusty pathways of rural backwoods, or the endless wastes of trackless deserts – can crawl to the waters of this sea of love and be washed clean and healed. They can come to this sea of love where the few, who have heard his voice and have come to a little place called Madonna House, are already encamped. And they can help one another become cleansed and healed.

As we look back at the past year, we must thank God for the increased gift of prayer, for the increased gift of understanding, for the silence and solitude of our poustinias. It is in his great silence that all of us will become pilgrims of the Absolute. His voice is heard most

---

*A reference to St Francis of Assisi's *Canticle of the Sun.*

clearly in that holy silence. Yes, as we look at this past year, we have much to thank him for. So let us begin the new year with a song of gratitude and joy.

The past year also increased our poverty. Each, according to his lights, has begun slowly or rapidly – this is a secret thing between each of our souls and God – to shed many garments, among them selfishness, self-centeredness, self-will. Our ears have been opened and our eyes have begun to see what his will 'looks like' and what it 'says' to us. And a greater peace has come into our hearts because of that. Yes, let us thank him for all of this, and for many more inexpressible gifts that each of us, in secret, knows has been received from the Lord. Yes, let's thank him for all of these.

Facing the new year, let us pray to grow in love and understanding, in tenderness and compassion, and to accept that poverty which is so rich. Let us leave behind our puny little human efforts which deal with 'the identity crisis,' 'interpersonal relationships,' 'sensitivity sessions,' and what-have-you. These modern-day terms are harsh and brittle words. They speak of human pride. Mere creatures think that by themselves (and with the help of various natural methods, lectures by psychiatrists, books by psychologists, etc.) they will achieve meaning and balance and unity in their lives. They hope against hope that they will achieve what only Love can accomplish – that mysterious unity which comes only from *the person of Jesus Christ, encountered and become one with us.* He alone leads us to the type of 'interpersonal relationships' that he means us to have with his Gospel. But really ... can you imagine Christ using such terms? I can't. So let us use his words. Gospel words like incarnation, love, peace, joy, service, suffering, death, resurrection.

Let us accept also the wounds of our own humanness. They are gifts to us. They are his wounds. He incarnated himself. He became one of us. He was a man, a human being, like you and me. Long before he was crucified, he had the same wounds that we have – emotional wounds of frustration, human wounds of boredom (it must have been hard for God to live with man, intellectually), wounds of fear (didn't he ask his Father to take the cup away from him?), wounds of rejection (wasn't he rejected especially by those who should have accepted him?). Yes, he suffered all of the wounds that we have. Let us accept them joyfully; for they make us share his divine life as he shared our human life. We are incarnational men and women.

But let us go further. Let us truly be crucified with him on the other side of his cross. For that is our greatest gift to our fellow human beings. That is the reason for our communities of love. In a mysterious yet obvious way, that is why Madonna House and each of our mission houses draws so many people (outside of those people we have been mandated to serve). Christ is asking us to show his wounds to the world. The world today, like St. Thomas, will not believe unless it sees for itself and touches those wounds.

While seemingly standing still in our given houses of the Apostolate, we become pilgrims of the Absolute. We become communities of love that constantly 'move on' to deeper, higher, wider, broader levels. And with his blessing and grace, these wounds of ours – which are so totally unseen – will become visible to the unbelieving, wounded Thomases of this world. Just by being, by loving, we shall allow God to heal this wounded world through us.

What am I saying? What am I trying to say in this long letter with stuttering words like those of a small child? I'm trying to say that we must plunge into the dark night of faith! While we cry out from the depths, our very crying becomes a stout cord, a sort of ladder, that brings men out of the pits of despair into the light of Divine Mercy. I'm trying to say that Jesus is using us as he used the uncouth, unlearned apostles and disciples, for whom he praised God, saying: "I thank Thee, Father, Lord of heaven and earth, that you have hidden these things from the wise and understanding and revealed them to babes."

I'm trying to say that we must have one desire – to become those little ones; to allow ourselves to be used by him as he wishes, no matter what the cost to us. He has brought us together, as it is becoming more and more evident daily, to do just that. The wise are confused. The wise are seeking their 'identity.' The wise are worshipping a thousand false idols. And we are asked by the Lord to go into their hearts so as to bring them to him, the living and true God.

But who of us would dare to venture into the caverns of men's hearts, unless as a child? A child ventures anywhere. So I finish my letter (incoherent, patched up, stuttering as it may be!) my dearly beloved in Christ, by imploring him to truly *give us the heart of a child and the awesome courage to incarnate it.*

Yes, let us become children, for "a little child shall lead them." The theme for Madonna House for the year 1969 should be just that: our *identification* with the Christ Child. We can give him (as I give you my own stuttering self) our poverty, our helplessness, all that we are and that maybe we shouldn't be. This Christ Child is so immense that, with just a glance, he will take away all of the dross and deformity, if we let him. He will form us into himself – a child!

Now I know the poverty that I bring you. It is the poverty of the Child in Bethlehem.

With all my love in him, yours,

I GIVE YOU JOY

Easter 1969

Dearly Beloved,

This year I have had a very hard time writing you my yearly Easter letter. When I say writing, I do not mean the moment when some words of mine fall on a piece of paper. No, when I say that I have a hard time writing, I mean finding the clarity of thought, coming to a definite understanding, praying for the assistance of the Holy Spirit to formulate those words that finally fall on paper and reach you.

Perhaps it is because Easter is a constant play of darkness and light. Good Friday is a very dark day, but its darkness is accentuated because it stands out so strongly against the rising light of Easter, seen on the horizon. As I said, my Lent has been filled with contrasts this year and hence are reflected in this letter. Yet my heart is full of tremendous joy and I sometimes feel as though I am a living *alleluia*.

Lent also encompasses the tomb; and some of us have to 'spend some time' there, as it were, before we can resurrect. For some reason I cannot explain, it seems as if I have spent quite a bit of time in a tomb this Lent. Yet joy predominates, and so I want to give you my joy. If I could, I would take the cross of your suffering upon myself in its totality, but this is not given to me to do; I can only share it. If you remember, I keep repeating throughout the years that, on Good Friday, one sees the light of Easter; and on Easter Sunday, one sees the shadow of the cross of Good Friday. This will continue until the parousia, until this interplay of light and darkness fills the whole world and especially us, the children of God, the brothers and sisters of Christ.

That is why I implore the Lord to give us a great gift now: the gift of forgetting ourselves and concentrating seriously, constantly, unceasingly, on the humble Apostolate of Madonna House which he has so gently and lovingly entrusted to us.

Yes, it is a hard letter to write because all I want to give you is my joy, just as I gave you my poverty for Christmas. So accept it, wrapped up (as the joy of every human being is wrapped) in the shadow of the cross and the blinding light of Easter. Alleluia! Alleluia! Christ is risen! Verily he is risen!

Lovingly yours in Mary,

MY GIFT FROM THE HOLY SPIRIT

December 23, 1969

Dearly Beloved,

The year 1969 has been a heavy and difficult year for me; yet it has also been a blessed, joyous, mysterious time.* During this year, I received a gift from the Holy Spirit. I received two words: *Fiat* and *Alleluia*.

I meditated long and hard on those two words. Finally, I understood that they contained our whole faith – from the Incarnation to the Resurrection, from the first *fiat* of Our Lady at the Annunciation to her last *fiat* at the foot of the Cross. There was also that first mysterious *Fiat* from the Son to the Father (the one that no one heard except the Trinity) to the last *Fiat* (which everyone has heard about) in the Garden of Gethsemane. I understood that God was giving me those two words, not only to build my life upon now, but also to give to others, especially to the family he has built on me.

So for your Christmas gift, dearly beloved, I give you *Fiat* and *Alleluia!* They are tremendous words, though very small; for the *Fiat* contains the Incarnation and the *Alleluia* contains the Resurrection (his and ours!). Yes, dearly beloved, when it comes down to hard brass tacks, I can only express my love by giving you those two words, having nothing else in my poverty.

Lastly I bow low before you, according to the custom of my people, and ask you to forgive me any way that I

---

*In 1969, Catherine stepped down from her position as Director General of Women so that others could be trained in the job of leadership. She retired to her hermitage to spend more time in silence and prayer. Her husband, Eddie, spent much of the year in Israel, studying for the priesthood. He was ordained in the Melkite Rite on August 15, 1969.

264

may have sinned against you, either by commission or omission. So please forgive me for these.

Fiat! Alleluia! Let your soul be a lifelong manger for Christ the Child. Pray that he may give you the heart of a child, and the awesome courage to live it out.

Love,

Catherine

HANDICRAFTS

April 20, 1970

Dearly Beloved,

I have spoken to you about handicrafts, but I want to add a few more observations. Let us consider the word itself. This is the way they spoke of something made or 'crafted' by the hands long ago.

It all began when men and women needed tools to hoe the ground, to grind the corn, to do various things. Gradually these tools began to be more polished and became adorned with designs. Houses and temples started to be adorned also, and the word began to embrace a totality of 'things made by hand' – whether a crude spoon or a nicely finished chest of drawers or a large mural. They finally developed into the fine art that we display in our museums today.

Eventually, the term handicrafts came to be relegated more and more to what was *not* considered 'fine' art, i.e., to simple articles made by underdeveloped countries or in small farming communities of developed nations.

Now, however, the term handicraft is having a resurgence. It is beginning to grow upon us slowly and quietly (and yet, in a sense, almost explosively). This is because human beings, having lived with modern technology, are realizing now that they must return to handicrafts in its many forms, or else their souls will shrivel up and perish! People need desperately to feel that they have created something with their own two hands – things they can touch and look at, and show to their friends. Men and women are beginning to revitalize the arts of mosaics, weaving, leather craft, candle making, silk screening, and many other crafts in order to have a feel, a touch, for their own work. Even more, they are searching for a 'communication with one another' as they used to have years ago when they worked together and were proud of their craftsmanship.

The loneliness of human beings today seems almost to have reached a point of no return. But in craftsmanship they make not only artifacts; they can make *friends* through their common interests. And today, *friendship is the most precious possession that a human being can share with another.* In our century, people are truly 'islands.' Even youth talk of 'doing their thing' ... doing it for themselves, instead of for others. Friendship has become a rare commodity.

Handicrafts, however, will open the door to both friendship and creativity. These two words go together, because friendship is always creative in one way or another. Handicrafts can also build bridges. For instance, a missionary can establish a means of communication with others and form friendships through crafts, even before he learns the language. As he creates something with his hands, he is forming – with God – creative relationships.

All creativity pertains to God; he alone is the one who creates.* When we get together in a creative endeavor of any kind – from the crudest drawing of a little child to the awesome art of some extraordinary artist – *it is still the Lord who creates in us.* And we create in the Lord! Alleluia!

---

*Cf. *Everybody Steals from God: communication as worship* ... written by Edward Fischer. University of Notre Dame Press, 1977.

The concept of 'handicrafts' – a word I have used so often among you, and a reality I have waited for in Madonna House for so long – need not remain in Combermere alone, in the hands of a select few. It should belong to each one of us in the Apostolate, in all of our houses. We all desire to have the Lord create in us and to create in the Lord! Even more should we desire this because these handicrafts are going to be one of the means that we shall use throughout our present and future technology as a tool to help people.

Let us not confine ourselves to only one type of craft, however. Let us remember that two or more people, talking in truth, are 'creative.' In fact, *every* form of creativity could, in a sense, be embraced by the word handicrafts. After all, it was the main avenue of creativity which started in our ice-age forebears tens of thousands of years ago.

But the term handicrafts could go still further. It could penetrate deeply and widely into the whole of our earth, for handicrafts can be a part of what we call *ecology*. An essential part of human beings, the very heart of human beings, craves to return to the earth and the simple things of earth. At the moment, however, that is beside the point of our discussion. The main point of this is that we of Madonna House should be involved in ecology. We must bring to our little Apostolate, in a manner of speaking, what Ralph Nader* is bringing to the world. We cannot do it on a big scale, but we can do it on a small scale. We can make our farm organic. We can help to preserve Canada, not only from the pollution of its water and air, but from the pollution of our very bodies that were made to serve God in simplicity and uprightness.

So many youth today are using drugs because they feel there is nothing else to do, or so it seems to them. We can show them that there is a back-to-the-land movement. We can show them handicrafts. We can show them how to be creative with God. The Lord has given us this earth to use, not to abuse; to manage, not to destroy! This we must do by every means possible, before it is too late!

---

*Lawyer and advocate on behalf of the rights of 'the little people.' He became a leader in the consumer movement in 1965, when his book against the automotive industry *(Unsafe at any Speed)* was published.

We of the Apostolate are truly God's handicrafters. We must become acquainted with all the handicraft skills, with their various tools. Remember that *nothing should be alien to us* except sin. We must go forth and do research and learn how to make this present world more bearable for the people of today and of the future. We must, by God's grace, learn how to change this age of cold hearts and lonely souls into the age of love and friendship.

It is strange how the word handicrafts, which I so casually used at first, came back to me. Thus unified and yet fragmented, the concept begins to make more sense to me, for I realize anew that it is from the creativity of God that all handicrafts stem. May his holy name be praised!

Lovingly yours in Mary,

ON BEING A FOUNDRESS

May 5, 1970

Dearly Beloved,

I have not written to you much in the last year or so. I see that there is a difference between 'acting as a director general' and 'being a foundress.' And it is because I needed time to think – to ponder and to contemplate this difference – that I have refrained from writing to you before now.

The insight came to me quite slowly. And to be absolutely truthful, I don't think it has yet come to me in the fullness of God's will. (There are times when God seems to 'move exceedingly slow'... or so it appears to me, and probably to the time-perspective of most mortals.)

Then again God seems at times to 'hasten mightily' to accomplish his Plan, and to plunge us constantly, relentlessly, into new dimensions! By his infinite mercy and grace, I have experienced quite a few of these dimensions over the course of my life, but until recently I had not discovered the aspects of 'being a foundress.' Why is that? Mostly because I generally didn't look at myself in that light. In day-to-day life, I seemed to have been not so much a foundress as a sort of 'leader' – the type of person who went about *stirring up things!* Mostly for God; and for those who deserve from us the same justice, compassion, and tenderness that God gives them – the 'poor ones' of the world. (In my mind, that phrase sort of embraced 'everybody' ... the poor rich, the poor middle-class, the poor religious, the poor professionals, etc., but especially the poor poor!) I frankly never considered myself a foundress. An organizer, maybe, but not a foundress.

So it came to me as quite a surprise that, when I decided to hand over the director generalship, I had to face up to a *role!* I seemed to have suddenly fallen into the same puzzling problem that others struggle with, the world over. For isn't everybody looking for their 'role' these days, their 'identity'? Well now, that didn't suit me at all! I twisted and turned in that 'role' or 'business' or whatever you want to call it, until one blessed morning I laughed aloud and said to myself: "Katie, my pal, that's errant nonsense! As far as you are concerned, you have never played *any* kind of role. You just tried to be what you are or what God made you to be. Let's face it, this business of roles and identity crisis ain't your cup of tea!" So that was that! And I could relax.

But now I really had to get to the bottom of this situation. What *was* it that God wanted me to be? Of course, you all know that my whole idea was the poustinia. I wanted to enter into the poustinia for many reasons which have been deeply imbedded in my heart for a long time. Some of those reasons you know from the *History of the Apostolate,** some my spiritual director knows, and some

*An unpublished work by Catherine, detailing her apostolic work from the 1930s through the 1960s.

only God knows! Among my desires, one was to be a sort of 'resource person' to the next director general, or to anyone else in the Apostolate. I knew from the beginning that I was going to have to adapt to many things (or perhaps the word is re-adapt). With the grace of God, I was ready for this too.

But once I got into the poustinia, I found out that God's dimensions were not quite my dimensions! What is more, I found out that I had a tremendous lot of trash to get rid of, or so it seemed to me. I thought (how pride does ride before a fall!) that I had a fairly empty soul – one in which God could, once in a while, if not stretch to his full height, at least to most of his height! Yes, I found a lot of trash in that soul of mine, and perhaps even in that mind of mine. I had to do some powerful housecleaning! I'm not done with it yet; I'm only beginning. It seems that there are all kinds of trash tucked away in various nooks and crannies of my soul, or along the endless corridors of my mind. So I found out that 'being a foundress' means this thorough cleansing of oneself.

I also discovered that it means being truly *nothing!* Very slowly, so tremendously slowly, as if drop by drop, God reveals the true essence of things. It is as if he were right there, sitting at my table, and saying very simply:

"Catherine, now you must begin to understand that everything that has happened to you thus far has been because of Me. Now you must begin to realize that you are indeed 'nothing' and that I AM WHO AM. You also have to begin to understand that this 'nothing,' this 'emptiness,' is there to be filled with Me, and it is beginning to be. Do you remember how I said, "Without Me you can do nothing"? In other ways, you are 'many things' ... but of this I will speak another time. Right now you are trying to figure out what it is to be a foundress; and I realize that you want to know this in order to serve Me better. That is why I'm here to explain things to you."

Of course, dearly beloved, all of this is a supposed conversation. Nevertheless, it is true; for God's dimensions are always true. And I do begin to understand what a founder or foundress is: it is someone whom God has plucked out from *nowhere* and has brought him or her from that nowhere into *somewhere*. That somewhere might be in one spot, or it might be in hundreds. This is not important because, whether the founder or foundress stays in one place or goes across the world for Christ, he or she remains a cornerstone, and a cornerstone always *stays put!*

So I discovered that I come from 'nowhere' to go into the 'somewhere' where God wanted to send me, day by day, hour by hour, minute by minute, second by second. (Yes, now I know a little bit better the dimension of being a foundress.) A cornerstone carries the weight of the whole building. So the Lord showed me that a founder or foundress equals, in some way, a foundation on which he puts his 'building' (whatever it may be) and that the person who becomes that cornerstone must never rely on himself or herself, but only on God. If even for a moment, one split second, this person chooses to be self-reliant, the foundation begins to crumble and the whole building will fall down.

God's dimensions are ever-expanding. I began slowly to discover that my love for all of you is taking on new dimensions of its own. It's as if God has pushed away walls that I never knew were there. It had seemed to me that I loved you, each one of you, deeply, profoundly, with my whole mind, heart, and my whole soul! But now I have discovered that I did not know the quality of my love, for the Lord did not deign to reveal it to me. He is just beginning to. It is a strange love, a unique love, which I think many of you will not understand until I am dead. (Perhaps not even then, for all things lie in the palm of God's hands.)

My love for those whom the Lord has brought unto this lowly cornerstone – myself, whom he has brought from nowhere to somewhere and added each one of you unto that cornerstone and thus made up a building (our Apostolate) – is a love of impenetration. It seems as if I know you now in ways that I have never known you before. It seems as though your pain has become my pain. It seems to me as if through me and into me go all your doubts, your hostility, your love, your secret longings, your moods, your pleasures and sorrows. Whatever they are, I begin to feel them in a new, tender, compassionate, and understanding way. It doesn't seem to need any work on my part; *it is just there,* if you know what I mean.

Yes, this has happened to me in the last year. Perhaps that was one reason why I wasn't writing, for you have to be very still when God, holding you by the hand, leads you into these new dimensions of his own!

So I discovered slowly, a little painfully (yet joyfully, in a manner of speaking), what it is to be a foundress. It is to be a foundation stone. It is to be 'nothing' – a nothing that God wants to fill. It is someone who still has a lot of trash to throw out from one's heart in order for the Lord to really feel at home there. A foundress is also a foundation for an edifice, and carries in love all those who have come to be part and parcel of the building that God has planned. To be a foundress means to have a new dimension of love. Yes, all of this I found out.

I also discovered that I haven't even begun. And here I beg you – in fact I implore you – to pray for me. All of these thoughts that have come to me through the Lord are but an entry-way into the Land of Prayer. Of this I cannot speak, for I know little of this new landscape. It is one thing to talk about prayer and its many aspects, during spiritual reading or whatever; it is another thing to enter even a few steps into its portals.

It is one thing to talk about poverty and to discuss the Friendship Houses of Harlem, Toronto, Hamilton, and what-have-you; it is another thing to enter into one's own poverty. Of this I am unable to speak as yet; not now ... and maybe never.

Some of the things which pertain to being a foundress I have knowledge of, a weak kind of knowledge, given to me by the grace of God. Being a foundress, after all, is but being a follower of Christ. So I know that I have to love, to serve, to be available, to come and go as God wants me to come and go. These are simple little things.

But at the end of it all, my dearly beloved, with all that I have tried so clumsily to put down on a piece of paper for you, the people with whom I have shared so much for so many years, I still don't really understand what a foundress is. I simply know that I am *someone from somewhere* whom God has put in the place where he wanted me to be; that all that I have had to do is to live between a *Fiat* and an *Alleluia;* that I have had to rely totally on his mercy and goodness; and that whatever happens to me or through me is of him.

Perhaps a foundress is just simply a lover and nothing more. So with my ever-growing love, I send you this letter.

Yours in Mary,

Catherine

PARADOXES OF THE SPIRIT

June 2, 1970

Dearly Beloved,

My secretary brought me an excerpt of a spiritual reading discussion that we had a while ago. The staff told her that it was 'exceptional' and was worth sharing with everyone. And if my secretary says so, what else can I do!

Someone: ...[reading from the Gospel of Mark, chapter 8]... "Anyone who wants to save his life will lose it. But anyone who loses his life (for my sake, and the sake of the Good News) will save it."

Catherine: I think we should stop here, Father, and contemplate this passage from Scripture. This seems to be a key mystery that continually escapes us all; or rather, it is a paradox from which we try to escape! We are not ready to have an inner battle with ourselves, sixty minutes of every hour, twenty-four hours a day, all of our lives. And that's what this Bible reading amounts to.

When I read this part of the Gospel, I feel within myself, very deeply, a sort of *cutting,* a pruning. Christ is a husbandman who carefully prunes and trains his vineyard, but only in order that it may bear more fruit. If this be so, why do I not have peace? God gave me his peace, just as he promised; but look at me now! I'm in turmoil. I'm a contradiction to myself. I spin like a top, around and around and around. The only thing that saves me is that God attracts me to himself. But outside of this, I am just like a spinning top. Now I go this way; now I go that way. I want everything all at once; to lose my life *and* to save it. I want to dedicate myself to you and to the Apostolate, and all that entails; and I find myself dreaming of the comforts of life – silk sheets and caviar, or whatever symbolic images come to mind.

You are always asking yourself, "What is my role right now?" When God brings you to this Scripture passage and you enter this different dimension of the Living God, *that* becomes your new role – being a top! You know how a boy takes a top and puts a string on it and pulls it. That's what God does to you. And you go through a sort of dizzy situation. It wouldn't do at all to go there immediately or and stay there constantly; you couldn't take it. You have to go there gradually. You have to enter into it slowly, slowly, because *the essence of prayer is not a place; it's a state.*

You have to *allow all those things to happen and not be astonished at them,* because these two opposing forces are going to live in you – the urgency to lose your life and the panic to save it. You don't have to be a hermit (or pretend to be a hermit) to have this occur; it will happen in every Christian. The two forces are going to meet in you, and you are going to spin around crazily, as if you were being pulled by two ropes, or were one top trying to go in two directions, begun by the same rope. Don't be astonished.

Here's another thing: Whenever you experience inwardly any annihilation of yourself, you will feel an overpowering urge to assert yourself outwardly, to imprint yourself on life. "Look, folks, I exist! I'm here. I haven't disappeared. I'm a person. Listen to me!" The Holy Spirit seems to annihilate your spirit, you see; or so it will appear to you. Sheets of flames and raging wind and all types of symbols will come into your imagination. You see they are terrible, *terribilis,* in their power to overwhelm you. You suddenly feel like this: "Where is that Kingdom which he calls me to, which he has promised *now,* for today? ... It is not true, what's happening to me! ... This can't be right! ... It's too heavy ... Make it go away and come gently."

It never comes quite as gently as you hope, and you're devastated inside ... utterly devastated. And it is in these devastations, and in this being touched by God, that you feel dizzy. You feel like a top, because you don't know where a top is going to end up. The top doesn't know where it is going; and there is this seeming annihilation of your personality; and all the time the Spirit of Evil is around, looking for a chink in your spiritual defenses. It's not a pretty picture, but this is what happens ... at least I think so.

Underneath all of this, what is taking place? What does it do to you? Well, it goes something like this: You're praying or you're just doing your job (whatever it may be), and this weight of turmoil starts to press upon you. Suddenly, inside of your soul, inside of yourself, you feel that you 'just can't take another step' so you want to drop somewhere and settle there. Slowly, slowly you sink down to the floor because it gets harder and harder to move. This is all while you're sorting jewelry, or dictating letters, or scrubbing a floor, or doing some other outward task. This is what is happening inside of you. All that your soul can do is moan ... and maybe pass days like that.

Now the grace is that you are on that floor, that you haven't turned your back to God and walked away. *That's* the grace. That's the beginning of your growth in faith: you're there! He was on a cross, and you are on the floor. After you get up, your soul feels like a thousand sponges that have been squeezed out, but it doesn't matter. Grace can go through inward sponges like water goes through outward ones.

There comes a day (I speak symbolically; there are no

days in this, or nights, or anything; there's no time in it) ...
there comes a 'day' when you wake up and find that a new
dimension of Christ has opened itself, and now you can
take some steps in his Kingdom. He has a vast Kingdom to
show you. And all he asks is that you are faithful. He asks
you one thing: to stand still, inwardly. All of this is inward;
it's in the dimension of the soul.

This inner dimension of which I speak has no
geographical boundaries, but that is where this happens.
And later, when that operation of the Holy Spirit 'sifts
through' into the other dimension where you are, that is to
say, where you exist in your outer life, then you begin to
know his Kingdom both ways, in faith and in your senses.
This may seem like a paradox to you, but it is all part of
being human; it's inevitable.

The Paradox of Divine/Human Actions

And to ask *why* all of this is happening to you is
useless. It is the will of God for you. You are the elect of
God. He has called you to this special place, and all you
have to do is to stay there. Don't ask yourself why; just
stand and bear it! Bear it and know that in time you will
walk further and further and further. The desire to imprint
your personality on everything (simply to show that you
have life and meaning) may continue to be violent, but you
will have learned to reduce it a good deal. God has to
increase and you have to decrease; and then, strangely
enough, you find that you also increase. Again the paradox.

There was St. Francis who virtually abolished himself,
let his life be lost. He called his body a donkey, an ass and
all the rest of it; but he is regarded as immortal. As he
became small, he became immense. That is why it is
important to get to the essence of these Gospel passages
and not just see the superficial aspects. The French have a
wonderful word for it, which I don't know how to translate
into English: "Quand on se donne au bon Dieu, on est
terrassé par Dieu. ... When you give yourself to God, you
are 'terrassed' by him."

Someone: Struck down, crushed, overwhelmed.

Catherine: Yes, that's right! I could say, "Mon amant

m'a terassée" which can mean "My lover has struck me down" or "My lover has embraced me." You see, when he embraces me, he crushes me; it has two meanings in French. And I think that there lies the essence of God's Kingdom. It's strange. We are still the thing created; and yet..... Well, now, what do you think of this paradox?

I have a sense that many of you understand very well what I am saying because you have (I can only imagine it or perhaps think intuitively) ... you have had some of these experiences yourself and you are wondering about them. Don't wonder; with God, never wonder. Just stand still; just let the storms rage and the tops spin and everything just go. It isn't easy; but it is essential to the inner struggle. And all the rest will flow from it.

The Paradox of Stillness/Activity

The person who lies there prostrate is the person who can go into the ghetto and understand the suffering of the other. The person who lies there, in stillness, under this will of God – I mean this way of God – is the one who can talk to his neighbor. Understand? This is where communication begins. It doesn't begin in all kinds of studies, techniques, or what-have-you. It begins when you lie there flat, or spin like a dizzy top, because you know that the hand of God is upon you; and he who is touched by the hand of God can do almost anything for the other.

We can't articulate it always. It's great when we can do so, but it's so difficult to put into words. And I think that one of the 'aspects' (shall we say) of prayer life is that sometimes you *must* articulate it in order to help somebody else. But you will know the time and the place to do so. And when it is necessary to articulate it, you are absolutely required to do so – no matter how painful it may be for you! – because it often helps somebody else. Does it, or does it not?

Someone: You've touched upon a very important thing, Catherine. For me personally, your words have helped a great deal. I think we all go through this struggle at times, and it often comes up by our questioning what our role is. We go around asking each other: "What is our role? ... What is the role of the men? ... What is the role of the women? ... What is the role of the priests?" And oftentimes it is this terrible searching for who we are; and as we do this (I certainly speak for myself), we're desperately reaching out for something – anything! – just to be able to say what's going on inside of us. I think it takes something to be able to 'speak out.' It has taken 'guts' for you to say what you did; but it is important to us because I think that almost everybody in this room must experience, at one time or another, the very same things.

A simile came into my own mind. Sometimes I go to the workshop and I see the guys doing some welding. They use a welding torch, and it's glaringly bright. It is so hard on your eyes that you have to wear thick black glasses for protection; and when you do so, all you see is a tiny pinpoint of light. But if anyone else comes in, not wearing glasses, their eyes could be burned by the light. I think God does that to us. He is so radiant that we are blinded by his Presence. But if he gives us some sort of goggles to wear, then we are able to focus our attention on His Will for us in the Duty of the Moment, and let everything else remain in darkness.

Catherine: That's true. And it is so easy to go off that very narrow spot of fire, which is in the very center of our being. Everything outside that center calls us to ... well, to go and do this and this and this ... to look at this and that and so forth. But God has told us to go without fear into the depths of *our own being.* So we must be without fear, and trust his Presence within us.

For instance, the hippies are starting to come to us. I can see this happening. Well, what can we give the hippies? What can we say to them? We can take their prayer methods or their fasting techniques, and so forth ... their search for a meaningful life, and put it into the right channels, if we have the 'guts' to tell them the truth. But where are we going to get those guts? Only by focusing on the presence of Jesus! He calls out to us through the Little Mandate: "Be hidden, be a light to your neighbor's feet. Go without fear into the depths of men's hearts. I shall be with you!"

After this, he adds: "I will be your rest." That's true; he will be our rest. But he first demands from us *action, movement, involvement.* He says in this respect: "Arise and go ... Go without fear." Why is he so specific here? Because he knows that we have fears – terrible fears, nightmarish fears – of going into the heart of the other. It's not easy.

Someone: You know, I really think that the plain fact of reading the Mandate shows us that.... I mean, Our Lord promised us that if we'd give up our homes we'd have a hundredfold increase. That's interpreted by many people that they'll be physically given a hundred more dwelling places. But I think these 'homes' are the hearts of other people: where he is, you know. I think it's important to say this because we are on pilgrimage, and I think that's where these two things come together – this giving-up and getting-back, this leaving ourselves and pilgriming toward the other.

The Paradox of Hidden/Open Lives

Catherine: Well, this is again a thing of the soul, this pilgrimage. It's the pilgrimage of detachment and it is so painful ... so painful that it's difficult to talk about it. *With God, you see, everything is always twofold:* painful and delightful. Like terraser: My lover can terrase me; God can embrace me, and strike me down; and, factually, this act is the same because he is my Lover. It's paradoxical.

It is the same with this business of pilgrimage. To be a pilgrim is to arise and go forth, to 'expose yourself' to the world. Not to be physically naked. In our time and age, we cannot walk through the streets without any clothes on. We would be arrested; we would be put in a psychiatric hospital. So the Mandate says, "Be hidden." In other words, don't be obvious in what you do. This relates to another Gospel passage where Jesus says that, when you fast, you are to put on whatever it was they put on in their times – oil or whatever. Today, it would be lipstick for a woman, or dressing neatly for a man. So, do not show yourself as what you are. (Don't take me literally.) What the Scripture means here is that you must adapt yourself to every age, so that you are not obvious.

To be a pilgrim is ... Well, for instance, let's take one thing: the desire for comfort. Now I'm not talking about anything very immense. I'm not saying that we all dream of having silk sheets, and a Bentley or a Rolls Royce. No. I would say that, in Madonna House, we desire *privacy* above all things. St. Teresa's cabin, for instance, is sort of everybody's goal for a holiday. To get rid of that desire is very difficult, but that is part of the pilgrimage. Now, it doesn't mean that you shouldn't accept a private cabin if it were offered to you. But you're not going to waste your time hankering after it, because you have surrendered all of yourself to the crucified Lord – all of your needs and desires, your compulsion to say Yes or No to life's situations.

The very moment that you are detached from this "Yes, I must have ..." or "No, I refuse to ..." God may grant you your desires. I think of the time when we didn't have any holidays, and then who walks in but Cardinal Spellman, along with Father Furfey.* Cardinal Spellman asked, "How many holidays do you take?" I replied: "None. The poor don't take them, so we don't." He said that was stupid! Since we got up at about 6 a.m. and retired at about 12 p.m., we needed to have some sort of holiday. When I pointed out that we didn't have any money for it, he said that we should beg for it and go. Only on the order of the cardinal did we do so. It took that much to make us go away for a while, to 'vacate' the premises.

You see how God was working – pretty well, eh? At first we were too ashamed to 'take a vacation' because the poor didn't have them. Eventually, deep inside of ourselves, we had reached the point where we didn't even want to go away for a holiday. At the moment when we were ready to give up holidays, God handed them to us. We had six weeks for the director and four weeks for the staff. And we returned refreshed and better able to serve. God is never outdone in generosity.

Someone: Just to follow your line there, Catherine, how do you see that we can 'pick up' on our brothers and sisters when they get caught up in emotional needs and desires. That is a very very delicate area. Should we just

*Professor of sociology at the Catholic University of America, Washington, D.C. He was Catherine's spiritual director for a time.

pray for them, and *not* stretch out our hand to correct them? Maybe it is a question of timing.

Catherine: Well, that is something that is on my mind. You remember the choir rehearsal we had the other night. Some of the music was atrocious, and Ray Gene had to stop and correct us on it. Singing, writing, dancing, and so forth, is an emotional experience. If people's emotions are upset, they are going to be 'off-key' in some way. Good singing is not something you can legislate into existence. You can only show people the proper musical notes, let them hear it from you, and then pray.

Now there's something else here. We have to be 'open to' each other about the spiritual life. (God knows I hate the word 'openness' because it usually introduces a lot of emotional 'baloney.') But we can really help each other, if we are honest and say what we truly find in our souls, not hiding behind some facade. We can share our experience of God, and the rest of it; not just 'talk about' the mystical life; you know what I mean.

We have an obligation to tell people when they are 'on-key' and when they are 'off-key,' and to remind them of the proper rhythm. We need to correct each other, not simply uphold but to correct as well. I think we get sloppy about that, just like we do with our singing. (We can get sloppy about anything.) This is where we need to say to one another: "Now, what do you think? Is this or isn't this in the spirit of the Mandate?" We can speak this way to each other when we see something that is not good, or hear a note that is off-pitch.

Then there is the question of tempo. We are not always sure when something is good and when it is not. When to work? When to play? When to study? Remember that we are always 'on pilgrimage.' Suppose we come to a village and find a dance being held in the marketplace. Do we go to that dance? Or should we travel on? There's nothing wrong with music and games. Recreation is good. We enter a room at teatime. Do we stop to chat, to play cards or mah-jong? "But I have promises to keep ... and books to study!" Well, maybe we should go in a corner and read, I don't know. You see how delicate it is. What is our inner attitude here? We need to listen to God and to consult our own hearts, but we should also bring the question up with a group of staff workers and say: "What do you think about this?"

So how are you going to talk to the other members about something? Your personal fasting and prayer might make others talk about things when they are not going well. That is one way of approaching others. There is always that radical personal detachment from people and from things, which is like tearing off your very skin. And the strange thing about it is that, just when you think that you are totally detached, you suddenly discover an whole abyss of attachments. I am in the process of doing this. It hurts; it hurts very badly. I really am afraid to open my mouth right now to correct anyone because I am discovering the amount of my own inner attachments. But I am speaking to you like this because I think these are words you want to hear.

Love,

Catherine

ADVENT MEDITATION

December 1, 1970

Dearly Beloved,

This Advent I have been praying intensely, praising God perhaps a little better than I have before, because my heart is so filled with gratitude for the things that God has given each one of us in this Apostolate. I have been trying to touch those gifts! But somehow I haven't been able to do so, for they are so very many!

As I was sitting there in the late evening when everything was quiet in my house, I tried to pick up his gifts one by one. There was the gift of faith given to each one of us so beautifully, so magnificently, so incredibly, so wondrously, at such a price! For aren't we baptized in the life and death of Jesus Christ? I pondered that and it brought me to the gift of his Incarnation, and almost without any volition, I fell to my knees. How else could I touch that gift, the gift of God, the Second Person of the Most Holy Trinity who became a Child, born in our midst and of our flesh?

The immensity of that gift – its mystery – enveloped me, and I began to think of the vocation of Christ. A strange thought, I grant you; not that it has never come to me before, but suddenly that thought became luminous. It came to me that 'the vocation of Christ' was his listening, his total absorption in the will of the Father! He was the Word that the Father wanted to 'speak' to us. Christ listened and obeyed. He descended and became that seed in the womb of Our Lady – that Child whom I just mentioned! In a word he became incarnate, one of us human beings, like us in everything except sin. That was the first part of his vocation, so it seemed to me.

That was Christ's vocation – to listen to the Father and to obey him, to become the Word of the Father; to show us the Father and to give us the Holy Spirit; to teach us how to love by loving us recklessly, passionately, until the very end; even unto his death. In doing this, he also brought a woman into our spiritual life: hidden, immense, simple, a woman of the people, and yet, because he was her son, he made her our mother, our sister, our friend. Through her, he united himself even more intensely with each one of us who are (or ever will be) born of women. Yes, those were the first gifts that I dared to touch with my heart as I was meditating on Advent, this time of waiting that was coming.

Then I went on, and a deep gratitude welled up in my heart because Christ had given us faith. He has given us the faith to understand a little what his vocation was, which is ours also; for we know that we too must listen to the Father. We must blend with Christ in doing the will of the Father as Christ did it. That simply means to incarnate, to 'flesh out,' the law of love. That alone will truly unite us with Christ. We will be united then in that immense unity that love gives us.

I thought of our community. Do you realize, dearly beloved, that we really are a community? We are united by the Holy Spirit who, like a golden thread, binds us one to another in the infinite beauty that comes from loving God and loving one another! In our tremendously lonely world where everyone seems to be an island, it is a grace beyond computing, our being together.

I looked again at the gifts of God – those he has given us. I saw priests, laymen and women holding hands, lifting them up together, as we do for the *Our Father* at Mass. I saw them singing with an infinite gladness. And the joy around them was as a great light – the light of gratitude, the light of love, the light of gladness. Consider, dearly beloved, how wonderful it is to be the people of God. There is Archbishop Raya and all of our associate priests. How beautiful it is to be this 'totality of Church' in a humble group, to blend with the Church in this unity that I call *sobornost* and that also is called *the Mystical Body of Christ*. Yes, I thanked God again and again for this gift!

Then I looked at each one of you separately. I cannot tell you how much I love each one of you. You were all there, and each of you and passed before me so clearly. I just fell prostrate before God because I felt so overwhelmed by it all. I felt like shouting, dancing, singing, for each of us is a gift to the other, and I love you so much. Each of you separately and together are a gift of God to me.

I wish I could express that love in words. But you know how I have always said that only 'the great silence of contemplation' expresses in fullness the love of one's heart. So this Christmas I am beholding, and I will behold, each one of you as a gift of God to me. Each one whom I love in a way that only silence can express. My humble love covers you like one of those beautiful capes that were worn throughout the centuries. It holds you warmly and securely and covers you with my simple blessing as I hold you in my arms. Yes indeed, I love you deeply. Perhaps you do not yet understand how much, but it will grow on you, for love does such things.

At that moment, my eyes fell on another gift: your love, not only for each other and not only for me, but for those whom you have gone to serve. And I saw you, each of you (wherever you are) kneeling by the crib. Each one of you was as a king, as one of the magi. Each one of you has heard the word, as if rising like a star in your hearts. That word is hidden in his heart and yours forever, for no one knows or will ever know how he spoke to you, how he told you to arise and come to Madonna House. *That is a secret between you and him,* and it will always remain that way. But it is a gift to all of us.

Yes, I saw each and all of you kneeling at the crib, bringing your gifts. And the gifts were your lives, which were blending with his. You were following the vocation of Christ. You really were listening to the Father. You were incarnating his word. You were obeying his law of love. You were also servants washing the feet of mankind and, in the process, bringing them with you to the crib.

The night of my meditation was closing. The dawn was a penciled light against the horizon. I didn't realize the time. I knew that there were many more gifts that I should be touching and be grateful for, but I didn't look any more. The ones that I had looked at and touched delicately with my heart were so overwhelming that all I could say was: "He loves us! He has come to prove it! Let us arise all together, hand in hand, and go to Bethlehem ... singing psalms of love, praise, and adoration ... alleluia!"

With love,

LET US CONSOLE HIM

December 13, 1971

Dearly Beloved,

I wish that we could be together and that I could express to you the constantly growing joy, the infinite gratitude, and the love that never ceases (not even for a moment), before the incredible sight of each one of you. Each one of you has been brought to Madonna House by the Lord, and I have watched your surrender and the mystery of your love answering the mystery of the love of God.

I realize, with grave humility and not too clearly (for such mysteries as ours are never clearly realized), that in order for you to answer his desire that you be here, there had to be a 'here' for him to bring you to; and I know that I am that place. I don't really understand how I came to be that 'here' – that place to which he brought you, and continues to bring so many of you. All that I know is that it is so, and knowing it, I marvel, rejoice, and praise him.

He has made us a humble, small community; and this year, this Christmas, he has given us a vision of the community that we are: a community of love, a community of forgiveness, a community of conscience, a community of praise, a community of suffering, a community of joy. We are a community which exists because he has drawn it together for one purpose: that we might love one another as he has loved us, and love his Father as he did.

With God, *every moment is the moment of beginning again;* and this is such a moment. It is time for us to go on a pilgrimage all together. Though divided as we are by sometimes thousands of miles, let us go together on that pilgrimage which knows no frontiers. Let us arise and go to Bethlehem, for this is the hour of waking up from whatever sleep we might be indulging in. This is the hour of arising, no matter how many pains and aches each of us may have.

This is the hour of going on a pilgrimage to the Cave of Bethlehem.

Yes, let us arise and go. None of us, and I least of all, have anything to bring to the Child except, perhaps, our poverty, our chastity, and our obedience. These are humble gifts of poor people – gifts which he, the Poor Man, will understand.

But this year we can bring him more; so let us hasten, for we can and must bring him *our consolation.* Behold the Christians of the diaspora, as the Jews were in Babylon. So many have been torn away from the faith. So many have left it deliberately. So many are confused. Priests are leaving – priests, the dedicated ones he has appointed to shepherd us! Yes, we can bring the Lord our consolation, our tenderness, our love, for this is the hour of his need for them.

It is a strange Christmas, this year of 1971. Bethlehem itself is in the midst of rumors of war. All around the world that Jesus was born to save, the world he died to save, this world to which he gave his beautiful Light of Love, there is hatred. Christians are not dying *for* one another; they are killing one another, and so, it seems, is everyone else.

Dearly beloved, let us arise and hasten together on this pilgrimage to Bethlehem to console him who is the consoler; to give our tenderness and compassion to him who is all tenderness and compassion, who is Love.

For each and every one of you, my Christmas wish is that you may be what he was on the night he was born: a Child who was a Flame of Love. Let us, you and I, dearly beloved, be childlike; let us be a burning bush that constantly lights the path of those who seek him.

Lovingly yours in Mary,

POUSTINIA AND DISPOSSESSION

July 8, 1972

Dearly Beloved,

I have been praying very deeply and seriously about the whole aspect of poustinias. They have been constantly in my mind. The reason for this is that such a constant stream of priests, nuns, and lay people (both Catholic and Protestant) come here often, to discuss the matter of poustinia, and specifically prayer houses. I have also been gathering what would be called fairly good data on the various faces of poustinia and the differences between the poustinia and prayer houses as such.

But let me first talk a little bit about poustinia. Before going into any of the physical aspects of it, I want to share with you the fact that when I introduced the poustinia concept some ten years ago, at Marian Meadows, I was walking in a sort of twilight. I was trying to adapt from one ethnic heritage to another; gently and tenderly, I took into consideration the great differences between those two cultures, East and West, especially regarding the spiritual approach to life.

Yes, quite a lot of time elapsed, and now I can begin to assess the whole idea of poustinias. I beg you to pray for me especially these days, because I am going to write about those poustinias. It will probably be a sort of booklet,* but now I want to put down in black and white what poustinia really is. I think that this is the time to do so.

Before I talk about any kind of a physical setup, the ways and means, ideas, and goals of the poustinia, I want to make one thing very clear: *The poustinia is a very direct way of dispossession.* We shall talk about the physical dispossession later; but now I want to bring before you the

---

*It developed into a book over 200 pages long. *Poustinia: Christian Spirituality of the East for Western Man,* published in December 1974 by Ave Maria Press, Notre Dame, Indiana.

'true' dispossession for which one enters the poustinia – the dispossession which is one of the fruits of poustinia (or should be) and certainly is part of its goals ... a very vital part.

What do I really mean by dispossession? Factually I mean what the word means. As I have often stated in writing and speech, dispossession is the essence of true poverty, obedience, and chastity. It is both the base and the apex of the spiritual life, for it will take the whole of our lives to implement this dispossession.

To dispose of one's wealth or goods is very laudable, and even holy if it is done for God's sake. But to dispossess ourselves of *self* is an entirely different matter. For what stands between myself and God? One or two little words – *I* and *self*.

To dispossess ourselves, or to be dispossessed, is to become selfless. It is to use the word *I* only in regard to the service of God and of man. To do this, one has to employ every possible means, and one of the great means is the poustinia. There, face to face with God in that solitude, fasting, and praying, one finally confronts this great obstacle that prevents us from 'making straight' the path of the Lord. Poustinia is a wonderful place to get the rocks of the *I* and the *self* blasted out, allowing us to make a path for the Lord to walk upon, even though it might be a very narrow one.

Poustinia also teaches us, as we proceed toward this dispossession, to understand very clearly that *without him we can do nothing;* that this dispossession, this making even a narrow path for him, is a true way for us to become the icon of Christ; that by doing so, we are allowing people to follow *him* – never us, but always him! Poustinia is one of the great means leading toward this end.

It becomes obvious, therefore, that anyone who is in the 'poustinia of the marketplace' or in a poustinia-cabin on our island (or wherever else it might be) must 'live out' this dispossession daily. Its primary form takes a complete denudation of the soul, becoming as naked as Christ's body was on the Cross. It begins with a premise which is starkly simple: there are to be no pictures on the wall, no cute arrangements of furniture – none of that stuff. The plainness of a Trappist cell should prevail. It even goes beyond Trappist cells. Slowly, increasingly, it should become the reflection of the person living there, a mirror of a soul that strips itself of the *I* and the *self.*

Obviously, those people who enter into a poustinia must be people of peace, of humility – grave humility – and *without guile.* They must be people who truly see Christ in their neighbor and can say, without hypocrisy or equivocation: "My brother is my joy."

The hospitality of the heart and of the house, poor and humble as it might be, is total. The poustinik is truly a person of 'the towel and the water.' In the dining room of Madonna House, just over my head we have a beautiful little towel, along with a basin and pitcher made out of copper. It was sent to us by the Israel Team because lately I have been referring so often to the fact that we must become 'the people of the towel and the water.'* That means that we who touch God in such a special way, by his invitation, are dedicated to the service of our brethren, even as Christ was dedicated. He showed this dedication by washing the feet of his apostles. We are, therefore, people of the towel and the water, standing ready to wash the face and the feet of each person we meet.

Forgiveness, peace, hospitality of heart and house, a total lack of hostility or anger, a deep and grave humility – these should characterize the dweller of the poustinia. If these characteristics are not forthcoming, then dwelling in a poustinia is useless, for dispossession is not taking place. And when dispossession does take not take place, the poustinia is not fulfilling its role, its goal.

That is why we are going to take a long time, a very long time, before we accept anyone to dwell on our island as a poustinik, that is, one who plans to make it a life's vocation. People who aspire to this special vocation within Madonna House are going to have to go through the usual procedures of becoming a member, and must be a member for at least two years. During this time, he or she will be 'tested by God and man' in a manner of speaking. We cannot accept for this strange vocation just anyone who may 'think' it is their calling.

*A book of meditations by Catherine was published in 1978, using this phrase as its title.

I speak, as I said, of anyone who desires to make a lifetime vocation of this specially accentuated, contemplative part of Madonna House. I am slowly coming to the conclusion that the 'poustinia in the marketplace' will not be feasible for us. This type of poustinia, better called an 'ashram,' is more suitable for the mentality and spirituality of the Hindu than for that of the American (or even the Russian soul). We are discussing this profoundly in Madonna House, especially with our priests, but also with all of the community. Pray for us, for this is an important part of our Apostolate. The more so in that many people are clamoring for answers regarding these matters.

Lovingly in Mary,

MORE ABOUT MISSIONS

August 19, 1972

Dearly Beloved,

For a long time I have been wanting to talk to you some more about missions. You understood some of the ideas that I have presented to you; but others have been shrouded in mystery, I think. I hope that, through sharing various letters and sharing my thoughts with you, this mystery will slowly be dispelled.

Let me begin at the beginning. I never took very kindly to 'activist' missionary endeavors such as being engaged in catechetics, in teaching, in working for a big hospital, etc. This never interested me that much. I agreed to small dispensaries where medical help was hard to get. I agreed, under duress I must admit, to the teaching of catechism. I was more interested in the line of action such as co-ops and credit unions, as an exponent of social justice and freedom from want. My background, my culture, everything in me, cried out for it.

What I wanted most of all has always been the *chitchat apostolate;* the kind that my mother undertook when she was a young woman studying at the academy of music in Petrograd. But besides the chitchat (which to me expressed the essence of friendship, of brotherhood), I felt that the main job of the missionary was *prayer,* and that he or she would attract many just by those two factors – prayer and the chitchat apostolate.

These ideas were exemplified by Russian missionaries. I challenge you to tell me how many Russian priests or monks you know about who spread the Word that Christ told us to spread, and who preached the Gospel everywhere. You would know very few, not because they were absent, but because of their unobtrusive method of entry into foreign lands. This entry usually was very quiet, practically without any repercussions on the side of either the missionary or the people he came to serve and instruct.

For instance, take St. Herman of Alaska, the Russian priest who came one hundred years ago to bring the Good News to the Indians there. He has just recently been canonized by the Orthodox Church. He arrived, built a log cabin such as we have on the island, and proceeded to say Mass outside whenever it was possible. He did this winter and summer, knowing that the Indians were a free people who liked to worship in the open air.

But he didn't approach them with catechetics right away; he just went on offering the liturgy – the Holy Mass. He had a wonderful voice, and he sang. The people gathered around him. And through friendship and the normal chitchat apostolate and the acceptance of their ways and customs, he had a tremendous effect on the Indians of Alaska.

Fundamentally, I believe that "a missionary does not bring anything to his mission land, but rather goes there to find the Christ who is *already* dwelling there and reveals him to others," as I read recently in a book by Father Jacques Loew.*

In the book, he discusses a priest who had been a missionary in Africa for a long time. Humorously and yet with some sadness, that priest describes the mentality of the Western missionary, just arriving in that African land; it is a mentality that I feel can be transposed to all Western missionaries of today. He says that most European missionaries come with an 'organizational' type of mind. They are concerned about the numbers of meetings to have, the number of people to have at each, what kinds of groups, etc. Many of them start with very elevated projects. They are like 'talking books' on the subjects of philosophy, theology, etc. What they should have done was contact people, one by one, telling about themselves and asking about the other, all very simply and delicately. If they had, they would have discovered a universe where God was *already* truly present. A missionary must listen to the poor very carefully and allow himself to be penetrated with their misery. And he must be filled with respect for the ones whom he has come to serve.

The priest went on to say that we cannot allow our own enthusiasm to carry us away, to cause us to strive after quick solutions by bringing our mission to some obvious and tangible conclusion. He says that we must divide our missionary activity into three parts. And for each we need to be well prepared, by prayer and fasting. Those parts are:

(1) a Time of Friendship;

(2) a Time of the Word;

(3) a Time of the Sacrament.

This friendship-time is a form of Nazareth – a shared life of working together, forming the bonds of kinship. Have you thought about this time of friendship for us here in Madonna House? The time of the hidden life? The time of silence in which cultural differences and difficulties are confronted and assimilated? Time used in a special way so that anything and everything can contribute to 'blending' us

*As If He Had Seen the Invisible: a portrait of an apostle today ... published in 1967 by Fides, Notre Dame, Indiana.

with the people whom we are called to serve? A time of 'uselessness' when the secrecy of the Father is at work? For he deals with missionaries as he dealt with his Son; he wants to send us into his Bethlehem and Nazareth.

Before we proceed any further, we must also understand that, although we are discussing foreign missions primarily, we must always remember that *every* Christian is an apostle, a missionary, one who is sent by God to others to proclaim the Good News and live the Gospel with his life. That means that Christians, apostles, missionaries, must be lovers of men as well as lovers of God.

This time of friendship is not just a chunk of time taken out of our lives so we can prepare for some *future* missionary activity. No! This time of friendship, like the rhythm of the seasons, accompanies our missionary life *always,* wherever we may go. Without it, we are not missionaries. We shall not be lovers of God or men, since friendship is the fruit of love.

Nor, as I said before, does Nazareth time consist in hiding ourselves in a poustinia. No. We must live friendship outside of our poustinia. We must 'live it out' where men live – in the marketplace if need be. And we go about it very quietly, without any hurry. If God wants to bind us to himself in this precious friendship, we must take root where the other person roots himself, and become 'all to all' in our love and service. In a word, the missionary must become a person of the towel and the water (as Christ washed the feet of his apostles), for this truly represents love and friendship.

When this time of friendship has taken root, now comes the time of the Word. Having formed friendship with others, we can begin to speak the Good News. We do so slowly, gently, changing the phraseology and semantics so that it 'fits' each person and every background. Above all, we must 'speak' that Gospel *with our lives.*

Then comes the time of sacrament. All of these were the stages which Jesus went through while he was on earth. For him, the time of sacrament was the time of the Last Supper, of the Cross, of death and resurrection, of giving and forgiving. When we sum up his life, we find that there are thirty-three years spent in the time of Friendship. His time of the Word (his public life) was three years long. But the time of the Sacrament lasted only a few days.

Without having read Father Loew's book, I had started my idea of the chitchat apostolate many many years ago, and I continued it throughout my whole life. It is funny that, when I say "I started it long ago and far away," I don't mean that I started it only when Friendship House was opened forty-two years ago. No. It was part and parcel of a my Russian culture; for my mother, as I have often told you, 'went to the people' as their servant. Russian spirituality recognized that we are all missionaries, apostles to one another. Each one of us is meant to proclaim the Good News to the other; and *repeatedly,* for the application of the Good News is none too easy! So, in a sense, I began that chitchat apostolate long ago and far away, and it was rooted in prayer. I still continue it today in Madonna House, which is so thronged with people constantly.

The time of the Word is one of continual growth; my incarnation, your incarnation, develops and grows until it becomes an icon of Christ. The Lord performed miracles of all kinds, including healing; and finally he gave us the Last Supper, with Wine and Bread that continued unto the end of time. To me, then, it seems that our life, our missionary life together – during the time of the Word when we really preach it fully, and with absolute faith – is a time of challenging trials for us.

Let us not be worried, even for a moment, about our thousand-and-one inabilities – our impotence, our lack of education, etc. It really doesn't matter, for it is not *we* who shall speak; he will preach if we but open our mouths 'in his name.'

We know who we are. We know that the seed must die to produce the fruit. And when we allow this to happen, then 'faith in action' comes and dwells in us. Daily we realize more clearly that we are preaching God's Word, and never our own. St. Paul tells us that we carry this treasure in a 'vessel of clay' to show that this abundance of power belongs to God, and not to ourselves. Because of this, I feel very strongly that we must realize the necessity for accepting our weaknesses, and God's strength, and to show them to the world. In my mind, these are the ways of preparing the time of the Word.

As for the time of sacrament ... well, there is very little to be said. Here, in our own small way, we undergo the agony in the garden and the crucifixion. This is the time that we walk in a desolate land. This is the moment when we get detached from the judgment of mere creatures. We are not moved by approval, or disapproval, from any individual or strata of society. We are indifferent to evil reports and good reports. In my estimation, the joy of the missionary – first, foremost, and last – is in this resemblance to Jesus Christ, in being an icon of Christ.

Perhaps St. Paul gives the best definition of a missionary.

> In everything, we prove ourselves *authentic servants of God:* By resolute perseverance in times of hardships, difficulties, and distress; when we are flogged, or sent to prison, or mobbed; laboring, sleepless, starving; in purity, in knowledge, in patience, in kindness, in the Holy Spirit, in a love free of affectation, in the word of truth and the power of God; by using the weapons of uprightness for attack and for defense; in times of honor or disgrace, blame or praise; taken for imposters and yet we are genuine; unknown and yet we are acknowledged; dying, and yet we are alive; scourged but not executed; in pain yet always full of joy; poor and yet making many people rich; having nothing, and yet owning everything. (II Cor. 6:4-10)

This is exactly what I mean when I talk about this chitchat apostolate of ours. It should apply to all of our active Apostolate and to those who are in the poustinia. It is so simple; and yet, because of its simplicity, it is intensely complicated.

These are some of my thoughts on missions.

Lovingly yours in Mary,

Catherine

SOBORNOST

August 29, 1972

Dearly Beloved,

Recently I received a copy of the minutes of a meeting at one of the houses. It was a very good report. Part of it I want to share with you so that you know what I am talking about when I speak of *sobornost,* so here it is:

> So much of our year has been a grappling with sobornost and trying to live it out. As we try to discover what it means, we move between two extremes: that of total dependence (say, of staff on authority) and that of total independence (of staff doing too much as individuals, without having a sense of 'community conscience' or of the need for communication). There is a fine balance – which we have not yet achieved – between operating from 'authority downwards' in a rigid way and 'moving in freedom' too individualistically. What we are seeking in sobornost is neither total dependence nor total independence; and this demands communication among us all.

As I kept reading and rereading this, I began to pray earnestly and deeply. It seems that sobornost is a difficult concept for Roman Catholics to understand, probably because their spirituality is so heavily based on hierarchy, on 'law and order.' That is because Catholic Rome was historically the inheritor of pagan Rome's legal traditions. Sobornost has very little to do with any "total dependence of staff on authority" or "total independence of staff, doing too much as individuals." Sobornost lies at infinitely greater depths. Its incarnation into the life of the people is like an artesian spring that wells up from the very heart of the Most Holy Trinity! Perhaps sobornost can be found, in its full perfection, only within the Trinity itself;

for here a *complete and total unity* of minds (if one can express it this way) reigns!

So it isn't really a question of dependence or independence, authority or subjects; all these things fall away, as if they were old, worn-out garments. Sobornost begins within the heart of people whose prayer-life is spent before the Trinity; and it becomes, as time goes on, a reflection of the Father, Son, and the Holy Spirit.

If, by the will of the Father, such people become 'bound together' into a community, they will assume upon themselves the obedience of the Son, and will rely on the Holy Spirit (the Advocate which the Father sent to remind them of all that the Son taught) for total unity of mind, heart, and soul.

Sobornost, you see, is a unity that includes mind, and heart, and soul. It is neither dependence or independence, nor even interdependence; it is far more than that. Neither is it a hierarchical setup as commonly understood. Nor is it a group of people 'doing their thing.' No. It is none of these.

Before I go any further, let me explain this Russian word etymologically. *Sobor* means a cathedral, a very special type of cathedral. St. Peter's of Rome would be such a cathedral; St. Isaac's in Petrograd would be another. But spiritually speaking, a *sobor* means a church which gathers all the people into one assembly (*sobrania* means 'assembly'). Such a sobor is a place where bishops, priests, and the People of God gather to offer the Eucharistic sacrifice (the Liturgia), as if all those people were one – totally, completely one! – one in mind, one in body, one in soul, one in heart.

This oneness in the Body of Christ is so totally united to him, and hence to the Father and the Holy Spirit, as to create in truth a Trinitarian Body, i.e., as Christ must have been during his incarnation. I don't know if I make myself clear, or if I mix you up all the more! But one thing I want to put across: Sobornost is achieved *only* by intense and constant prayer.

Perhaps it would be clearer to you if I spoke of it as 'total openness to one another.' It is an openness so great that it would be completely natural for each person to speak honestly about himself, allowing even the flow of the unconscious to move easily, openly, simply, from one person to another in the community. Perhaps even that is muddling, for no matter where I turn to try to explain that incredible unity which fills the heart of a community, and which in turn is filled with Trinitarian Sobornost, I find myself bereft of words.

Here is another paragraph from the meeting that I spoke about:

> Will we as a community use the fruit of our prayer and meditation of last year? We all seem to agree that we should sometime share our reflections about this last year ...

To the Russian mind, that sort of question and answer would appear utterly superfluous. *Of course you should!* Use the fruit of your prayer, meditation, and experience of every minute, of every day, of every year, sharing the same with one another constantly. I mean *constantly,* not 'sometime.' But do it spontaneously, because sobornost, when all is said and done, is a union of love between the Father and the Son and the Holy Spirit, which takes place in our own bodies. Remember, we are the temple of the Trinity. And this Triune God who dwells in us (if we only let him take over) will make us a sobrania (a gathering or assembly) of lovers of the Triune God and of one another.

Dearly beloved, if we love one another with the love of the Most Holy Trinity – or as close as we possibly can through constant prayer and meditation – I ask you, "Would there be any questions about dependence, independence, or interdependence?" No, there wouldn't be. For none of those things would be important. Not even interdependence. For interdependence would flow simply and naturally from this constant communication of people loving one another.

What would be important is this: that those in authority love as the Father loves, and give themselves as the Father has given the Son, for our salvation. So any 'authority' in a setting of sobornost would act both as the Suffering Servant of Yahweh and as the Person of the Towel and the Water – Jesus Christ! Authority would be the servant of all, willingly crucified for the need and the salvation of all. Authority would be in true sobornost, loving both God and men, especially with those who belong to the community.

The members of such a community, functioning within this ideal of sobornost, would likewise be lovers and servants of one another. Authority and members, all united, would be constantly on the alert, concerned about one thing and one thing only: that they be not 'many' (in a manner of speaking) but 'one' in the Lord. Therefore, all questions of any type, from the most routine problem (how to arrange the picking up of donations, how to organize the clothing room) to the most grave situation which might confront the Apostolate, must in this sobornost, in this total unity of love, achieve a total unity of opinions.

This might take time at first. But as we more and more become 'one' with that stream which issues forth from the depth of the Trinity, time will cease to exist. To put it another way, we will resolve our problems faster and faster because we will love one another more and more, and be ever more closely united.

Have I explained anything? Have I given you yet another glimpse on what sobornost is? I don't know! You will have to tell me. Please ask more questions if you have any.

Lovingly yours in Mary,

OUR APPROACH TO FOOD

September 12, 1972

Dearly Beloved,

Although we are in the midst of the local directors' meeting, I want to drop you a line. We are talking about many things, and some of us have discussed quite a bit our approach to food in Madonna House and in our fieldhouses. The reason why we mentioned this was that we were evaluating our approaches to various things.

We were discussing hippies and poverty, and how the younger members of Madonna House (but everyone factually) are talking about 'the Pilgrim Church,' and prayer, fasting, hair shirts, and what-have-you. All around you, you see the hippie youth and other youth passing to and fro 'on pilgrimage.' You see them with knapsacks on their backs, going in search of God or Yoga or Buddhism or whatever. Fundamentally, they are in search of God.

They are, perhaps, the St. Francises of today. They are the poor who have made themselves poor. Like St. Francis, who had a rich father in the clothing business, they too often have rich fathers and mothers in suburbia. But filled with a search for new values, new guidelines, new ways of life, they have arisen and crisscrossed the earth, just as St. Francis traversed the Mediterranean countries, even allowing himself to be taken prisoner by the Muslims.

So we have been faced with much discussion about poverty and simplicity and such things. Come mealtime, however, we find ourselves asking: "What's for dessert?" (As if this were important!) We continue to pick and choose from what is on the table, and the old days of Friendship House and Madonna House are totally forgotten. Because of the charity of our good benefactors these days, our meals are getting to be pretty good. So we forget about the days when a cup of coffee, or tea, was a luxury; when for years we had nothing but pea soup; when butter was something we couldn't remember the taste of; and margarine was not yet in existence (and if it had been, we probably could not have afforded it); when an *ice cream cone* was practically a Christmas gift only! Yes, all of this has somehow gone down the drain. When your local director returns, perhaps you will have prepared an answer to all of this because the directors are perturbed about it.

In our abundant society, there are benefactors who help us with all sorts of foods. Could some of these gifts be given to the poor around us? Could we stop selecting things and 'eat what is put on the table' without any questions about what's in it? And whether we like it or not, is it possible to do some of that fasting which everyone is talking about these days?

Think about it, my dear ones. Pray about it. And when your directors return, talk with them about it and drop me a line.

Keep praying for us.

Love,

Catherine

THE FRUITFULNESS OF POVERTY

September 23, 1972

Dearly Beloved,

I seem to have a great need to write to you before I go to Israel. I feel very close to each one of you. And because the directors' meetings were so beautiful I feel a fantastic desire to keep sharing with you all that is in my heart.

There is no denying that our meetings this year were deeply spiritual, and they dealt a lot with the subject of poverty.

But, to be absolutely truthful, I am obsessed by something that goes beyond poverty. Perhaps it is part of it; or perhaps it is the heart of it. I really wouldn't know. I just share it and call it *dispossession*. Now, what do I mean by that? Well, the first thing I mean is contained in the words that you find in a book called *The Struggle With God*.* Evdokimov defines poverty in one short sentence: *When the absence of 'the need to have' becomes a need NOT to have!*

Imagine yourself being really poor in spirit, as poor as we were in Harlem and in Toronto. Imagine any one of us walking down Fifth Avenue. We really reached a stage when we looked at the beautiful display of dresses, jewelry, and various *objects d'art* quite indifferently; we did not desire to possess them. Poverty had cleansed our hearts and our souls of such cravings.

But time went on, and months and years passed. And if any of us were walking down Fifth Avenue now, we would not only look at these beautiful things with indifference, but our souls would cry out as we walked, longing for that other depth of poverty called *dispossession*. Not only would we not desire to have any of the lovely things, we would passionately desire only one thing: to have nothing at all!

When indifference changes to passionate longing, then somewhere in our inward depths, we desire to be poor as St. John the Baptist was poor. We desire passionately to identify with the most abject poverty available to us. Not only that, we also desire to possess a deep interior poverty, a total *emptiness* of heart and soul – an emptiness in which a naked Child could be born, an emptiness big enough to contain a naked Man on the Cross. That is the meaning of the words of the sentence: When the absence of the 'need to have' become a passionate need NOT to have.

On August 15th, when everyone was asking me what the theme for this beautiful Feast would be for the year 1972, I blurted out *dispossession*. That is how all of these

*Written by Paul Evdokimov; published in 1966 by Paulist Press, Glen Rock, New Jersey.

things I am writing about became posters which were placed in the little fireplace library and in the community room and on the way upstairs.

Let us look at those posters and see what they tell us. One read: "Dispossession is *freedom*."

Does it seep down, down, into the deepest parts of your heart, mind, and soul? It is such a simple sentence. If you dispossess yourself for Christ's sake, for God's sake, for Love's sake, you become as free as the air. You have nothing to worry about; worry passes you by without a backward glance at you, or your looking at it.

You possess nothing. You are empty, hollow, ready to hold a naked Child, or a naked, crucified Man; but also you will hold anyone in need, for all that you can give them is yourself. Maybe you have a match somewhere about you so that you can light a fire to warm someone. Maybe you have a piece of bread that someone gave you (for the dispossessed eat, too), and you can share it with someone. Maybe you have a corner where you sleep; corners can be shared too, you see.

When you have that freedom that I speak about, you will no longer worry about approval or disapproval. And others will sense it. No one will feel they are 'below' you, for the dispossessed have a way of making others feel 'superior' in some way. When people feel themselves to be free from worry, free from the desire for approval, free from the fear of rejection, don't you regard that as true freedom and true wealth? A dispossessed person 'possesses' all these things.

Another poster read:

Remember how *generous* the Lord was: he was rich, but became poor for your sake, to make you rich out of his poverty. (II Cor. 8:9)

Yes, let us remember his generosity. And remembering, we can really plummet into dispossession as the stones plummet into the depths when hurled from the heights; as a hawk plummets to catch its prey. Yes, let us plummet and catch dispossession in its totality. It is not going to be easy, however, because this demands not only identification with the poor of spirit, the pure of heart, the whole gamut of identification with the Beatitudes, it demands *identification with Jesus Christ.*

It means that into the garden of our souls will enter some strange words: "Learn of Me for I am meek and humble of heart." And dispossession will blossom there. The dispossessed for Christ's sake are meek and therefore are peacemakers. They are the gentle ones who use their poverty, their dispossession, to wipe the tears of others. They are humble ones, because they know that the greater their dispossession, the deeper they are in the Truth of God; and therefore, they become totally humble.

The next poster read:

As for me, the only thing I can boast about is the *cross* of Our Lord Jesus Christ, through whom the world is crucified to me, and I to the world. (Gal. 6:14)

What a beautiful poster! St. Paul boasts only about one thing, the cross of Our Lord Jesus Christ! I ask you, dearly beloved, what else *can* a dispossessed one boast about, except the cross of Jesus Christ, through which the world is crucified to him, the dispossessed one; and through which the dispossessed is crucified to the world.

Perhaps I do not give it exactly the same accent, shall we say, as St. Paul; but where else can a dispossessed one 'rest' except on a cross? Those of us who really desire to be dispossessed wouldn't wish for any other 'bed.' It is not only a question of having a bed with boards (which doctors recommend today for our aching backs). No. It is rather that the dispossessed, the poor ones, the meek ones, the humble ones, are indeed Christbearers. And what better bed for a dispossessed person than to take 'the cross of someone else' for a spell, and use it for his bed, while the suffering one, the tired one, has a chance to rest on some soft and pleasant cushion!

The next poster said:

Poverty is the treasure of the Most Holy Trinity, reserved for the soul of man. When, in the stillness of the dark night, it grows into a mighty branch of the Tree who is the Son. Then, bedecked with all the richness that poverty and *obedience* possess, that branch becomes the bride of Christ and enters into his kingdom while yet on earth.

Ah yes, this is from my own writings. I must admit that I had forgotten that I wrote it. But as I reread it now on the poster, it becomes clear that a new word is added to dispossession. It is *obedience*. Did it ever occur to you that, to be totally dispossessed, one must be totally obedient? Obedience is the crown of poverty ... or is it the base? Whatever it may be, it is bound up with poverty as if they were Siamese twins.

That 'hollowing out' which dispossession must make in our hearts and souls to hold that naked Child once born in a cave, to hold that naked Man once crucified on a cross, is done by obedience. Without it, poverty would be but a shallow word; it certainly would have nothing to do with total dispossession.

The next poster read:

You have stripped off your old behavior with your old self, and you have put on a new self which will progress toward *true knowledge* the more it is renewed in the image of its creator. (Col. 3:9-11)

Strange how dispossession (such a humble word as you meditate upon it; as you become that little stone which God has plummeted into his own depths) becomes immense. You really wonder how it is possible for so tiny a word to become that immense, to blend into eternity, into the infinity of God.

We have moved beyond the word *poverty* to dwell on the term *dispossession*. And somehow it acquired *freedom*. And then it called for *identity* – not with other men, saints, or what-have-you, but with God himself. And then it gathered, somehow, a *cross* to sleep upon; and *obedience* rose out of it like a vivid light; and now *true knowledge* comes into dispossession. Yes, he who dispossesses himself totally for love of God is mysteriously visited, and the knowledge of the Most Holy Trinity is given to him. This happens in God's own time and place, but it is inevitable that it should happen. For he who dispossessed himself to

306

become a human being will share the 'true knowledge' of himself and the Father and the Holy Spirit with one who his dispossessed himself totally for the love of that Three-in-One.

The next poster read:

God has made me *fruitful* in the land of my poverty. (Gen. 41:52)

Fruitfulness is another gift that will come. But of course the dispossessed one is fruitful! What else can he be? He has received the fruits of God's own garden, given to him by God himself. And in his dispossession he never dreamt of touching the forbidden tree. And so his empty hands are full of God's fruits – God's harvest – and all he wants to do is to share his bounty with others. For only the dispossessed have such wealth.

And the last poster read:

But you *happily* accepted being stripped of your belongings, knowing that you owned something that was better and lasting. (Heb. 10:34)

This last poster seems almost anticlimactic; yet it is a perfect ending, a sort of 'period' that punctuates the rest. For it shows to all those who love the Great Pauper that poverty is Divine. If you meditate on this, happiness will be yours at every stage of your dispossession.

With much love,

HUNGER AND FIRE

December 12, 1972

Dearly Beloved,

This year I approach the writing of your usual Christmas Letter hesitantly! I think the reason for it is my visit to the Holy Land. I hope that by now most of you will have heard my tape on that visit. It has had a profound effect on me, and it seems to continue its work, its inspiration, long after I have left that holy place.

As I explained on my tape, when I got to Lod Airport, even before I put my foot on the earth outside of the plane, I had an encounter with Christ which, for lack of other words, I expressed as *being possessed by Christ, and possessing him.* All of this in an instant. From there on, it seemed as if my life had been changed. Yet I cannot find words to express that change.

As Christmas approaches, the moment of his Incarnation, I feel a great need to try to share with you the thoughts that are in my heart this Advent. There is in me a hunger that doesn't seem to be assuaged by anything except the Holy Eucharist, and the food that you alone can give me. It seems to me that I am at Mass and that I receive the Lord. And then I come to you, praying, looking, hoping for an *agape feast.*

You know something? You give it to me beautifully and constantly, for an agape of this type to me is your unity, your love, your trust in one another. In a word, the implementation of our Little Mandate, which can be done only by prayer. Yes, you give me a quite beautiful agape feast; but here and there, occasionally and quite unexpectedly, a part of the food is missing. This is only natural because we are human beings; but the moment it happens, I hunger again (and I believe that God shares that hunger). I wonder if I serve an agape food for all of those in Madonna House and outside of it. So here is hunger!

Then I cannot get rid of the idea of a *burning bush*. I was thinking that, in a manner of speaking, Our Lady is a burning bush. Out of the flame of her love, her humility, her submission, and the fact that she is full of grace, came the Lord Jesus Christ. And who is the Lord Jesus Christ? He is Flame and Fire. And I meditate on his birth. What a hidden fire was burning in Bethlehem!

I followed without following (if you know what I mean) his life in Nazareth. When I walked into that town it shook me. I sensed that this town still contained The Triune God – Father, Son, and Holy Spirit. It still was filled with the love of the Father, who so loved us that he gave us his Son ... with the love of the Son who so loved us that he gave his life for us ... with the love of the Holy Spirit who comes as the Wind and the Fire to make us sparks of that Fire. Nazareth is an awesome town, but so is Bethlehem and so is all of Palestine. God walked there!

How can I share hunger and fire? Hunger that never is assuaged, for I desire with a passionate desire – even more passionate than before – to show people the face of Christ. That kind of hunger cannot be explained in words; even prayer is silent before it. Perhaps it is the silent prayer that spiritual writers talk about. You just sit and hunger, as it were, for men to come and be filled. Put that together, dearly beloved, if you can! I can only state it in faltering words; words that, perhaps, make no sense at all. And the same is with the fire. As I contemplate the burning bush and other symbols of the Scriptures regarding light and fire, I realize that I, too, am a fire – on fire with desire for the Desired One.

Yes, from Palestine I bring to you somehow a gentle Christ – the One who is so meek and who is so humble that he lay as a child in a manger. I bring you 'the Lord of the Dance,' a song that people sing now. Having been in Palestine and having seen the Jews and Arabs dance (especially the men), I can understand why this song came to be. Yes, I bring you the dancing Christ, who asks you to join him in the dance which leads eventually to Calvary. But what does it matter? For Calvary is the door to the resurrection. But right now, don't you feel like dancing around the creche of a Child? If I were in your houses on

Christmas Day, I think I would dance around the altar.
Fire ... Hunger ... Light ... Dance ... Gentleness ... Humility ... Meekness ... These are the gifts I think God wants me to give you this Christmas, and I want to add to them a prayer that you may all be united in trust of one another.

I pray that this coming New Year, after we have visited Bethlehem, will be one in which every one of us will empty himself or herself so as to carry the Christ Child comfortably and warmly in one's heart. And the Christ Child will be comfortable and warm only if we love and trust one another.

Perhaps what I really brought back from Palestine is best expressed in a poem that I wrote long ago, in Advent 1961:

> *A loosing of all moorings, all reality and being known*
> *   to man.*
> *A tearing, an uprooting – like a meteoric star*
> *Shooting into unknown and awesome depths!*
> *Thus with my soul.*
> *Why this upheaval, Lord ... on the gentle threshold*
> *Of your quiet coming to us –*
> *A Child?*

> *A gift of sharing My descending ... My emptying ... My*
> *   clothing*
> *With flesh in a pure womb ...*
> *Yet remaining terribilis and God –*
> *A feeble image of the darkness I found in flesh*
> *Whilst yet keeping*
> *The divine knowing*
> *That for so many my incarnation would be in vain! ...*

> *Your descending, your emptying, are beyond my*
> *   kenning,*
> *O Awesome God!*
> *It is for me a thousand dyings, while still alive*
> *Upon this earth!*
> *It is like entering a thousand stormy seas ... or winds*
> *in fury,*

And I a leaf, drenched in those seas, dry-boned
In winds of light so dazzling..
That they are to me dark nights! ...

I sought a woman's womb to become Man. Now I seek
*   a soul*
To bring My Love to them!
A soul – to be My stable, My manger, My Bethlehem!
So I take thy poverty into my descending
And fill it to the brim.
Have faith. Have love.
Let my winds and waters fill you up ...
You will return and find me within your soul and
*   heart,*
Simple and humble – a child.

With much love,

OUR INTERIOR MISSION FIELD

January 11, 1973

Dearly Beloved,

Greetings! And a wish for the New Year to all of you: May the Lord set your hearts on fire! May the Holy Spirit, the Wind, make of your fire a bonfire full of love, the incense of which will reach God the Father! Alleluia!

At the beginning of this New Year, it came to me that my letter on the missions was incomplete. I explained to you all about our foreign missions and my attitude to them, but I didn't cover that vast and unknown territory which lies within one's self. For each of us is an immense 'mission field' which we must explore, cover, attend to, if we want to be of any use to our brothers and sisters anywhere, but especially in the Apostolate itself. The realization of the fact that *we ourselves are a mission field* begins, of course, with the commandment of God: Love your neighbor as yourself.

Unless we love ourselves, we cannot love anyone else! Here begins the first step of surveying our own mission field. What does this mean, this loving ourselves in order to love our brother or sister? The answer comes quickly if we pray over it. It simply means answering another question, or set of questions: "Do I wish to manipulate myself; or do I wish to leave all manipulation in the hands of God? ... Do I have a wrong image of myself; or do I see reflecting in me the image of God, the One who created me? ... Do I worry about the approval of men (my need for human respect); or do I concern myself solely with the approval of God? ... Am I full of fears (which, of course, will inhibit any ability to love others, or even to love myself); or have I understood that 'perfect love' casts out all fear?" This briefly would be the appraisal of my mission field.

It would be like someone going to Peru and arriving there and, after settling into a hut, would begin to examine the neighborhood, the little roads, the big roads, the back roads, etc. In the same way we all should examine our own mission field, our own mission roads into this uncharted territory!

If we choose to do our own will instead of God's will, while outwardly mouthing pious platitudes about that submission to God's will which we are not doing, we shall be utterly incapable of loving our neighbor. It would be as if we were locked up in a room where each wall is a mirror, and so are the ceiling and floor. No matter where we turn, our so-called exploration of this mission field will clearly reflect ourselves back into ourselves and into no one else, not even into God.

The next point in surveying this inward mission territory, the one that is so deep in our own hearts and souls, would be to look at the manipulation of one's self

312

and others. What does that mean to manipulate? The word is from the Latin word *manus* – for 'hand.' It means to deliberately 'handle' the arrangement of our lives, and the lives of others, *so as to suit ourselves;* and to use all kinds of natural, medical, psychological, and spiritual methods of achieving this manipulation, in order to make us feel as though we were the 'top man,' and consequently more comfortable with ourselves.

For instance, a factory can manipulate its workers by high wages and a deadly assembly line. By this manipulation it 'controls' people, in a manner of speaking, by letting technology dehumanize men and reduce them to the state of machines.

I needn't go into the possibility of medical manipulation with drugs, pills, or what-have-you. Man is already being manipulated almost into being an automaton without a will.

Psychological manipulation is so obvious that it is frightening. The knowledge of genetics opens a fantastic field for future manipulation! Then there is psychological manipulation such as Hitler did, and I need not go into that.

Spiritual manipulation is becoming rather more evident these days. Many are setting themselves up to be gurus of various sorts. There is astrology, voodoo, witchcraft, various superstitions. There is a renewed interest in all of that stuff. One can hear the voice of Jesus Christ saying:

> Take care that no one deceives you, because many will come using my name and saying, "I am the Christ!" And they will deceive many... (Matthew 24:4-6)

> If anyone says to you, "Look, here is the Christ!" or "Over here!" do not believe it; for false Christs and false prophets will arise and provide great signs and portents, enough to deceive even the elect, if that were possible. Look! I have given you warning. (Matthew 24:23-25)

But that is exactly what we are doing. We are allowing people to manipulate us, but we also want to manipulate them. We use so many ways to do so that *our own mission field* gets overgrown with coarse grass and prickly cactus instead of yielding a fine harvest for the Lord. How many of us try to escape from plowing, harvesting, and seeding our own mission field by taking recourse in sickness, psychologically induced or otherwise?

How many of us refuse to do real plowing and seeding because we have manipulated ourselves into a series of 'works' which are not too important (if we really examine them deeply and seriously). Work can become an escape, medically and psychologically, and can be a deadly thing supernaturally! Occupied in one corner of our field, we refuse to see the rest of it, including our brethren in the Apostolate. Of course, all this amounts to *doing our own will;* so the mirrors are still around about us reflecting only ourselves; and God is absent.

We seek approval. For what? God has given each of us a mission field of our own, an interiorized mission field, which is to be plowed with charity and harrowed with courage, in order to seed it with the seeds of faith. We should await the harvest in hope and in patience, seeking only the approval of God. Let each one of you, my dearly beloved, examine your own conscience as to how you are being a missionary to this mission field that the Lord has given to you.

Whatever your conscience comes up with, it should not come up with human respect or conformity. Words like that have nothing to do with any mission, or any missionary. For all missionaries – be they assigned to Peru, to Honduras, to the West Indies, or to the hidden fields of their own hearts – must totally disregard human respect (in the spiritual sense of these words) and seek only God's blessing (which is his divine respect for creatures). If you were given a mission to deal with in the Caribbean or in the Yukon or in Arizona, what would you do? Would you become the type of 'missionary' who would hide himself (or herself) within the cozy framework of his little or big mission house? One who would seldom go out, and who would establish around himself a series of fortress-like walls that say in effect: *Leave me alone! I am busy!* What would you think of anyone who acted that way? Actions like that factually spell out fear of involvement with fellow staff members and with anyone who comes to the door. Could you act that way and still call yourself a lay missionary? Would you act that way if the mission field were your own heart?

For some unaccountable reason, I dreamt not long ago that the Lord was sending me down into the mission field of each one of you. This corresponds with our Little Mandate to "go without fear into the depths of men's hearts ... I shall be with you." So in my dream I went where the Lord had sent me. Strangely enough, however, he kept stopping me and asking me to read the signposts along the road. I did so, and these signposts I just wrote out for you!

Perhaps this is a foolish letter; perhaps not; but these days I share everything with you, my foolishness and my 'unfoolishness.' So here is a letter that comes out of a prayer and a dream.

Love,

Catherine

A DEEP QUESTION

February 15, 1973

Dearly Beloved,

I approach this letter with a deep sense of compassion, of understanding, of pity, all of which are the fruit of love. I am not expressing myself in order to judge anyone. But I must present a life situation – a very ordinary one that happens to all of us – and ask you a question which I hope you will answer, so that each of you will know what the other thinks, feels, and prays for, about it. This is a heavy letter because all I wish (and I know that you wish it too) is to love God more and more.

Members of Madonna House are getting older and older. As people grow older, their parents die or become incapacitated and need help. Until recently that was all clearly defined for all of us, with very few exceptions. When parents die, there is the question of going to the funeral. Normally speaking, of course, Our Lord himself in the Scripture tells us that burying the dead is a work of mercy; there should be no difficulty about this. If one is far away on a mission, however, then one can let the funeral go, and remember a father or mother as he or she last saw them.

But what are we to do when parents become ill with lengthy sicknesses, and there are many-faceted problems arising? Perhaps the mother might have cancer and the father is in his eighties. There might be other family members who could take over, but they themselves are physically or psychologically incapacitated. What is a member of Madonna House to do? Should he or she go and look after the one parent until that person dies? And then what about the surviving parent? If there is one of our fieldhouses nearby, should the member of Madonna House divide his or her time between the house and the parents? Is this possible? Does it create a divided heart? All of these things are deep questions.

If money isn't a problem, then it seems simpler to hire someone to look after one's aged parents and to visit them occasionally. For it seems to me that we are coming up against certain 'utterances of God' that just cannot be totally disregarded. Personally, I fear the dilution of those utterances. I fear the rationalization of them. I feel there must be some kind of simplicity in us that accepts the words of God as read. I might be mistaken. In fact, I wouldn't know absolutely; that is why I ask. Should we allow one of our members to go to nurse a parent who has had a stroke, if there is no one else to look after the person? Or should we try to find alternative modes of acting to get the parent cared for, such as in a senior citizens' home?

There are many variations on the theme, but as I sit

here in my poustinia, I wonder about it all. Chapter 14 of the Gospel of Luke has a paragraph that I read and reread endlessly:

> Great crowds accompanied him on his way, and he turned and spoke to them: "If any man comes to me without hating his father and mother, wife and children, brother and sister, yes, and his own life too, he cannot be my disciple. Anyone who doesn't carry his cross and come after me cannot be my disciple."

Jesus would never ask for hate as we understand it, for he is love personified. He asks for total detachment. There are other examples of this detachment that he asks of us.

In Luke 8, Jesus was told that his mother and brothers (meaning his cousins in those days) were standing outside and wanted to see him. Jesus said: "My mother and brothers are those who hear the word of God and put it into practice."

In Luke 5, the first four disciples are called while they were fishing. We are told that Jesus said, "Do not be afraid. From now on, it is men you will catch." And Scripture tells us that "they left everything and followed him." We have those words 'left everything.' Presumably that included father, mother, wife, children – even mother-in-law, as far as Peter was concerned.

Then in Mark 10, Peter wanted to know what would happen to the apostles, especially to himself. "What about us? We have left everything and have followed you." And Jesus replied:

> I tell you solemnly, there is no one who has left house, brothers, sisters, father, children, land, for my sake and for the sake of the Gospel, who will not be repaid a hundred times over, houses, brothers, sisters, mother, children, land – not without persecution – now in this present time. And in the world to come, eternal life. Many who are first will be last, and the last will be first.

I have given you some of the Scriptural quotes about leaving father, mother, earthly possessions, and so on.

There are many more which you can look up ... the eye of the needle, and so forth. Scripture shows us a greater dimension of 'the problem of poverty' than just our parents and their needs. There is a dimension of our personal poverty which consists in our becoming ever more dispossessed and detached. The way I understand it (and I stand corrected at any moment), dispossession means a giving up of *things* (ideas, and such); and detachment means a giving up of *relationships* (with people, etc.). Dispossession and detachment I consider to be like two friends, or like husband and wife. They go, hand in hand, into the heart of Christ. There they are totally purified and healed. And now they can return, as it were, to the world of men with a complete freedom and an infinite joy.

I did not start this letter to preach, however, but to ask you a question: What do you think members of Madonna House should do when their parents are ill and unable to take care of themselves? In the old days, health insurance, social security, pensions, etc., were unknown. The matter was clear then, because it came under the commandment of God: "Honor thy father and mother" (which is in the Old Testament). Christ speaks of it also.

We stand before a mystery here. A child is conceived by a man, a woman, and God. He (or she) is baptized, which is a great grace of God; and by this baptism, he immediately enters into union with God because the Trinity has entered his soul, into the very depths of his being. It means that the child now has *a destiny to fulfill,* and this requires a totality of obedience to God's commandments.

One of those commandments is to 'honor' his parents. In previous times, that also meant that the child might have repay his parents for the Gift of Life by 'laying down' his own life. If the parents lacked food, clothing, shelter, or medical care, the child had a duty to provide it for them. He could not marry, nor could he enter a religious vocation, unless he attended to that primary duty first. If he had many brothers and sisters (as in those days, people did) or other relatives who could take over the parental care, he was released from this responsibility. (There might also have been a pressure for young unmarried children to stay home and look after the parents, whether or not they really needed care.)

In our days, the circumstances have largely changed. Medicare, social security, welfare, homemakers, visiting nurses of various kinds, public health workers, meals on wheels, etc., are available to people who need them. So the question becomes twofold: Is it necessary, unless the circumstances are exceptional, for a son or daughter to go home and care for parents who are in comfortable circumstances, financially speaking? The second question is: Is it necessary to go and care for parents who can be well looked after by any or several of the helps available today?

Having answered those questions, we come to another crucial one: What does it really *mean* to 'give up' father, mother, brother, husband, wife, children, as Christ said? The word of Scripture seems very clear. Are we rationalizing then? Do we want to water it down? What is it all about? It seems a strange situation, and I am not quite sure why. On one side, we have the statements of Christ; on the other side are the questions we are faced with.

As I stand before Love Personified and ask myself what is the place of love, I come to the conclusion that it comes ahead of everything else. Love is the essence of the spiritual life, and that love means an interior and spiritual identification with our neighbor, and that neighbor includes our brothers, sisters, parents. *Love means far more than sentiment, however.* We must love others not as objects to whom we 'do good' or as authority figures whom we are obliged to serve. We must love others *as ourselves.* We must die to self (which is very hard for most of us) and learn to live for others. We all try to resist that death! It demands our loving in such a pure and detached way that all exploitation, domineering, authoritarian brutality, or condescension is absent from our hearts. In a sense we have to 'become' the person whom we love.

Now this applies to both sides, you understand. Parents can use authoritarian attitudes. I know of a case where the mother (who was perfectly well) kept feigning illness and writing to her daughter in a convent that she had a 'heart condition' and needed her. The daughter left the

Order and came home only to find that the mother didn't have any heart condition at all. When the daughter joined another Order, it happened again. Each time, she felt guilty that she was not keeping the fourth commandment, not 'honoring' her father and mother, so she was never able to follow her vocation until it was far too late.

Let's look at both sides of the question. Do we really love our parents in the way I have tried to describe love? Do our parents love us with true love, or selfishly? Which is it? We must pray about these things deeply and profoundly because, you know, if we really love our parents, really want to do them 'good' in the full sense of the word, we have to bring them to understand that the Kingdom of God is very close to them, and they too will be judged on love – on unselfish love.

I remember my own mother saying to me, "You were given to me by God and to God I must return you." I felt the same way about my son, George. Perhaps it results in a tragic wounding of the psyche, of the emotions; but, strange as it may seem, it eventually brings an immense peace. The question, however, is still before us. With all of these explanations, puny as they might be, simple as they are, primitive perhaps; but even with these explanations, the question is still yours to answer.

I have an answer; but I give it with, not a divided heart, but an unsure heart. It is true we send people to the poor to nurse them for short periods. Then why shouldn't we send people to their own parents to do the same? It is a good question; and yet somehow my heart is not quite satisfied with it. I am uneasy and I don't know why. You see, I look at us and see that we *are* an Apostolate. The essence of our being together makes us an Apostolate. People today call it community, a Christian community; that's a good name too. When the Lord sent his disciples out two by two to preach the Good News, there were no strings attached to these people. They left everything to go forth and preach that Good News. God has gathered us together in a place called Combermere and to sit at the feet of Jesus, as it were, and learn a little of what he has to say. And then we are told to go forth and to preach this Gospel of his with our lives, and we have been sent about his business far and near.

Now what would happen to the Apostolate if, as we grow older and our parents grow older, many of us went back to our parents to look after them? What would happen to this Apostolate that God has created? That looms before me like a big question mark! And behind it stands Christ; the Christ who said that he didn't have any mother or brothers, but that *we* were his mother and brothers; the Christ who gave up his mother to someone else, there under the Cross; the Christ who died as naked as he came into the world; the Christ who had nowhere to lay his head; the Christ who said that if we want to follow him we have to give up everything – relatives, friends, our goods, our life – and become naked, in a sense, and follow his nakedness. This bothers me.

Could the answer be that each case should be examined on its own merits? This would be wonderful and I would be very happy to accept that kind of judgment. And yet, deep down, my Russian heart hungers for a sobornost answer to the question. But I don't think that I will get it. So perhaps we can just pray that East joins West in this case, and that each personal problem along those lines will be examined individually. Perhaps the day will come when all will understand – parents and children – what love is in its total surrender to the words of God.

With much love,

THE SONG OF A CHILD

December 7, 1973

Dearly Beloved,

We are celebrating once again the birth of Our Lord Jesus Christ. I wrote a poem about it for the Christmas issue of Restoration. It is to take the place of the editorial I usually write. (I will append a copy of it to the end of this Staff Letter.)

The poem was veritably wrenched out of my heart. I wrote it in the middle of the night. Besides the pain that you can sense in that poem, I want you to understand that there is an infinite joy in my heart too, for that is what the love of Christ is. That's what Christianity is all about – the crucified Christ and the dancing Christ. (You remember the song: I am the Lord of the Dance, Am I.) The cross is but the path to the resurrection.

In the Eastern Rite, alleluias are sung on Good Friday because Easter is already overshadowing the darkness of the Cross. It is a beautiful symbolism that we should accept fully and make our own. Yes, let us make it our own because the Lord has called all of us to bear the burdens of our brethren. We wish to wash the feet of others as Christ washed the feet of his apostles.

But carrying the burden of our brethren, washing their feet, means entering into *every* phase of their lives: spiritual, political, economic, what-have-you, It means for us tension, anxiety, lassitude, and a host of other emotions. But let us stop for a moment and think. Only a corpse is devoid of all emotions. Do we wish to be the living dead? Do we wish to serve God as if we were zombies? Of course not! We have to begin to understand that all this anxiety, all this tension, is only natural and normal. We are human beings dealing with other human beings; and they are shot through (if our faith is deep enough to see it) with infinite joy.

That joy should sing inside our hearts, for if our faith does not sing it is a kind of dead faith, isn't it? For love is a song – the echo of God's voice – and we must make it available. We must make it heard by all of those with whom we come into contact, for a song attracts more than a sob.

Listen! Do you hear the gurgle of a baby? It holds a song already within its sound; it holds the first smile of a child. Almost none of us can resist the gurgle that really isn't a gurgle but a series of fantastic things. Yes, listen! It is his gurgle. He is in the manger and he is happy to have become a man – a human being. Consider the incredibility of what has happened. God entered the womb of a human! God stayed there as every child of man stays – nine months! Then he was born. That, my friends, my dearly beloved, is the Incarnation!

And he was happy to be incarnated because he loves us. Hence that funny little gurgle is the song, the smile of a Child. Come, let us arise and go together to Bethlehem. We shall be all one around his crib, though seemingly divided by space. But when we love, neither time nor space matters. So we shall all be together and we shall behold his gurgle, his song, and his smile.

So let us remember it forever and forever, until we meet him face to face. For it will assuage our depressions, our anxieties, our tensions. From his smile we are going to learn to smile and sing ourselves, no matter where we are and what we have to do because we shall know as we already know that our life is an eternal pilgrimage to Bethlehem.

Happy arriving at the crib! May he bless you with himself.

Lovingly yours,

The ox and
The ass
Are a bloody mess!
There is no manger.

The Child is
Somewhere –
Where a thousand
Refugees
Are gathered
On a dump.

There is no cradle.
Just a torn
Hammock
Rescued from
The junk
Left over
By some soldiers.
(So many
passed this way.)

The woman who
Rocks the
Hammock
Is gaunt.
There is
So little food.
Yet she sings.

Suddenly
Her song
Is shattered
By screams
Of bombs
Dropped
From Heaven.

And as suddenly
All is quiet again.

A lone woman,
A hammock,
A Child,
Are still
There.

The refugees?
They are
No more.
The dump heap
Is filled
With blood
And pieces
Of human flesh.

Happy Christmas,
Christian People!

———————————

HELPS FOR THE READER

A number of people who have read Volume One of this series have written to say that they have found the book very nourishing. However, they wonder if we can give them any hints as to how to absorb Catherine's words more deeply into their lives.

Here are four suggestions. They have to do with listening to the word; pausing in silence; seeing the complexity of human personality in all its depth and roundness; and going forth in mystery, with great confidence in God.

* * *

Normally, Catherine would keep two or three secretaries — in rotation — busy each day with the transcribing and the typing of her many ideas. She could 'speak out' a chapter for her next book, dictate a twenty-page Training Outline for a Madonna House department, compose an article for her monthly newspaper column, and then (when the afternoon mail had arrived) respond to the many letters she received that day. She would switch back and forth between secretaries as needed, for Catherine was rarely at a loss for words. Her assistants were sometimes hard pressed to keep up with the flow of sentences.

It is important to realize that Catherine did not really *write* the letters in this series called *Dearly Beloved.* What she did was to *dictate* the letters, usually to someone who was speedy enough to type her spoken words directly onto a master stencil. The letter was then cranked off on a duplicator, and the inked sheets stuffed into envelopes and hustled off to the post office. There was no time for editing. No time even to put in the proper punctuation, since the typist couldn't always be sure when one sentence ended and another began. (Punctuation remained something for editors to add in, at a later date.)

Thoughts poured out of Catherine's mind, laying themselves down in sentences on the printed page, following her rhythm of speech — which was that of a professional lecturer, one accustomed to using words or phrases to catch the audience's attention. At times, there were some redundancies. (The editors have kept them to a minimum, but did not remove them entirely, since to do so would have damaged the rhythm of her words.)

Just as Catherine did not 'write' these letters in silence, neither did her followers read them in silence. For the most part, they read the words aloud in small groups, or whispered them half-aloud to themselves, to catch the sound of her spoken voice.

If you find it difficult to understand any of Catherine's ideas, we suggest that you slow down the pace of your reading and try to hear the words as they are being 'spoken' in your mind. Imagine that Catherine is sitting at your kitchen table, having a cup of tea or coffee with you, and talking with you.

This is the first suggestion — 'listen' to the word, don't simply read it.

* * *

Remember that, in these letters, Catherine is speaking primarily to men and women who have lived with her, day in and day out, over a period of years. They are people already conversant with her ideas. She often makes a passing reference to a Biblical phrase or to some familiar saying, and assumes that her listeners will understand its implications. (Since many readers live outside North America, the editors have put a number of 'words' in single quotes to point up familiar references, or to indicate Madonna House sayings and informal American phrases.)

Catherine is aware, of course, that her thoughts may not always come out as clearly as she intended.

Some of her own staff may have trouble grasping their full import. To counter this problem, she offered the following technique:

> Please do not feel that you have to read all my Staff Letters, at once, as they come to you. I presume that the local director of a given house opens my letter and decides when, and at what time, and with how much spacing, to read a given letter with the rest of you.
>
> I definitely want you to have plenty of time to discuss, to consider, to write to me for clarification if need be, to tell me where you disagree, etc. Obviously, when one letter after another arrives at your doorstep — 'one on top of the other' so to speak — it doesn't mean that you should read them as soon as they arrive. Read them one after the other, but with due spacing ... slowly!
>
> I am sharing with you not only my own ideas but those of many others here at the training center. Like every writer, however, ideas sometimes crowd me and clamor for expression. That means I am practically compelled to put them down on paper lest they vanish. For it would be too bad if a good idea disappeared because of my laziness!
>
> So I put them down and my lovely secretaries mimeograph them and send them out immediately. They do so for practical reasons — so as to have them 'out of the way' as it were, and to let us go on to the next job (of which we have many, as you know). So you'll have to bear with me and my cycles of letters, which may suddenly come to you in great numbers and then taper off for a spell.

Readers who follow this 'spacing' method tell us that they have found it very effective for unlocking the secrets buried in Catherine's writings. They may gather each evening around the dinner table, as a family; or else meet with friends once a week in someone's home. They read aloud portions of a Staff Letter. They take time to reflect, to discuss a letter at a time, perhaps a paragraph at a time. There is no sense of hurry. They do not rush. They give God some 'elbow room' so he can work profitably in the depths of their souls.

Catherine's technique of 'giving the word due spacing' is valuable for any of her writings. But it is especially appropriate for a series like *Dearly Beloved,* where each volume spans many years of thought.

We recommend to all our readers this second suggestion — pause in silence. Give God time to 'work things out' for you.

* * *

Some readers are not so familiar with Catherine's prophetic vocation. They are, perhaps, people who know her only through her quiet meditative writings; or they have met her after she had become a quite aged, and somewhat mellowed, person. So they find it an unexpected challenge to meet — on the pages of this book — such a strong-spoken woman, with ready answers for any situation, who appears to be (and is!) a decisive, organized administrator.

This is not surprising. No single book or personal encounter can reflect all the sides of Catherine's many-faceted personality. In reading this printed collection of letters, you cannot hear the laughter and good humor that sometimes punctuated her conversations, or catch the wink or smile or knowing look that she sometimes bestowed on her listeners during pauses in her talks.

You do not smell the aroma of tea, or perhaps coffee, as she slowly sips a cup of it and marshals her thoughts before dictation. You do not notice her momentary grimace as she 'gears up' for the painful duty of having to 'preach the word' to us. You do not sense her quiet sigh of relief when the lecture is over, and she can turn to more amenable duties.

And it is rare — even for us, her closest daily

companions — to get a glimpse of that ever-present 'shyness of soul' which lurks underneath her self-assured manner. That is part of her private being ... as is the quiet stillness that comes over her when she glances out her cabin window to see a wild flower in bloom, or to watch a lingering sunset reflected in the clouds.

Catherine's words are often prophetic. And not always gentle, or genteel. We who have lived with her, and have seen close-up this resplendent facet of her personality, want to share with our readers all the vibrancy and full-blooded robustness of her words. We want to give you in unadulterated form her 'direct speech.'

If, at times, you feel overwhelmed by this directness, we ask you to remember her other qualities as well, the hidden ones that are not revealed in her words. In this regard, quiet prayer is always helpful.

By doing so, you are following the third suggestion — to see the complexity of a human personality in all its depth and roundness. Not only Catherine's personality, but your own personality! And to appreciate the unique gifts God has placed there.

* * *

Some readers ask if there is a one-page summary of Catherine's spirituality, and whether it is possible for non-members of Madonna House to participate fully in that spirituality. The answer to both questions is: *Yes!*

It is true that these letters were written primarily for Staff Workers, those who have taken promises of poverty, obedience, and chastity, and who express this commitment within the family of Madonna House.

Even so, those who wish to be 'spiritual children' of Catherine, and are not called by God to be with Madonna House in an official capacity, will find no barrier to following her teachings and to 'living out' her spirit. While Catherine herself does not address this question specifically, she does give generous hints to 'non-members' by the way she discusses *the spirit of Madonna House.*

In Volume One, page 120, she mentions four key elements: Gospel Living, Childlike Simplicity, Duty of the Moment, Little Things Done Well. To these she adds two more words: Peace (pax) and Love (caritas). These half-dozen 'words' can be practiced by anyone, anywhere: rich or poor, married or single, imprisoned or free, old or young. It need not require joining Madonna House as a member.

In Volume Two, page 123, she adds the word 'family' and the Gospel image of 'Nazareth' to the word Love (caritas). On page 153, she expands on the theme, this time using the phrase 'community of love' and fastening upon three Gospel images — Bethlehem, Nazareth, Golgotha. She speaks of a commitment that is 'personal, individual' and is extended to others on the same basis, 'one-by-one.' This commitment is not to an institution, such as Madonna House; it is a commitment to God alone. (See pages 70 and 72.)

Catherine (who founded a group called Friendship House before she started Madonna House) often speaks of the value of 'friendship' with others. On page 265, she says that "today, friendship is the most precious possession that a human being can share with another." In many of her letters, she talks of being 'available' to others, of 'going into the marketplace' where others can be found, of engaging in the 'chitchat apostolate' there, of being a person of 'the towel and the water' who offers 'service' to others. (Again, this work of friendship can be done by anyone, wherever opportunity avails itself.)

On page 278, Catherine brings together a rather strange combination of ideas, that of 'going forth as a pilgrim' and being 'naked, stripped, exposed to the world' yet 'little, hidden, unobvious.' For most of us, it is an acceptable challenge. It is possible to risk a pilgrimage into the unknown, following wherever God leads, as long as we know it won't be 'obvious' to those around us.

The harder part is mentioned on page 193. God may call us into the valley of secular activity, *without* showing us what we are to be or do there! We will need a great childlike confidence in God (this applies equally to a member of Madonna House as to a non-member) to simply be present in the 'marketplace' and to peacefully look around until we find the 'pitcher and basin' God wants us to use.

On pages 179-180, all these 'words' of Catherine will be found, gathered together and placed in a definitive form, which she calls her *Little Mandate*. This is the one-page summary where the spirit of Madonna House can be found.

How shall individual readers incarnate this spirit in their daily lives? On pages 153-154, Catherine says: "Although the essence of this spirit can never be tampered with, the techniques of its application, the ways it can be presented to the world, must be *intensely flexible.*" In other words, we must couple a profound faithfulness to that spirit with a response that is fitting to our particular stage or state in life.

Volume One, pages 18-19, echoes this plea. Catherine asks us to be "flexible like rapiers, malleable like wax" and not to get bogged down in this or that customary method of operating, even if it seems like a hallowed Madonna House technique; else "we will become hidebound, dead wood, and of no use to the Lord."

So then, the fourth suggestion is a simple one, though not always an easy one — arise and go forth, in the mystery of your being, with great confidence in God. *Listen to the Spirit; he will lead you.*

Writings of Catherine de Hueck Doherty
Apostolic Farming
Dearly Beloved – Vol. 1 & 2
Dear Father
Dear Seminarian
Doubts, Loneliness and Rejection
Fragments of My Life
The Gospel of a Poor Woman
The Gospel Without Compromise
I Live on an Island
Journey Inward
Lubov
Molchanie
My Heart and I
My Russian Yesterdays
Not Without Parables
Our Lady of Combermere
Our Lady's Unknown Mysteries
The People of the Towel and the Water
Poustinia
Re-entry into Faith
Sobornost
Soul of My Soul
Stations of the Cross
Strannik
Urodivoi

by Eddie Doherty
Cricket in My Heart
Gall & Honey
The Secret of Mary
Splendor of Sorrow
True Devotion to Mary
Tumbleweed

by Fr. Emile Brière
I Met the Humbled Christ in Russia
Katia
The Power of Love

Available through Madonna House Publications
Combermere, Ontario, Canada
K0J 1L0